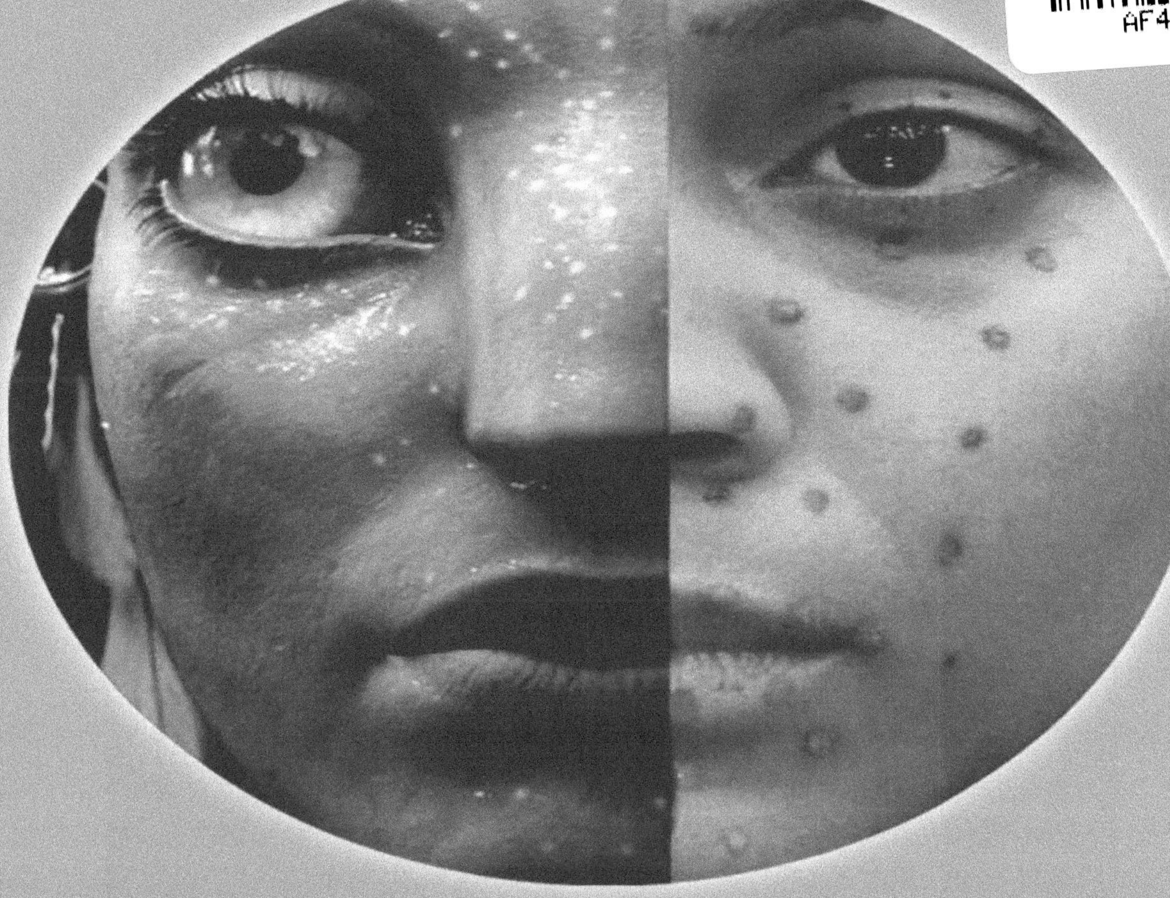

Teach Yourself Autodesk
MAYA

Cromosys Publication

NIRANJAN JHA SHOWMAN

Founder - Niranjan Jha Showman

cromosys®
Corporation
Education and Technology Research Center
Patankar Park, Nallasopara (W), Mumbai. +91-9561450045
Education, Technology, Publication, Healthcare, Newsmedia, Realtor, Filmmaking
www.facebook.com/cromosys

+91-9561450045
Learn Advanced Skills
And Get Job Instantly
GERMAN
Python
FRENCH
C++
SPANISH
Java
ENGLISH
HTML5
RUSSIAN
CSS
JavaScript
Cromosys
Education and Technology Research Center
Nallasopara (W), Mumbai

Learn Web Programming
Demo-Class Free
HTML
CSS
React
JavaScript
Typescript
Bootstrap
Cromosys
20 Years of Experience
Nallasopara (W), Mumbai
+91-9561450045

+91-9561450045
Learn Software Engineering
Demo-Class Free

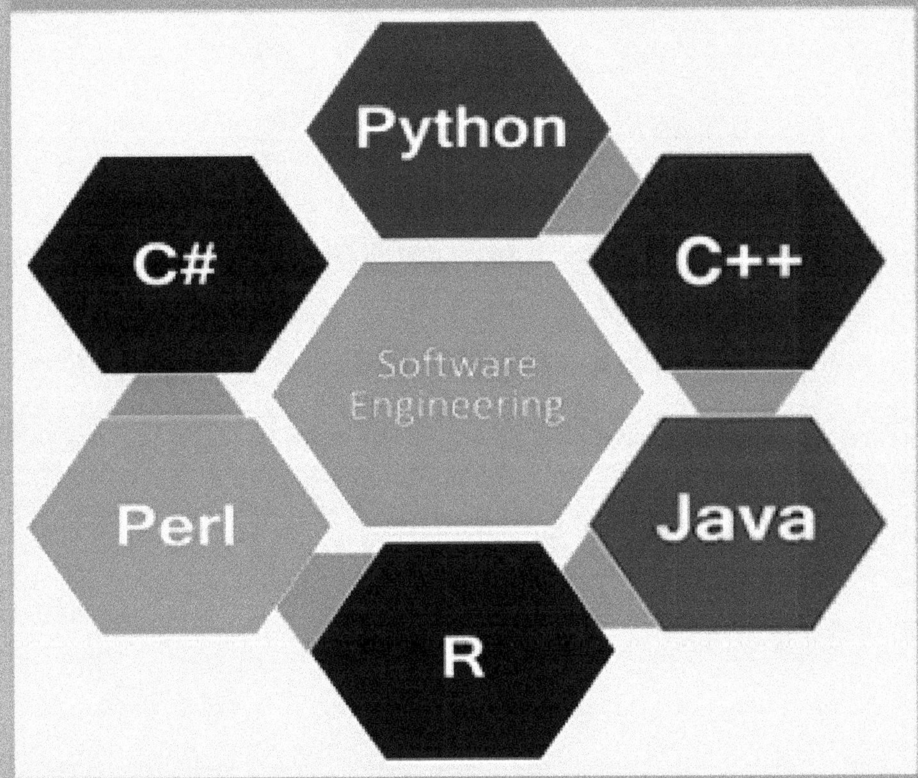

Python
C#
C++
Software Engineering
Perl
Java
R

Cromosys
20 Years of Experience
Nallasopara (W), Mumbai
+91-9561450045

25 Years of Experience
Learn Visual Multimedia
Animation VFX
Movie Editing
Game Development
Cromosys
+91-9561450045
Education and Technology Research Center
Nallasopara (W), Mumbai
www.facebook.com/cromosys

Jobs Available
For Candidates Who Know

German
French
Spanish

Vacancy in Germany, France, Spain

For Hospitality, Engineering, IT Sector
With Free Visa, Airfare and Accommodation

Cromosys
Education and Technology Research Centre
Nallasopara (W), Mumbai
+91-9561450045
20 Years of Experience

+91-9561450045
Foreign Languages Institute
German, French, Spanish
Basic and Advanced - All Levels
3 x 6 = 18 Courses
FRANCHISE
Business Offer
Teaching Materials Provided
We have 1 Million Students Globally
Great Income Assured
Global Exposure
Cromosys
20 Years of Experience
Nallasopara (W), Mumbai
+91-9561450045

Book: Teach Yourself Autodesk Maya
Author: Niranjan Jha Showman
Publisher: Cromosys Publication
ISBN: Acquired
Category: Computer Education
Subcategory: Animation and VFX

Preface

Cromosys Publication's **Teach Yourself Autodesk Maya** book is an optimal quality guide to the beginners and advanced learners of Maya. We are the leading eBook publisher of languages and technology. Our research and education center working for last fifteen years has made tremendous efforts to simplify the learning of Maya, and so, we assure you that this book will walk you through in the simplest way in your entire course of learning, and will make you a master of it in just one month of time. Academy Award winning Maya software is the world's most powerfully integrated 3D modeling, animation, effects, and rendering solution. It also adds to the quality and realism of 2D graphics. That's why film and video artists, game developers, visualization professionals, web and print designers turn to Maya to take their work to meet the demands of next generation productions. The tutorials in the chapters will lead you step-by-step giving pictures of every move and will help you create and design models from scratch, not like other books that tell you to copy things and make shallow editing. We do not encourage such misguidance because the learning of Maya is not a child's play. Today's world is the world of 3d design, visual effects, animation, and so everyone wants to create a moving, talking, and interacting visual expression. If you are interested in editing movies, games, architectural designs, earning a way to Hollywood, or impressing your loved one, Maya can serve all your purposes, as it does all the works of this kind. The lessons conceived and prepared by us will let you start your learning from real basic making your move amazing, astonishing, and exhilarating for you. And soon you will feel that you have got a new horizon to show your creativity. It's cool, simple, and sublime!

Niranjan Showman, the author of this and twenty other eBooks available online, is the founder of Cromosys Corporation. His dedication in technological and linguistic research is significantly known to the millions of people around the world. This book is the creation of his avowed determination to make the learning of Maya easy to the people. After you install this program on your system, you just have to follow the instructions doing the same on your computer, and you will see that you are quickly learning everything. Just an hour of practice per day, and in a month of time you'll get a lot of knowledge, tips and tricks to work with this software. This is an unmatchable unique book of its kind that guarantees your success. The lessons are magnificently powerful to bring you into the arena of visual effects. It is the need of time, and that's why many people have been sharpening their knowledge to be good in it. The still-image creation software like CorelDraw, Photoshop, Illustrator and 3D design software like 3ds Max and Shockwave are where you create the image of your choice and animate them, but when you wish to add visual effects, there you need Maya. What Maya does, no other software can do. It is totally different. For instance, if you want to create a real-looking rain effect in a particular scene of a video, do you think any other software can do? No, absolutely not. Only Maya can do that and it can do in just a few minutes of time.

From the year of 2013, with the industrial growth, the accurate and profound knowledge of this software has influenced zillions of minds; therefore we conceived the idea of making this book a guideline for those who want to be perfect in it starting from real basic. One thing is important to say that nobody can learn Maya playing around it, and even nobody can play around also. People do learn other software like CorelDraw and Photoshop in casual efforts, but Maya cannot be cowed down in that manner. It is dynamic, resolute, vivid and vivacious and that's why we salute Maya a thousand times. If you dare to be inattentive, you'll experience your own failure because you will not learn anything. It needs your attentive, continuous, controlled and patient efforts. Don't get carried away at the first lesson and start doing irrelevant things of your own, as it happens because of the vivaciousness of this software. You'll burst into laughter or start dancing when you'll see your creation coming out of computer screen, but believe me, there would be still more to learn.

Cromosys, our education and technology research center, saving human efforts from being wasted, is committed to help you gain profound and contemporary knowledge. The world growing with density has brought enormous opportunity to animation talents irrespective of their geographical boundaries. We strongly believe that this book is useful for the people working for art and design, web creation, media houses, entertainment world, and obviously for those who love animation. After you start the lesson, you don't need to worry about anything but just follow each and every step carefully. This eBook is designed to fulfill the instant need of learners in a very economical way, as it is easy to find on internet and affordable to buy and share. Cromosys, our path-breaking pioneer training institute for Computer Courses, English Speaking, Mass Communication, Foreign Languages, and Competition Coaching, is dedicated to enlightening human mind with educational endeavors, and we are doing the same for last successful fifteen years. And recently we have come up with 'Worldwide Online Teaching System' for languages and technology. We not only hope but believe that your success is in your hand now, as this book will take you miles ahead in your expectation. We always respect the views and comments of readers, so for any communication with regards to assistance, enquiry or collaboration, we are always there at your reach as it helps us improve our quality.

Niranjan Jha Showman
Founder: Cromosys Corporation
Web: facebook.com/cromosys
Contact no. +91-9561450045
Email address: cromosys@yahoo.com
Facebook link: www.facebook.com/niranjanshowman

Books by the same author: Teach Yourself Adobe Flash, Teach Yourself 3ds Max, English Voice Accent and Pronunciation, Teach Yourself Spanish, Teach Yourself French, Teach Yourself German, English Word Power, Dynamic Grammar of English, English Dictionary of Modern Slang

Cromosys
Education and Technology Research Center
Education, Technology, Publication, Healthcare, Realtor, Filmmaking
Nallasopara (W), Mumbai, India

Caution: All the writing works that include all the educational, non-educational books, novels, and articles of the author Niranjan Jha, are the registered contents of Online Digital Services and also published contents of his registered magazine FACE OFF - Inventing Truth, which carries registration no. MAHENG12112/13/1/2009-TC and the endorsement no. 3244 28/5/2009 with the Ministry of Information and Broadcasting, Govt. of India. Any plagiarism in this regard will attract strict legal action. Any further publication of any of these books requires his written permission. Copyright certificate of this book is attached at the end of this book.

Lesson 1
Introduction

This book provides an in-depth approach to learn the skills of creating 3D content using Maya 2013. I focus on the key concepts of 3D computer graphics and animation. This lesson will also introduce you to the new and enhanced features of Maya, such as interoperability, nHair simulation system, Retime Tool, improved Viewport 2.0, HumanIK, Extrude command, and file referencing. I have laid efforts to make the learning easy and systematic. The lessons are supplemented with practical examples and screenshots to explain various concepts of Maya 2013. The lessons will also help you create your own 3D models, apply materials, add lights, and animate them. You'll also be explained about achieving realistic rendering effects using the mental ray. The contents are equally helpful to beginners as well as professionals.

Autodesk Maya is an industry-leading 3D computer graphics (CG) software used for creation and production solution. In the 3D entertainment content creation industry, Maya is extensively used by artists working in visual effects, animation production, and game development projects. Maya is also capable of mixing live action footage with computer generated footage. And so, Maya has become so popular that it is used by prominent companies, such as Walt Disney Pictures, EA Sports, Pixar Studios, and DreamWorks Studios. It includes new features like Open data and single step data exchange. Interoperability is a major feature which establishes live connection to Motion Builder and conversion of 3ds Max CAT characters to Maya HumanIK with one click. The Open Data provides tools to facilitate parallel workflows and better handling of complex files.

Launching Maya

You can install Maya either using its installation DVD or downloading a trial version from http://www.autodesk.com. But before starting the installation, you have to verify the system requirements, confirm local administrative permissions, disable antivirus, and close all running programs. In order to install Maya, you must ensure the system requirement. Maya 2013 is available for all major operating system platforms such as Microsoft, Linux, and Macintosh. The system requirements include both software (operating system and web browsers) and hardware of the computer. The table below lists both the software and hardware requirement for the 32-bit and 64-bit versions of Autodesk Maya 2013.

	For Maya 2013 32-bit	For Maya 2013 64-bit
Operating System	Windows 7 Professional with Service Pack 1, Windows XP Professional with Service Pack 3.	Windows 7 Professional, Windows XP Professional x64 Edition with SP 2, Mac 10.7 and 10.8, Linux 6.2 WS, and Fedora 14.
Processor Type	Intel Pentium 4, AMD Athlon with SSE3 support	Intel Pentium 4, AMD Athlon with SSE3 support, Macintosh computer with Intel 64-bit processor
RAM	2 GB	4 GB
Hard Disk	10 GB free space	10 GB free space
Browsers and others	Internet Explorer 7, Safari and Firefox. OpenGL graphics card and three-button mouse.	Internet Explorer 7, Safari and Firefox. OpenGL graphics card and three-button mouse.

When you open Maya After installation, it appears with the **Essential Skills Movies** window. The Essential Skills Movies window provides video tutorials to the basic features of Maya 2013, such as navigating in the interface, transforming an object, creating and viewing objects, selecting components, animating an object using keyframes, applying materials and lights, and rendering. This window opens by default every time you launch Maya 2013, but you can hide this by selecting the option at the bottom of the same window that says 'Do not show this at startup check box'. If you want to watch this video later, you can select on Maya screen Help> Learning Movies from the main menu bar. To start working with Maya, you can this window. The Maya 2013 interface (UI) appears, as shown in picture 1.1.

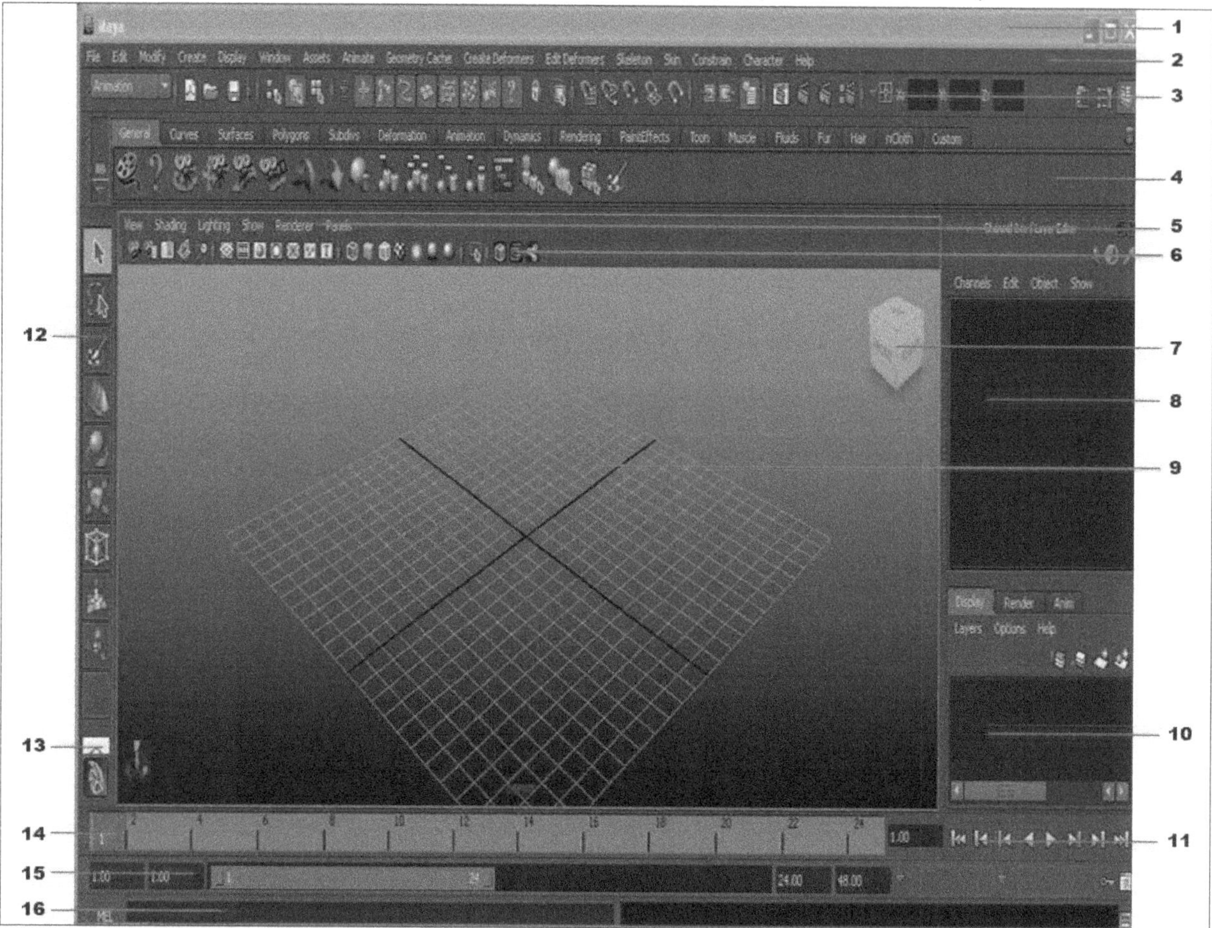

Picture 1.1

1. Title bar
2. Main menu bar
3. Status Line (entire row)
4. Shelf (entire row)
5. Panel Menu
6. Panel toolbar (entire row)
7. ViewCube
8. Channel Box
9. Viewport
10. Layer Editor
11. Animation Controls (entire row)
12. Tool Box (all nine buttons)
13. Quick Layout buttons
14. Time Slider
15. Range Slider
16. Command Line

The numbers shown with the bars and command panels in the picture are explained in the list above. Using these commands, you can create models, apply materials, and animate objects.

New and Enhanced Features

Maya 2013 has several significant new and enhanced features for modeling, file referencing, dynamic simulation, rendering, rigging, and animation. To facilitate non-linear workflows, it has Open data, which provides a high performance workflow to work with and manage complex data. There are other features also that help you to create highly realistic hair, assess you work in a higher fidelity interactive environment, simulate both soft and rigid bodies in a single system, and bind geometry to skeleton more accurately. You can also use the improved file referencing workflow and Alembic and Animation Transfer Object Model (ATOM) file formats. All the new features and enhancements facilitate in the developing 3D content more efficiently. Now you'll see a list of new and enhanced features of Maya 2013 below.

Interoperability: Allows live connection to Motion Builder. Maya 2013 also supports the conversion of 3ds Max CAT characters to Maya HumanIK with a single click.

Enhanced Viewport 2.0: Supports rigging and animation features, such as HumanIK, joints, motion paths, ghosting, and playblasts. Including the features supported in the previous edition (motion blur, depth of field, and ambient occlusion), the enhanced Viewport 2.0 gives an output similar to the rendered output without rendering or exporting to external software.

HumanIK Enhancements: Allows animators to map and retarget HumanIK animation to and from a custom rigged character using the bipedal character tools. You can also use a unified character for increased usability and customized character view to suit specific requirements.

nHair Simulation System: Supports hair generation system, which has been added to the Nucleus dynamic simulation framework. Dynamic nHair curves can self-collide and interact with other objects in the Nucleus system: nParticle and nCloth. The new nHair system has improved performance especially for hair systems with a large number of follicles and better collision accuracy and control.

nParticle: Determines how ramp attribute data is evaluated using a new Post Cache Ramp Evaluation attribute. This attribute is turned off by default. You can turn it on to reevaluate the ramp output using the cached input attribute rather.

The new ATOM Format: Supports reusing animation data. Using the ATOM format, you can transfer animation data between characters to repurpose an existing animation data for new characters. This format natively supports keyframes, constraints, animation layers, and driven keys.

The new Alembic Format: Allows you to exchange complex 3D data (animation and simulation) through application-independent baked geometry. Baking is the process of rendering lighting, shading, and texture data to an image file that is mapped onto a model or an environment. It also reduces the overhead and loss of interactivity associated with transferring fully editable scene data. It is an open source CG interchange framework format.

File Referencing Enhancements: Improves the user interface and underlying architecture for file referencing that helps to manage the work with complex scenes simultaneously. Outliner now includes a Reference Node display option that allows you to locate and indentify all file references in a scene. This option is enabled by default. In addition, you can view the hierarchy of the unloaded references in a scene without loading the reference using the new Preview unloaded content option.

<u>Trax Clip Matching:</u> Allows you to define and offset object that is used to align the movements in an animation sequence when manipulating clips of animation in Trax Editor.

<u>Retime Tool:</u> Allows you to directly adjust the timing of key movements in an animation sequence in Graph Editor. You can use this tool to work with pose-to-pose animation. You can retime an animation segment by adding retime markers in the graph view area. Graph Editor also introduces a stepped preview mode.

<u>Extrude Command Enhancements:</u> Incorporates a number of enhancements to the Extrude command, such as Thickness, Offset, and Division. Its precision settings are similar to that of Channel Box. The sliders that have been removed limits to a maximum or minimum value. Additionally, the background color is added to labels for improved readability. You can also use the CTRL and SHIFT keys to adjust values with varying speeds.

<u>Node Editor:</u> Allows you to view, modify and create new node connections in Maya. The Node Editor displays nodes and the connections between their attributes. The GPU Cache node converts Alembic files into light-weight, non-editable form directly on the GPU that allows you to create and work with more complex scenes.

<u>Playblast Improvements:</u> Supports the H.264 Quicktime output on Windows 64-bit along with audio and multi-track audio.

<u>Free Image Plane:</u> Allows you to create a free image plane, which is an image plane that is not attached to the camera. You can select and transform a free image plane in your scene.

<u>Mental ray Improvements:</u> Allows you to render GPU cached Alembic files using the mental ray renderer. The mental ray renderer also supports baked diffuse color information of the Alembic files that are created using the GPU cache. Maya 2013 now uses the mental ray renderer version 3.10.

Understanding the 3D Workflow

You need to know how 3D contents are used in movies. As you can understand, the scene that you can not create and shoot using conventional video shooting, you can create that in the 3D creating software. The second thing that even film producers do not let the people know is 3D creation reduces the cost of film making. 3D movies earn huge benefits because people love to watch those movies feeling virtual reality wearing 3D glasses. And even now-a-days, 3D enabled theatres that create some extra effects (rain, smoke, chair movements) inside the auditorium are attracting more audience exaggerating 3D movies as 4D.

The workflow for creating a 3D content is quite similar to live action movie. There are three main production stages in live action films, namely: preproduction, production, and post-production. Pre-production stage involves story boarding, casting, setting up the sets, and finalizing the locations. In the production stage, the actual shooting is performed; adding audio/video effects, editing, and composing are performed in the post-production stage. The 3D workflow follows a similar procedure with few variations.

Preproduction 3D Stage
The preproduction stage for a CG animation involves assembling reference materials, model sketches, layout drawings, and motion tests together to make the actual CG production hassle free. It is the most important in the line-up to develop 3D content of CG production. In this stage, you can create an outline of a project, including research and development, scope, conceptualization, storyboarding, and animatics (animated storyboards). It is already proved that a sincere approach in the preproduction stage ensures a good quality 3D content. Prior to developing the 3D content for a movie, you must create a theme or story called a script. As the script forms the basis of the story and includes the description of each of the characters, dialogues, and timings, it should be well defined and complete with all the details.

Production 3D Stage
As you know that all characters, backgrounds, props, and other objects are created using the 3D software, such as Maya and 3ds Max. The process of creating 3D objects, characters, and props is known as modeling and the created objects are called 3D models. Once the models are created, they are applied with appropriate textures and lights based on the story. After that, the live characters in the story are animated. At the end, the movie is rendered using the rendering process, which transforms all 3D representations to 2D images or image sequences.

Post-Production 3D Stage
This stage involves compositing, editing, and adding soundtrack to the final rendered movies. The process of combining or merging two or more layers is known as compositing. For instance, to create a scene in Maya to move a ball in a zero gravity environment; you can shoot the ball with a pure green or blue background and the space environment, separately. Using these two separate footages, you can create an illusion of the ball as part of the environment and include in the same scene. Using software such as Combustion or Final Cut-Pro (FCP), you can remove the green or blue background from the ball footage and composite it on the space footage.

Editing involves selecting and combining shots into sequences and ultimately creating a complete movie. It is the art of storytelling and crucial part of the 3D workflow that requires a substantial amount of time and a great deal of precision. The sound that you apply in the animation must complement the theme or story of the animation. Sound effects are artificially created sounds or enhanced sounds to emphasize the overall impact of an animation. In certain cases, dialogues are assigned to characters in an animation. The dialogues are included in the 3D graphical content by lip-syncing, which is a process of synchronizing the lip movements of the characters with the dialogues. To do this, you must first record the dialogues, and then animate the lips and facial expressions of the characters, so that they appear to speak.

Lesson 2
User Interface of Maya
To utilize the advantages of the Maya functionalities, a thorough knowledge of all the tools is essential. You can go ahead and launch Maya by selecting Start> All Programs> Autodesk> Autodesk Maya 2013. Maya UI includes various elements including Tool Box, editors (Channel Box/Layer Editor), Shelf, Status Line, Playback Controls, and the viewport. All the UI elements are placed around the centrally placed viewport. To make the UI less complicated, few elements such as Attribute Editor and Outline are hidden, by default. You can display these hidden elements when required. You can also access a special

context-based menu know as Hotbox. It refers to the method of accessing menu items and tools at the current cursor position on the screen. To access the Hotbox, you can press and hold the Spacebar key. You can also use the marking menu, which is a context sensitive menu to access specific menus. This menu appears if you press and hold the right mouse button. To understand to user interface of more efficiently, you need to do a lot of practice.

As you saw in picture 1.1 and now you can see on your computer screen, the Title bar appears above the Maya window and displays the name of the application and the name of the currently opened scene. The main menu bar, Status Line, and the Shelf are arranged in a sequence and are located below the Title bar. On the extreme left, there is Tool Box, and on the extreme right, there is Channel Box and Layer Editor. Time Slider, Range Slider, Command Line, and Help Line (last row at the bottom); appear at the bottom of the UI. At the center of the screen, you have a viewport or workspace. Apart from these elements, other frequently used elements are Attribute Editor, Outliner, Hotbox, marking menus, and Asset Editor.

Menus and Menu Sets

In Maya, you have two types of menu to make selections. The types of menu are – main menu and panel menu. The main menu (which is a bar) appears below the Title bar of the Maya window and the panel

menu appears on each panel. Menus in the options windows are also called panel menus or individual menus. The main menu bar contains context-sensitive menu items and submenus. The menu items and submenus on the main menu bar vary depending on the active menu set. Based on the kind of work you do, you can select the menu set appearing at the start of Status Line. For example, in the Status Line, if you click the first option Animation, the available menu sets that you will get are Animation, Polygons, Surfaces, Dynamics, Rendering, and nDynamics, as shown in picture 1.2.

Picture 1.2

You can also customize a menu set using the Customize option in the menu selector drop-down list which is a button beside the world Animation, shown in the picture 1.2. The menus sets and their respective submenus are organized based on the task they are designed to perform. For example, the polygons menu set includes the menus and submenus that are used to create and modify polygonal objects. You can also access menu sets using the hotkeys. For instance, pressing the F3 function key selects the Polygons menu set. The table below is showing a brief description of the menu sets and their hotkeys. Instead of going a long way, you can use the hotkeys (shortcut) to select the desired option, as animators like to do. Starting from F2 to F6, all the shortcut are mentioned with their respective options. In this Table, the word NURBS stands for Non-Uniform Rational B-Spline.

Menu Set	Description	Hotkeys
Animation	Provides menus to animate objects.	F2
Polygons	Provides menus to work with polygon objects.	F3
Surfaces	Provides menus to work with NURBS curves and objects.	F4
Dynamics	Provides menus to work with deformers, particles, and fluids.	F5
Rendering	Provides menus to render Maya scenes.	F6
nDynamics	Provides menus to work with nCloth, soft/rigid bodies, and complex deformers.	

Static and Specific Menus

Now we're going in depth to know about the types of menus. Maya has two types of menus in the main menu bar which are – Static and Specific. Static menus or common menus are always available as they do not change if you select another menu set. Static menus include File, Edit, Modify, Create, Display, Window, Assets, and Help, as shown in picture 1.3.

File Edit Modify Create Display Window Assets Animate Geometry Cache Create Deformers Edit Deformers Skeleton Skin Constrain Character Help

Picture 1.3

But Specific menus change when you change the menu sets. As you can see in the picture, the menus such as Animate, Geometry Cache, Create Deformers, Edit Deformers, Skeleton, Skin, Constrain, Character, Muscle, and Pipeline Cache are specific menus that appear on selecting the Animation menu set. In Maya, few plug-ins help to add menu items to the main menu bar. If the plug-in is turned off, the respective menu item is removed. Both the Static and Specific menus contain options and submenus. The menu item below the Specific menus shows two different demarcations: arrow head and rectangular box. The rectangular box is called Options box. Arrow heads indicate that the menu item includes submenus. When you click an arrow head, various submenus appear. But Option box includes options for a tool which appear in a separate window. For instance, if you select Create> Text> Option box from the main menu bar, the Text Curves Options window appears with various options such as Font, Text, and Type.

One thing that you may like is that you can also place menus on a floating window, by detaching the menus from the main menu bar. In these floating menus, you can place the frequently used menus without having to access the same menu repeatedly. Supposing you need to access the Polygon Primitives menu frequently to create various polygon primitives, so you can separate the menu from the main menu bar to create a floating window and place it anywhere in the UI. To tear off a menu, move the mouse pointer over the dashed line which is called the Tear off line above the menu or submenu, and click it when it turns blue.

Status Line

As you saw in picture 1.1, the entire horizontal bar just below the main menu bar is called Status Line. It contains logically grouped icons, which represent shortcuts for most menu items and tools. Status Line begins with the menu selector dropdown list for selecting a menu set. There are shortcuts to create new scenes, open existing scenes, and save scenes. In addition, there are tools that you can use to set up options for object selection and snapping.

Shelf

Shelf is placed below Status Line in the Maya window. There are number of tabs in Shelf, each representing an individual Shelf. They contain sets of frequently used tools based on different workflows for single-click access. Shelves save the last used preferences. So, on starting Maya, the shelf used the last time becomes active and General tab is selected by default. To select another shelf, you can click the other tab. You can also see that the last tab is Custom, which is empty by default. You can add the frequently used icons and tools into it. The guidelines mentioned below are important to work with Shelf. Even if you roll the mouse pointer over an icon, a tooltip appears with information (the name) about that tool. You can perform the steps mentioned below to understanding the basic functions of Shelf in Maya.

1. To add a menu item in Shelf, press Ctrl+Shift keys together and select the menu item from the main menu bar.
2. To remove an icon from Shelf, press the middle mouse button and drag the icon to the Trash icon located on the top-right corner of Shelf.
3. To see any hidden icon of a particular shelf, click the up and down arrows located on the right side of Shelf.

Tool Box
You can find the Tool Box on the far left of the Maya window. It is a set of nine buttons which contains the most frequently used tools including Select Tool, Lasso Tool, Paint Selection Tool, Move Tool, Rotate Tool, Scale Tool, Universal Manipulator, Soft Modification Tool, and Show Manipulator Tool. You can use the Q, W, E, R, T, Y hotkeys to toggle the selection between various tools. For example – Select Tool (Q), Move Tool (W), Rotate Tool (E), Scale Tool (R), Show Manipulator Tool (T), or access the last used tool (Y). Tool Box also provides Quick Layout buttons to quickly change the viewport layout. All these buttons are pre-configured based on the Maya viewport.

Viewport
The picture 1.4 is displaying below the large grey area in the middle of the Maya window which is viewport or workspace. The all types of creation and modeling works are done in this viewport selecting the desired options.

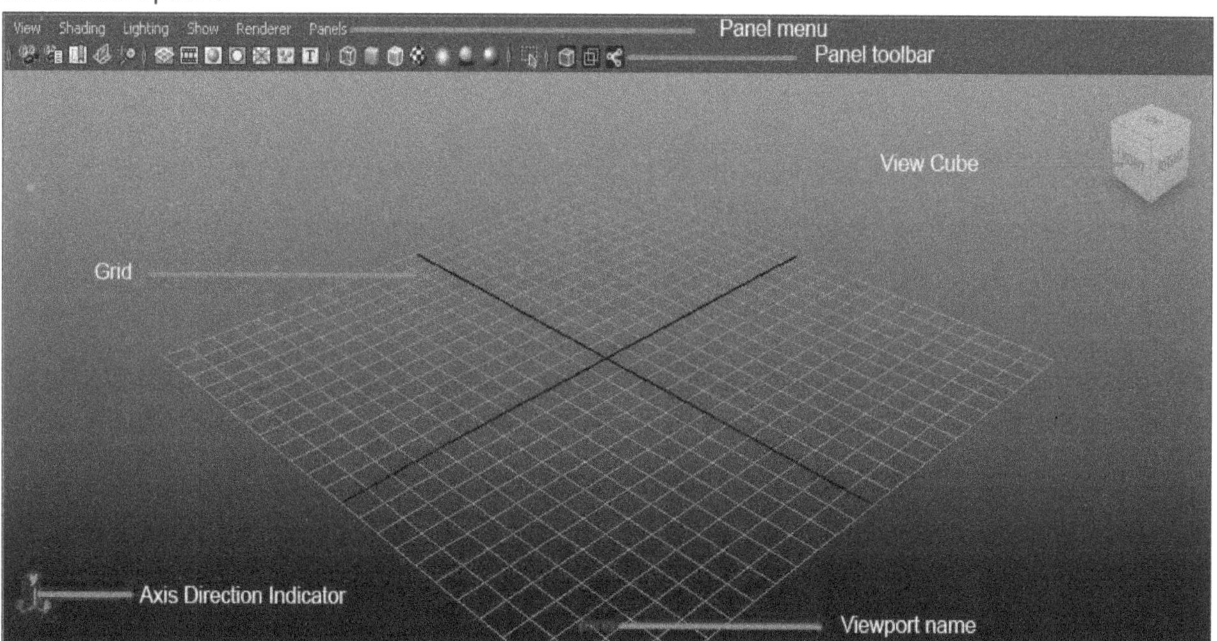

Picture 1.4

You can create and evaluate a scene or you can create, modify, texture, and animate objects in the viewport. There are two types of viewports in Maya – Perspective and Orthographic (top, front, and side). The orthographic views provide 2D representations of the entire scene. The scene is viewed from the Y-axis in the top view; from the Z-axis in the front view; and from the X-axis in the side view. Maya follows the 3D coordinate system that has three axes – X, y, and Z. Each axis represents a direction perpendicular to the other two axes to present a 3D view of an object. By default, the perspective viewport, which is named persp is selected on creating a new scene, as shown in picture 1.4.

If you want to display the viewport in four views, you can select Panel> Layouts> Four Panes from the panel toolbar, but that is only when it is required. The picture 1.5 shows the viewport in four views. It includes perspective, top, front, and side. On your screen, you'll also see all the elements such as panel menu, panel toolbar, ViewCube, and Axis Direction Indicator appear for each viewport.

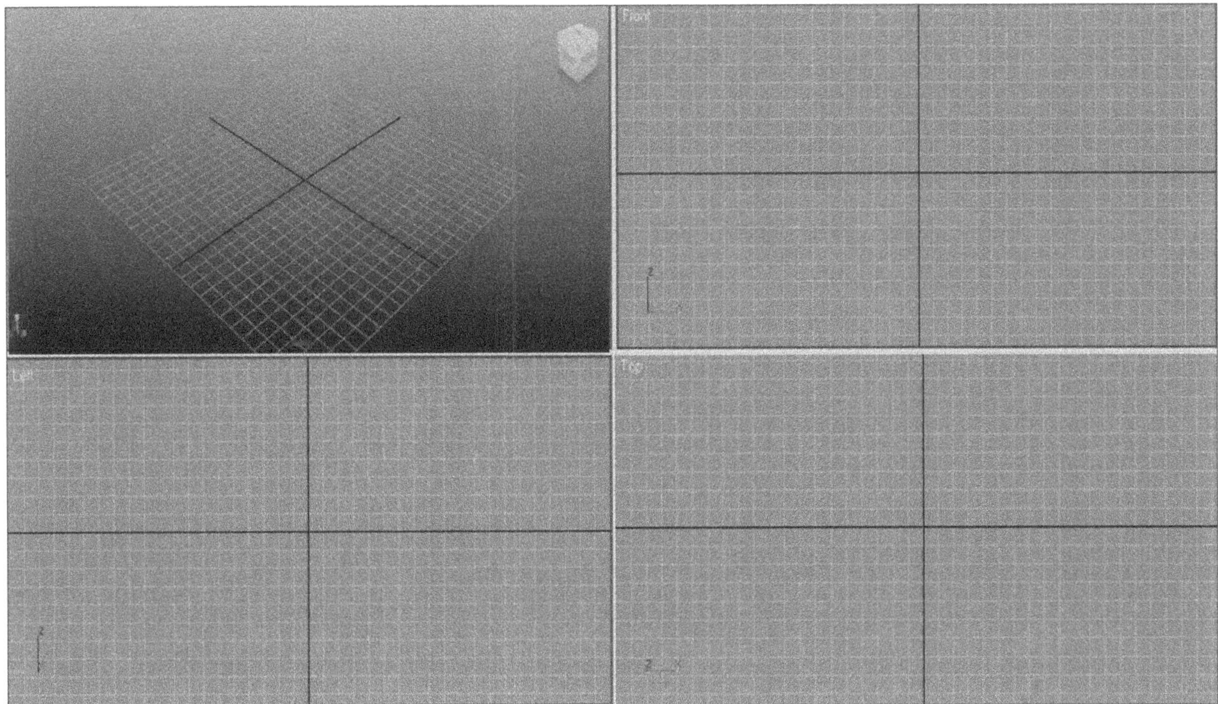

Picture 1.5

Panel menu includes View, Shading, Lighting, Show, Renderer, and Panels. If you don't see panel menu, you can enable it in the Preference window. In the Interface category, select the In Panel check box to display the panel menu and panel toolbar. One of the essential tools in Maya is ViewCube. It is a navigation element that appears at the upper-right corner of an active view. ViewCube provides visual display of the current camera content in the relation to the 3D scene and allows you to switch easily between scene views. To switch between camera views, click the faces, corner and edges of ViewCube. In total you can have 26 views on ViewCube (6 face views, 8 corner views, and 12 edge views). You can click the Home icon to move to the default active view. At the time of creating a 3D content, you may require a bigger monitor to have a better view of your content.

Channel Box and Layer Editor
When an object is selected, its name appears at the top of Channel Box followed by attributes. You can see Channel Box and Layer Editor on the right of your viewport, as shown in picture 1.6. It lists object attributes (also called channels) and input and output connections. These attributes are most commonly animated and used for keyframing. You can also rename an object in Channel Box. To the right of each attribute, a text box appears to specify its value. The shape node, input node, and output node appear below the attributes.

If you select a polygon cube in the viewport, the Channel Box will display the attributes of a polygon cube (polyCube 1) in three sections – polyCube 1, SHAPES, and INPUTS. The polyCube1 section represents the transform node of an object and its visibility. When you transform an object, the respective values in Channel Box change. You can also type values to modify an object. To hide an object, type 'off' in the visibility text box. The second section SHAPES is related to the shape node and displays nodes that define the shape of an object. The third section INPUTS displays the nodes that

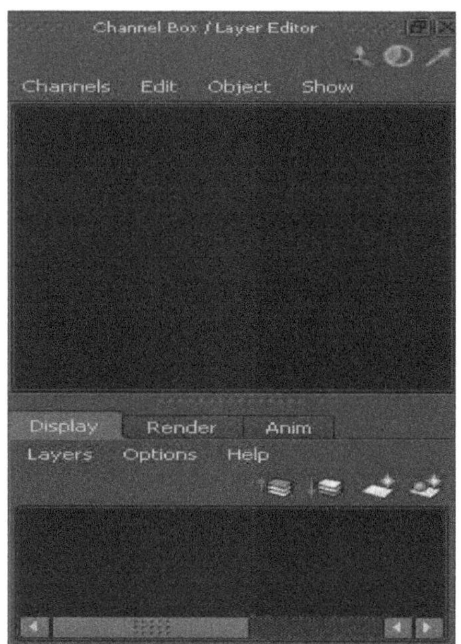

affect an object and contains various attributes specific to the selected object. In case you don't see Channel Box and Layer Editor, you can select Display> UI Elements> Channel Box/Layer Editor from the main menu bar to display them. Now we can discuss about Layer Editor which you can find just below the Channel Box, showing in picture 1.6.

Layer Editor organizes objects in a scene using layers. You can create new empty layers as well as layers with selected objects. You can also change layer stacking order using various buttons present in Layer Editor. There are three types of layers in Maya – Display, Render, and Anim (Animation). These layers are organized in different tabs in Layer Editor. The Display tab is selected in the Layer Editor, by default. The Display tab helps you to manage Display layers; the Render tab helps you to work with Render layers; and the Anim tab helps you to manage Anim layers. Maya uses Render layers to set up render passes and Anim layers to use separate animations on the objects.

Picture 1.6

Time Slider and Range Slider

On your computer, you can find Time Slider and Range Slider below the viewport and at the bottom of Maya screen. These two UI elements are used to animate objects and control playback options. You can also use Time Slider to quickly move through an animation. Time Slider shows the time range as defined by Range Slider, the current time, and the keys on selected objects or characters, as shown in the picture 1.7 below. You can drag these sliders right and left to adjust the animation speed and various other things.

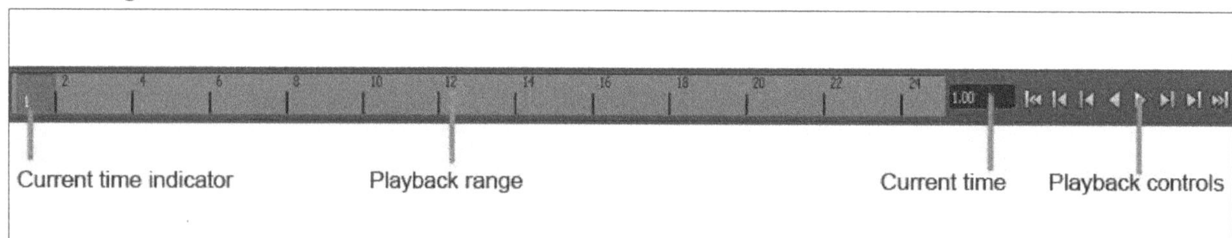

Picture 1.7

You can see in this picture that Time Slider has a playback range, current time indicator (CTI), current time field, key ticks and playback controls. Key ticks represent the keys to set for an object. The current time indicator is a gray block in the playback range showing the current frame in an animation. You can drag it to move forward or backward in the animation. The current frame can also be viewed in the current time field. Playback controls is located on the right of Time Slider and used to perform several actions, such as playing an animation, moving back to a previous frame, and going to the start of the playback range.

You can find Range Slider just below the Time Slider. It is used to adjust the range of animation playback. You can set the start and end time of an animation and playback range. Before moving ahead, you can have a look at some important elements of Range Slider:

Set the start time of the animation: Sets the start time of an animation.

Set the start time of the playback range: Sets the start time of a playback range.

Range slider bar: Displays the playback range of an animation.

Set the end time of the playback range: Allows you to view and enter the end time of a playback range.

Set the end time of the animation: Allows you to view and enter the end time of an animation.

Auto keyframe toggle: Sets the keyframe automatically, when you make any modifications in the scene, such as changing the time or an attribute.

Animation preferences: Allows you to specify the animation-related settings such as Time Slider settings and Playback settings.

Command Line and Help Line
Command Line appears right below Ranger Slider, and just below that you can find Help Line at the bottom of Maya screen. Command Line allows you to execute single MEL (Maya Embeded Language) or Python commands without opening Script Editor. You can toggle MEL and Python mode by clicking the MEL/Python button. Even action that you perform in Maya invokes an MEL command or script that runs a particular function. All the animation applications like Adobe Flash, 3ds Max, and Maya have their programming languages (script). In Maya, you can type a MEL command in the text box that appears on the left of Command Line and press enter key to execute the task. The output of the command is displayed in the command feedback area.

Help Line, which is at the far bottom in the last row, shows the information about a selected UI element or tool. For example, if you place the mouse pointer on Polygon Sphere Tool, the message displayed is Polygon Sphere: Create a polygon sphere on the grid. Help Line also shows different kinds of messages, tips, and instructions when you select a tool or action. It instructs you about the command that you select on Maya screen.

Outliner
Outliner is hidden by default in Maya screen. To open it, you can select Window> Outliner from the main menu bar. Outliner works as a scene manager and displays a hierarchical list of all objects in a scene. In a complex scene with hundreds of objects, it becomes very challenging to select objects. For that reason, you can use Outliner to select objects. It exposes every single object of a Maya scene. You can also use it to create a parent-child hierarchy between tow objects. The picture 1.8 shows the Outliner which when you open on your screen; will display the list of objects in the order that they are created.

Picture 1.8

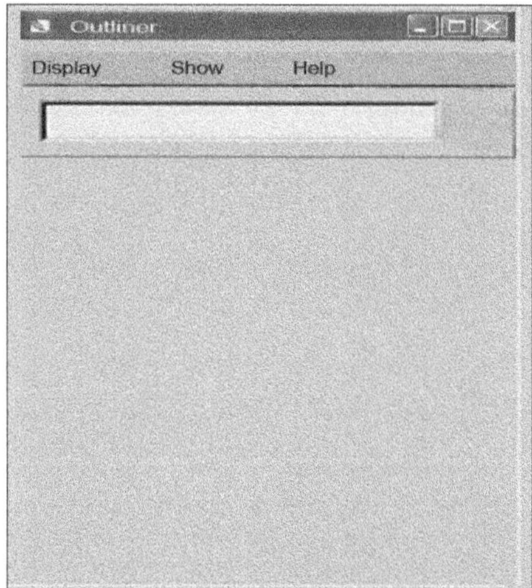

When you are working in a particular scene in Maya, you can activate Outliner which will show the list of all the objects of the scene. If you want to select an object in the Outliner, you can click its name. You can also rename objects in Outliner by double-clicking the name of an object. Using the divider bar at the bottom of the Outliner window, you can see the outline of an object in two separate views. By dragging the divider bar upward or downward, you can display two views.

Attribute Editor

Similar to Channel Box, Attribute Editor lists the attributes of an object. Attribute Editor is used very commonly in Maya. It helps to conveniently access all the attributes related to the selected object. However, unlike Channel Box, which provides access to only the important attributes of an object, Attribute Editor provides access to all attributes of an object. By default it is hidden, but you can display it by selecting Display> UI Elements> Attribute Editor from

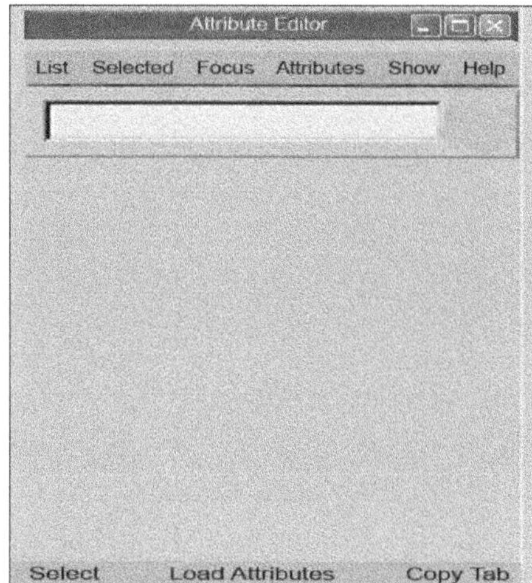

the main menu bar. You can also display it by going to Window> Attribute Editor from the main menu bar. And even clicking the Show or hide the Attribute Editor icon on Status Line also displays the Attribute Editor in Maya screen. The picture 1.9 shows the Attribute Editor which you can find on the right of the Maya screen replacing Channel Box/Layer Editor.

Attribute Editor shows the attribute of a selected object. It has a menu bar at the top and several tabs representing the available nodes of the object that you'll select. You can select any of the preceding tabs to view or modify attributes. And you can also configure Attribute Editor to open as a separate window by selecting Window> Preferences> UI Elements and deselect the Attribute Editor check box.

Picture 1.9

Now for example, if you go ahead and select a polygon cube in the viewport of Maya screen, it will show the tabs that are listed below:

pCube1: Represents the transform or Directed Acyclic Graph (DAG) node of an object attributes related to the transformation, such as the position, rotation, and scaling of the object appear in this tab.

pCubeShape1: Represents the shape node of an object. The attributes related to the geometrical shape of the object appear in this tab. But some objects like 'line curve' might not have the shape node.

polyCube1: Displays the poly cube history such as dimensions.

Initial Shading Group: Provides common attributes for the default shading material of an object.

lambert1: Shows Lambert shading material which is the default shading material of an object in Maya.

Asset Editor

Asset Editor does not appear in the viewport by default, but you have to select it by going to Outliner> Hypergraph Connections Editor> Asset Editor. An asset is a special type of node used to encapsulate sets of related nodes called container. For example, if a scene is with many nodes and attributes, assets become a key organizational tool. Using this tool you can package nodes together and expose only those preferred attributes. Asset Editor allows you to view, modify, and organize the objects in a scene in the form of assets. You can see it by selecting Window> General Editors> Asset Editor or Asset> Asset Editor from the main menu bar. You can find a menu bar at the top of Asset Editor containing menus to create container nodes, publish node attributes to the container nodes, assign new templates, and lock attributes, so that they cannot be edited. A template is an external file that specifies a common interface that can be applied to multiple assets and accessed from the Maya UI.

When you open Asset Editor on your screen, you can see two vertical panels in it. The left panel displays all the containers created for a scene along with the nodes of the objects and the attributes of these nodes. You can use the left panel to view the container, internal nodes and their attributes, and publish the attributes to the container node. You can use the right panel to bind or unbind the published attributes of the nodes from the published names.

At times, you may have to create a new container, and for that you can go to Assets> Create Container from the Asset Editor menu bar. The thing you can keep in mind that newly created nodes are automatically placed in the current container.

Hotbox and Marking Menu

When you are working in a complex scene, you may need a shortcut that can significantly speed up the work. For that, you have Hotbox and Marking Menus that enable you to assess menu items and tools at the cursor position. To display the Hotbox, you can press and hold down the Spacebar key, as shown in picture 2.0. When you do it on your system, the Hotbox appears with menus based on the currently selected menu set. The Hotbox has four thick diagonal lines on its periphery, which divide it into five different regions – North, East, South, West, and Center. When you click any of these regions, another set of menus called marking menus are displayed. If you want to hide the Hotbox, you can release the Spacebar key.

Now you'll notice one thing that Marking menus vary based on the selected Hotbox region. They help to conveniently access the commonly used features and tools. They also appear on right-clicking an object. You can also access additional features such as selection modes and shading materials using marking menus. I am sure you need to work on Hotbox to understand its basic functions, but just keep that in mind that it is only to speed up the work. Even if you don't learn about it, you can still work in Maya. For the professionals who love to work using Hotbox, here is a list containing a brief description of the marking menus in different Hotbox regions:

Hotbox Regions	Description of Marking Menu
Center	Allows switching between the perspective and three orthographic views of a scene.
North	Allows you to select a layout for a scene.
East	Allows you to show or hide different UI elements such as Status Line and Shelf.
South	Allows you to display a window (such as Outliner) in place of the current window.
West	Allows you to work with the different selection masks and selection modes.

The picture 2.0 shown below displays the Hotbox where you can lick on required option without going into menu bar and looking for the other sub-option.

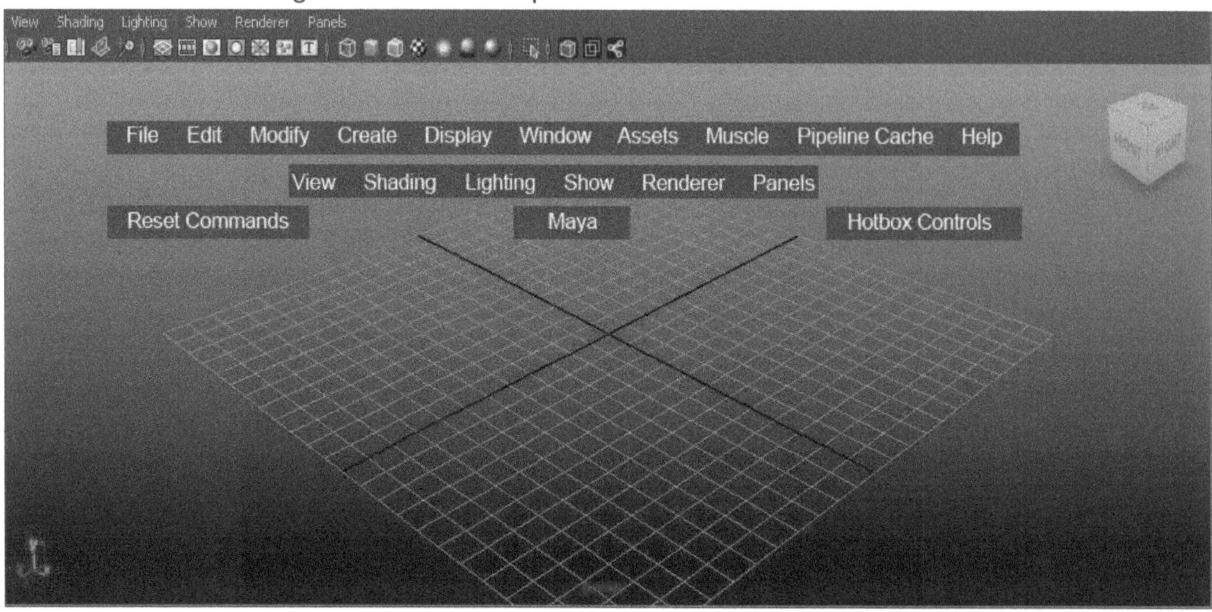

Picture 2.0

Lesson 3
Knowing about Maya Preferences

This lesson is going to introduce to you the numerous program-related settings of Maya. Till now, you have seen all the UI related settings. The program-related settings are known as preferences, which allow you to customize tasks performed in Maya. You can set these preferences as required to enhance productivity. Preferences settings are saved every time you close the application. You can also modify the preference settings using the Preference window. In the Preference window, click the required category of preferences on the left panel to display the associated settings. Then, edit the required settings. Customizing Maya is easy, productive, and efficient if you are familiar with the application. You must know the preferences settings, or else it might cause problems. If you find that the settings that you changed are causing problems, you can set default preferences to restore the original settings using the Restore UI Elements feature.

Changing Default Settings

Maya is such software that allows you to customize every tool and option. For example, you can tear off menus and change the settings of every tool using the Options box. To customize settings, you can select Window> Settings/Preferences> Preferences from the main menu bar. On the left of the Preferences window, there are various categories and on the right their respective preference settings. You can change any of the preference settings and to apply them, click the Save button. Changing default settings in your way makes the interface friendly to you. Now here is what you can do to change Maya default settings. As you read the steps, you must perform the same on your computer system without fully depending on the pictures shown in this book because Maya is such a huge application that giving pictures of every move is quite difficult. Let's perform these steps to change the Maya default settings:

1. Select **Window**> **Settings/Preferences**> **Preferences** from the main menu bar to open the Preferences window.

2. Select a category in the Categories pane. For now, we can select **Display**.

3. Make the required changes. In our case, we have selected the **Hide** radio button for the **Grid plane** setting in the **View** section.

4. Click the **Save** button to apply the change, as shown in picture 2.1. This hides the grid on the active viewport in Maya screen.

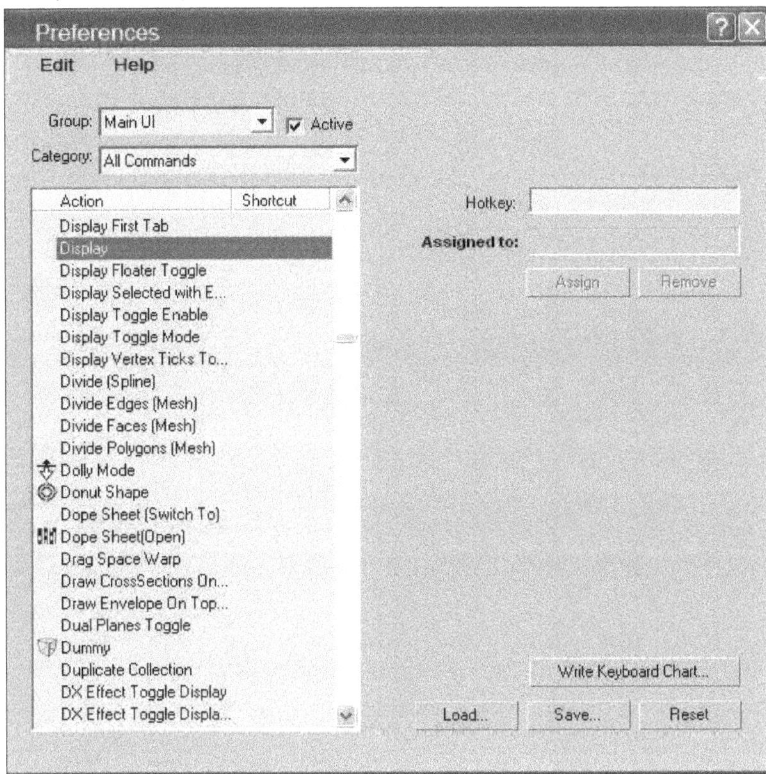

Picture 2.1

Restoring Default Settings

Now you are going to learn about restoring default settings. In few cases, you customize the default settings in Maya by defining a shortcut key for a particular command or changing the display of UI elements. But you can also restore the default settings using the Preferences window. Maya, the gigantic application has several tools, different menus, and submenus. So it is difficult to remember all the default settings. You can also revert to the last saved preference settings as it was when you launched Maya for the first time. It is a kind of undo command for default settings at the time when you are lost doing things that you were not supposed to do. Let's perform the steps mentioned below to restore Maya's default settings:

1. Go to **Preferences** window, and select **Edit**> **Restore Default Settings**.
2. Click **Save** button to save the default settings. It'll bring the grid back in the viewport and everything will look same as it was.

Stepping into Projects and Scenes

When you make a project in Maya, it saves with a collection of folders for different types of files. If you save a scene file to any location on your computer, it can be very complex because a Maya scene file might have separate source directories – such as textures and images. In that case, project management becomes critical. Whenever a project is created in Maya, different types of folders, such as Scenes, images, and Textures for different file types are created. These folders contain various types of files used in a scene. Maya provides a standard folder structure that helps to organize multiple scene files and files present in a project.

Creating a New Project

Maya is very specific about organizing files of a project that you create. When a project is created, all the files of the scene are stored in a separate folder. Projects in Maya assemble and organize the files pertaining to a particular scene. The reason is that, when you select Open to open a scene, Maya has to work in the background with all the assembled files to open the scene in the organized way. After you open Maya, here are the steps to create a project:

1. Go to **File** and select **Project Window** from the main menu bar. The Project Window appears as shown in picture 2.2.

Picture 2.2

The current project name is written as default that you can change by typing a new name. You can also change the location of the new project by clicking the Browse button (a folder icon). For now, you do not need to change the name or location for convenience.

2. Click the **New** button beside the Current Project text box. The Current Project text box becomes active and the project name is changed to **New_Project** by default.

3. Type a new name in the Current Project text box. In our case, we type **Race_Project** as the current project name.

4. Click the **Accept** button at the bottom of the window. By clicking Accept button at the end, you save your project in Maya.

If you want, you can specify the location by clicking the folder icon and select a folder in the Select Location dialog box to save the different assets of the project. You can leave it unchanged also which will use the default location and the names for the folders will be automatically chosen. When you go to find the Race_Project folder in the selected location, you'll see two more folders (scenes and images) with it. The scenes folder is used to store all the scene files and the images folder is used to store all the rendered images.

Creating a New Scene

Whenever you start the Maya application, an untitled new scene is created automatically. Scenes are entities that represent a task created in Maya. They are stored in the files with the extension .mb (Maya binary) or .ma (Maya American Standard Code for Information Interchange or ASCII). You can also create a new scene by selecting File> New Scene from the main menu bar or pressing the Ctrl+N keys. Let's perform the following steps to crate a new scene:

1. Go to **File**> **New Scene** from the main menu bar. It automatically creates a blank scene with the current settings. If you're currently working on a scene, and use the New Scene command, a warning message appears with a confirmation to save or discard the existing scene.

2. You can click **Don't Save** button on the warning to discard the changes. If you click on Save, you'll need to specify scene settings such as working units, Time Slider settings, and the end time that appear for the scene.

Saving a Scene

It is very important to save a scene in Maya, because if you don't save a scene or task, you cannot reopen it. Any changes in a scene are temporarily stored in the memory, until you save it. To save a scene, you can select File> Save Scene from the main menu bar or press Ctrl+S keys together. Let's perform the following steps to save a scene:

1. **Create** a Maya scene and make some changes. Then select **File**> **Save Scene** from the main menu bar which will open **Save As** dialog box.

The scene is saved in the default project folder. As we have created a project (Race_Project) earlier, it automatically opens the scenes folder of the project. If you want to change the path of the file, you can select it in the Folder Bookmarks section. You can also select the project in which you want to save the scene in the Current Project section.

2. **Type** a name for the scene in the File name: text box. In our case, we type **Race_01**. Then click the **Save As** button to save the scene.

It saves the scene with the specified name and format in the scenes folder of the project. When you save, it selects the file type Maya Binary (.mb). If you want to save the scene in another format, select the format from the Files of type dropdown list in the Save As dialog box. Alternatively, you can save a scene in Maya ASCII format. To access the Save Scene Options window, you can select File> Save Scene> Rectangular Box from the main menu bar. In the same Save As Options window, you can put a check mark on Incremental Save check box, which will save a backup copy of the scene every time you save it.

Opening an Existing Maya Scene

It is recommended that you should keep Maya scenes at a safe location on the hard drive, so that you can easily access them for further modifications. It is also necessary that the scenes are saved in a project folder. To open an existing scene, you can select File> Open Scene or press Ctrl+O keys together. It opens a dialog box where you can browse the directory and select the scene. In our case, we select the Race_01.mb scene to open. In order to close Maya 2013, you can go to File> Exit from the main menu bar or press Ctrl+Q keys together.

Lesson 4
Creating Objects

The dynamic application Maya has a virtual 3D space to create objects similar to ones existing in the real world. As whatever we see in real world is an object. Similarly in the virtual 3D space of Maya, everything is created using geometry objects which are represented by a collection of points in 3D space. There is a collection of predefined objects known as primitive objects or just primitives such as cube, sphere, cone, pyramid, prism, and cylinder. Using these primitives as the starting point, we create any kind of more complex models in Maya. For example, for creating a human head model, you can use a sphere or a cube as the starting point to modify. There are different types of primitive objects in Maya like polygons, Non-Uniform Rational B-Spline (NURBS), subdivisions, lights, and cameras. You'll learn several methods to create and modify these objects. After creating an object, you can select and transform it to modify its attributes. You can also create identical copies by duplicating an existing object. In the viewport, you can create and modify objects, and you can also navigate by dollying, tracking, and tumbling which are the important aspects in Maya. Apart from navigation, you'll use several other features while modifying objects.

Insight of Virtual 3D Space

If you can view an object from 360 degrees, then the object is considered in 3D space. The virtual 3D space is a geometrical model that represents the physical universe allowing you to measure every object by length, width, and height. In real world, you encounter several 3D objects such as books, computer, and 3D spaces such as universe. You can determine the position of an object by measuring it with respect to another object or to a point in space. In the digital world, artists create images and sequences of images using tools such as shape, form, color, texture, and time. In Maya, you can recreate real-world objects in 3D using colors, textures, and lights. The picture 2.3 shows an object defined in 2D and 3D spaces. The 2D space has two axes – X and Y, and the 3D space has three axes in which Z axis represents the depth of the object.

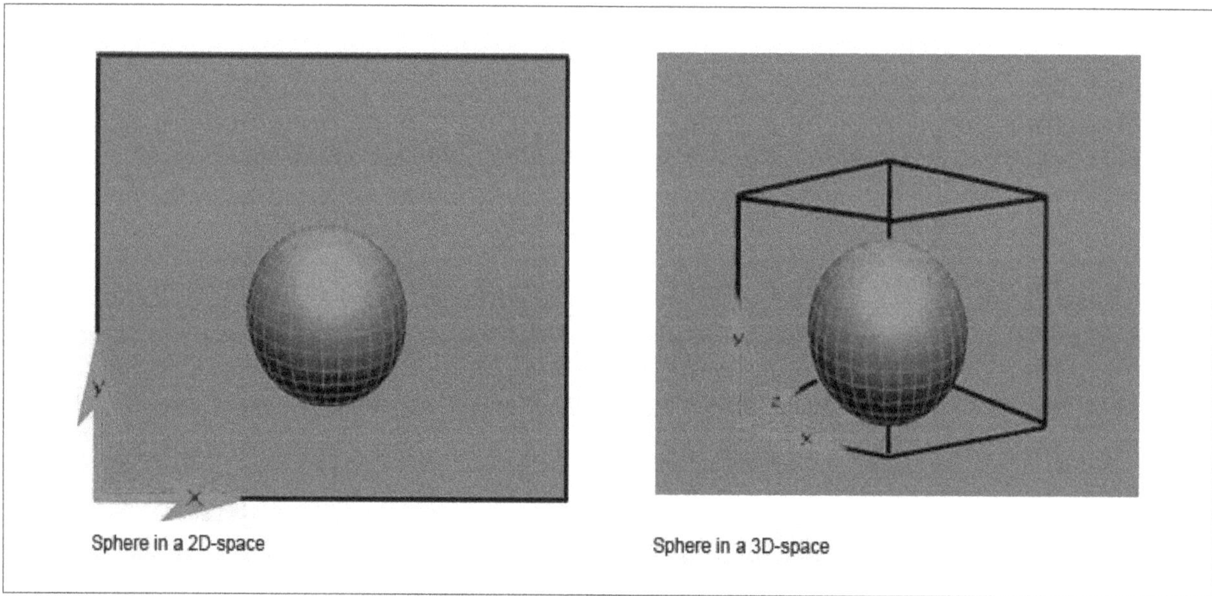

Picture 2.3

The picture shown above explains the 3D space. In the next section, you're going to learn about XYZ Coordinate System.

XYZ Coordinate System

In 3D space of Maya the width is represented by the X-axis, the height is represented by the Y-axis, and the depth is represented by the Z-axis. You can find any point in the 3D space by defining a coordinate for each of these axes. When you look at your viewport in Maya, you'll see different colors representing these three axes, in which red is for the X-axis, green is for the Y-axis, and blue is for the Z-axis. The picture 2.4 shows an object with axis indicators in the perspective viewport. The axis indicators help you to visualize an object coordinate. Points in a 3D coordinate system are measured against an origin, which appears at the center point of the grid. The origin is assigned a value of (0, 0, and 0); these are the values for X, Y, and Z coordinates, respectively.

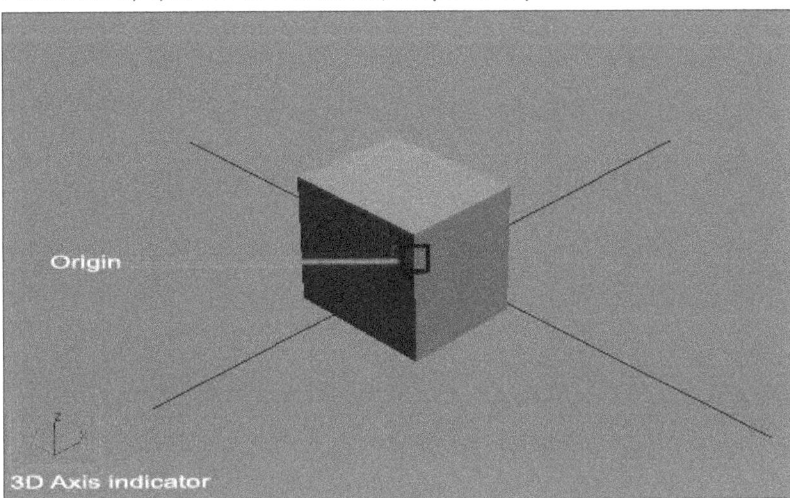

Picture 2.4

Perspective Projection

When you visualize objects in real world, you do not need to think about axes and 3D coordinates. You just see the objects in a perspective view; the farther you see them, the smaller they become. In 3D application such as Maya, using the perspective view, you can visualize a 3D space similar to the real world. The perspective view is automatically computed based on the camera position and the view angle. The perspective view is used to compose a final shot for rendering.

At the time of creating, manipulating, and viewing 3D objects or particles or animations, both perspective and orthographic views are used. In the perspective view, you can rotate, dolly (a technique used to smoothly move the camera in Maya), and pan a view. Navigation in these views involves a combination of mouse button and keyboard key.

To rotate the view, hold the Alt key + left mouse button and move the mouse.
To pan the view, hold the Alt key + middle-mouse button and move the mouse.
To zoom in and zoom out, hold the Alt key + right mouse button and move the mouse up or down.

Orthographic Projections

A perspective projection helps you to compose a shot but it does not allow you to calculate the dimensions of an object precisely. So it is not always the ideal projection for modeling and animating objects. To work efficiently in Maya, you need to use orthographic projections that allow you to analyze a scene using parallel projections of two axes simultaneously. Using these projections, you can accurately determine the position of an object. Professional animators use the perspective projection to compose a shot in Maya, while orthographic projections are used for references. In orthographic projections, you can see top, front, and side views that allow you to dolly and pan the camera view.

To understand the orthographic views more clearly, first you can select Panel> Layouts> Four Panes from the panel toolbar, and then, go to Main menu bar and select Create> Systems> Biped. When Biped is selected, you can go to its Properties Panel and under the category of Body Type select the option Male. Now draw it in one (perspective) viewport, and your screen will look like the picture 2.5. In case you don't find Male option under Body Type, still you can draw the Biped in the viewport making it taller so that it can occupy the good length of the screen.

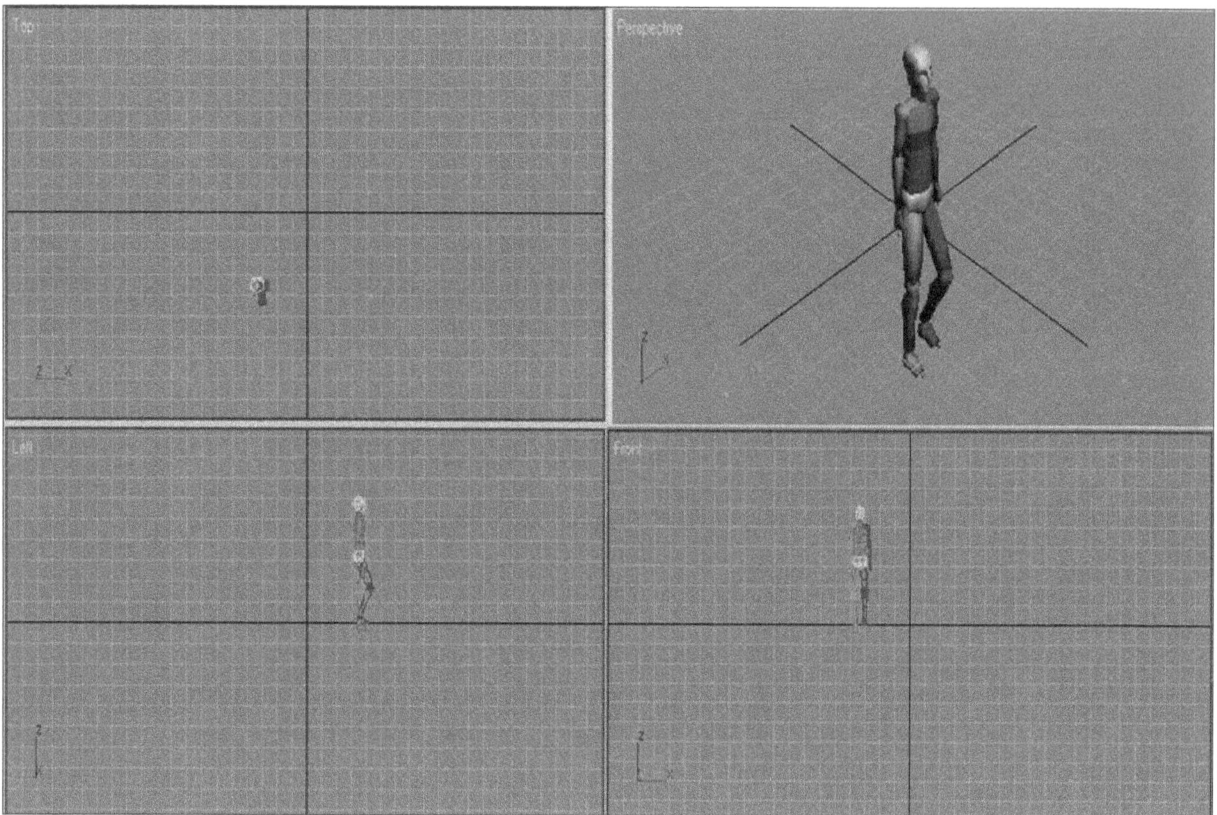

Picture 2.5

World Space and Local Space

The picture 2.5 will help you understand the world space, which is the most important coordinate system. It is for the entire scene with its origin in the center. In world space, all objects are positioned and animated in the grid, where the movement of objects and collisions between various objects are calculated. Grid is used as a reference to place objects in a scene. The picture 2.5 shows the grid in the world space axes. But local space is the coordinate system that uses the origin and axes of the parent node of an object to transform it. The origin of local space is at the pivot point of the object.

The fact is that both the world and local spaces are used for linking an object (parent) with another (child). This creates a hierarchy, where the parent objet determines the position of the parent-child group in world space. The attributes of a child object are controlled by its parent. A child object can be the parent of another child object. The child objects inherit this positioning from their parent objects and combine this with their own local space to determine their position. This parent-child relationship is used during the animation of an object, where keyframes can be set on both the child and the parent.

Lesson 5
Exploring Types of Objects

In this lesson, we're going to discuss about the basic objects in Maya. Almost all actions in Maya, such as modeling, texturing, animation, and rendering are performed on objects. Every object represents a geometry that exists separately in the 3D space. The most basic objects available in Maya are primitive objects. Primitives are the predefined objects that you can use to create more complex objects. For example, to create a human head model, you can use the polygon cube primitive object and gradually add complexity. With primitives, you can define the level of details, which is an advantage. For example, you can create a primitive with any number of subdivisions. When you select Create tab at the top in the Main menu bar, you'll have several options to create different types of objects by drawing them in the viewport. The primitive objects include – polygon, NURBS, subdiv (Subdivision surface), light, and camera. There are some objects shown in the picture 2.6 which may help you understand the basic of creating objects. You can try drawing some objects in your viewport and see how they look in different colors.

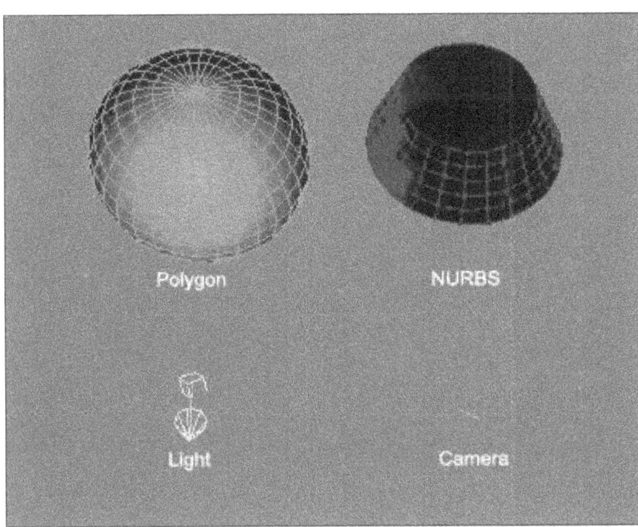

Picture 2.6

Polygons

A polygon consists of three components – vertex, edge, and face. It is a 2D closed shape made up of two or more points connected by straight paths known as segments. These segments are called edges or sides of the polygon; and the point where two edges meet are called the vertex. Polygons can be triangular, rectangular, hexagonal, or square in shape. You can create a polygonal object or mesh made up of a number of polygons. Modifying a mesh involves editing various components, such as – vertices, edges, or faces.

Vertex refers to the corner point of a polygon.
Edge refers to the edge of a polygon or the line connecting two polygons or vertices.
Face refers to the area covered by edges, and is the alternate name for polygon.

Polygon meshes are used to create models that require real-time streaming; for example, video games or Virtual Reality (computer-simulated environments that can replicate real world as well as the imaginary world environments). Polygons are important for polygonal modeling in Maya. In the next section you'll learn about NURBS objects.

Non-Uniform Rational B-Spline

The second type of objects in Maya is NURBS primitives. These objects are 3D geometric shapes defined using mathematical functions. NURBS is used to crate curves and surfaces. A NURBS curve or surface is parametric; the equations that describe it depend on variables (or parameters), which are not part of the geometry. The basic building blocks of a NURBS object are curves, as they help you to create smooth surfaces, such as a sphere or a tube without using many points. A NURBS curve has only one direction, which is U, while the NURBS surface has two directions – U and V. A NURBS surface contains different components such as CVs, isoparms, and hulls. Hull is a NURBS surface component that connects two CVs with a straight line. You can edit these components of a NURBS surface to transform it into different shapes. You can create models in Maya using NURBS curves and surfaces that you'll learn later from this book. You can convert a NURBS model into a polygon model selecting Modify> Convert> NURBS to Polygons from the main menu bar. You can also convert NURBS to subdiv, and polygons using same commands.

Subdivision Surfaces

Subdivision Surfaces are also called subdiv surfaces in Maya. Subdivs are surfaces created from a base polygon mesh in an iterative process (subdividing the polygon mesh). The modeling process uses the subdiv surfaces and is known as subdivision modeling. The iterative process makes the base mesh smooth by increasing its density. Subdivs are unique surface types that possess characteristics of both polygon and NURBS surface types. A single subdiv can have different levels of detail in different regions. For instance, you can add finer detail in case of a complex shape by adding more control points; add fewer control points for less intricate shape. In addition, subdivision modeling lets you create a high detailed polygon object from a low-poly object (lower number of polygons). The smooth subdivs can be calculated from the base mesh or surface by subdividing each polygonal face of the mesh into smaller faces. For example, you can divide a polygon cube into a sphere by repeatedly subdividing it. For real-time modeling tasks such as gaming, you need to keep the polygon counts (the number of polygons used to create the model) minimum to run the games smoothly.

Lights

In Maya, there are six types of lights – Ambient Light, Directional Light, Fill Light, Point Light, Area Light, and Volume Light. To create lights, you can select Create> Lights from the main menu bar and select the light type. Lights are objects used to make a scene appear realistic to a viewer. Lighting in Maya is similar, but not completely identical as used in the real world scenario. These lights are used to illuminate objects, create shadows, and other effects in a scene. To see the light effects in a scene, you need to render the scene. Rendering is the process of translating all information in a 3D scene to a final image or image sequence.

Cameras

If you have a camera in your home, you must have seen the certain basic physical characteristics of it. For example, a real-world camera has film format: 16mm, 35mm, and 70mm. You select a specific camera for its basic physical characteristics based on the plan to present the finished film or video. However, in Maya, you can create and change all characteristics of a camera any time. It is a good practice to set the basic properties when you create a camera for the first time. You can set these properties based on the plan to use the rendered images in post-production. For instance, if you want to render an animation and merge it with a live action video, you must set the Maya camera similar to the real world camera used to record live action.

Creating Primitive Objects

All primitive objects involve similar operations in all objects, including a NURBS object, polygonal object, or any other object type. You can create, select, deselect, and transform these objects in Maya. Primitive objects are used as base shapes for more complex models. Using NURBS, polygons, lights, and cameras, you can create variety of primitives. These objects are created in Maya using menus, Shelf, and commands. Using commands to create is a popular method for advanced Maya users, but the most common method is using Shelf. However, all primitive objects are not listed in Shelf by default. For example, you cannot create the Prism or Soccer Ball primitive objects using Shelf. In this case, you need to use menus and submenus to create them. The Create menu lists different types of primitive objects that you can select. To create an object using Shelf, select the icon in Shelf and then drag in the viewport.

For creating NURBS and polygon primitives, you must consider two options – Interactive Creation and Exit On Completion. The Interactive Creation option allows you to create primitive objects by manually clicking and dragging. The Exit On Completion option allows you to exit the object creation mode once you create an object. If you want to create multiple objects, you should have Interactive Creation selected. By default both options are selected and can be accessed from the NURBS Primitives and Polygon Primitives submenus.

Using Shelf

The users, at the time of creating primitive objects in Maya find Shelf the simplest tool. First you need to select an object icon in Shelf, and then drag it in the viewport. To create a primitive object, first select a primitive type such as NURBS or polygon and then select the icon of that object that you want to create. For example, if you want to create a polygon cube, first select the Polygons shelf tab, then select the Polygon Cube icon, and then drag in the viewport. You can perform the following steps to understand it practically:

1. **Launch Maya 2013** which will open with a new scene (untitled) by default. In case you're working on a different scene, select File> New which will ask you to save the previous scene.

2. Click the **Surface** tab in Shelf. It'll open various icons representing primitive objects, tools, and menu items such as Revolve and Loft.

3. We want to create a NURBS primitive object for now, so you can go ahead and click the **NURBS Sphere** icon on the Surfaces tab. The shape of the cursor changes and an instruction appears on the grid.

4. **Drag** the mouse pointer outward in the grid to create a NURBS sphere. Like this, you can create other objects in the viewport. The picture 2.7 shows a sphere created in the viewport.

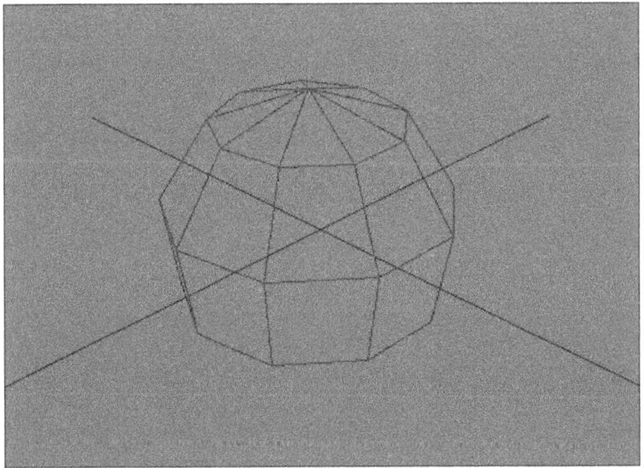

This way, you can create other primitive objects by selecting Create tab from the main menu bar. For example, to create a polygon cube, select the Polygons tab, and then select the Polygon Cube icon. You'll see the instruction changing depending on the type of object you select. If you select an icon in Shelf when the Interactive Creation option is deselected, the primitive object with the default dimensions is created automatically at the center of the grid. The dimensions depend on the dimension mentioned in their respective options window where you can change the options as required.

Picture 2.7

In Maya, the primitive objects appear in wireframe mode, as you see in picture 2.7. You can click the Smooth shade all button in the panel toolbar to view the primitive object in the shaded mode.

Using the Create Menu

The menus and submenus are used to create different types of primitive objects as they provide the

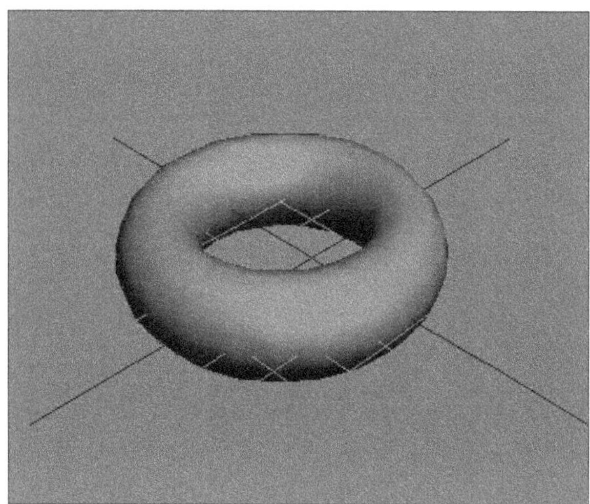

traditional method of accessing tools and commands. Using Create menu in the main menu bar, you can create primitive objects including cameras and lights. Now to create a torus using Create menu, let's perform the following steps:

1. Open a scene and select **Create**> **Polygon Primitives**> **Torus** from the main menu bar. The shape of the cursor changes and an instruction appears on the grid.

2. **Move** the cursor over the area where you want to create the object. **Drag** the mouse-pointer outward on the gird to create a torus, as shown in picture 2.8. Don't worry if the torus is in wireframe mode.

Picture 2.8

Using Command Line

Command Line also helps you to create primitive objects in Maya, which is generally used by advanced Maya users. To create an object, you need to type the Maya command known as script in the dark gray text box in Command Line. By default, MEL is selected as the scripting language. Maya has two built-in scripting languages – MEL and Python. You can switch between these two languages by clicking the name at the start of Command Line. You can also write your own commands or scripts using either Command Line or Script Editor. To create a primitive object using Command Line, perform the following steps carefully:

1. When Maya scene is open, **click** the text box next to <u>MEL</u> in <u>Command Line</u>. It will activate the Command Line.

2. Type in the text box: **polyTorus** and press enter. It executes the MEL command and brings a polygon torus in the viewport.

A polygon torus appears at the center of the grid and a message confirming the creation of the polygon torus appears in the command feedback text box. The polygon torus appears with default settings as set in the Polygon Torus Options window, which you can change if required. Like this, you can type: **cylinder** and press enter key to create a NURBS cylinder.

Lesson 6
Object Selecting Method

When you need to make any changes to an object, you click the object in the viewport to select, or draw a rectangular bounding box around the entire object or portion of it. If you want to select all objects in the viewport, select Edit> Select All from the main menu bar. To select multiple objects, hold the Shift key as you click objects to add them to the selection. During selection, the existing selection turns white and the new selection turns green. Holding Ctrl key and then clicking on a selected object deselects it.

Functions of Selection Modes

In a Maya scene, you have different levels of an object hierarchy. For instance, at times you need to select an entire group of objects, or only one of the objects in that group, or even points on the surface of that object. This is where selection modes help you as they limit the items to specific type such as objects, components, or hierarchical elements while selecting in the viewport. You can also select different objects in the hierarchy of objects. The hierarchy of an object is formed based on the parent object (group of the objects), sub-parent object (objects regrouped within a group), and child object (standalone object). By default, the parent object is selected which means all sub-objects are selected automatically. However, with selection mode you can select only child object, sub-parent object, and points on the surface of that object depending on the active selection mode. The selection mode buttons present in Status Line let you switch between various selection modes such as, Select by hierarchy and combinations, Select by object type, and Select by component type.

Select by hierarchy and combinations: Enables you to select groups of objects or parts of a group. This selection mode is important to work with groups as well as parent and child objects.
Select by object type: Enables you to select the entire object in the viewport, such as primitives, lights, and cameras. In this mode, you cannot select the individual components of the object such as vertex, face, and edge. When you first start Maya, the default selection mode is set to Select by object type.
Select by component type: Enables you to select an object's components, such as vertices, faces, or the CVs of a NURBS surface.

Many primitives are grouped, like the NURBS cube primitive consists of six square planes. When these plans are grouped together, they create the hierarchy. The Select by hierarchy and combinations selection mode allows you to items within a group. You cannot modify on the item that is a part of the hierarchy. Pressing the F8 key (hotkey) allows you to switch between object and component selection modes. The Select by hierarchy and combinations mode works on the whole object. For instance, you have grouped several primitive objects into a single unit and want to transform (move, rotate, or scale) a group as one unit, here you need to select the Select by hierarchy and combinations mode. A hierarchy is a collection of nodes or objects that are connected together to form one unit.

Using Selection Masks

Selection mask allows you to filter the selection to prevent the unintentional selection of objects or components. It determines the type of object or component that you can select in the viewport. The selection masks in Maya are All Objects, Animation, Polygons, NURBS, Deform, Dynamics, and Rendering. You can pick up one Set of selection mask from the dropdown list in Status Line, as shown in picture 2.9 here.

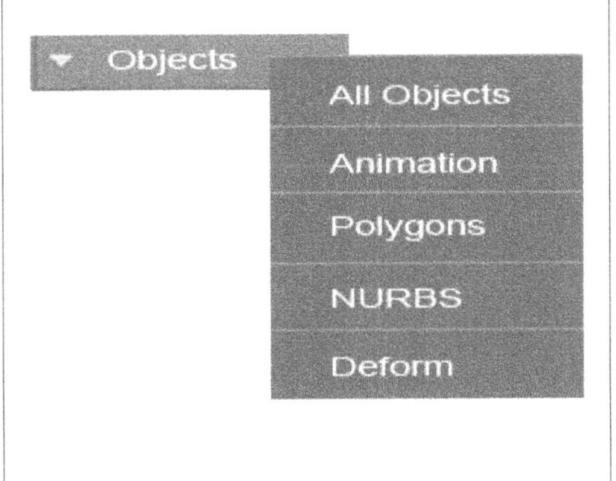

While working on a big project in Maya, you have a multiple layered scene in which you want to select only the polygon objects and not any other object or object component. That time, you can use the Set of selection mask to select the Polygons option, which only allows you to select polygon objects in the scene. You cannot select a NURBS or subdiv object when Polygons is selected as the selection mask. The All Objects option which is selected by default lets you select all types of object in a scene.

Picture 2.9

Using Pivot Point

The pivot point is generally located at the center of an object, but it is not visible. In 3D space, a pivot point is a specific point which is used as a reference for object transformation. Every object or node created in Maya has a pivot point set at the origin, by default. When you move an object the pivot point moves with it. When you group objects, a new node called a parent node is created for the group. The pivot point for the parent node is placed at the origin (0, 0, and 0). If you scale the group object, it is scaled from the center of the group. Pivot points play a key role in the transformation of objects. They control the rotation and scaling of objects in the space. As said earlier, the pivot point is not visible by default. If you want to make it visible, you need to select any transformation tool from Tool Box and press the <u>Insert</u> key on the keyboard. When the pivot point is visible, you can move it to any location you want. Let's perform following steps to change the position of a pivot point of a primitive object:

1. Go to **Create** in the main menu bar, select **Biped** or **Polygon head**, and draw it in the viewport. Select this object in the viewport for its pivot point to be repositioned. In our case, the object we have selected is Biped.

2. Select a **transform tool** in the <u>Tool Box</u>. In our case, we click on Selection Tool. When you do that, the origin appears at the center of the object you have selected, as shown in picture 3.0 A. You can also use the orthographic views to see and change the pivot point of the selected object.

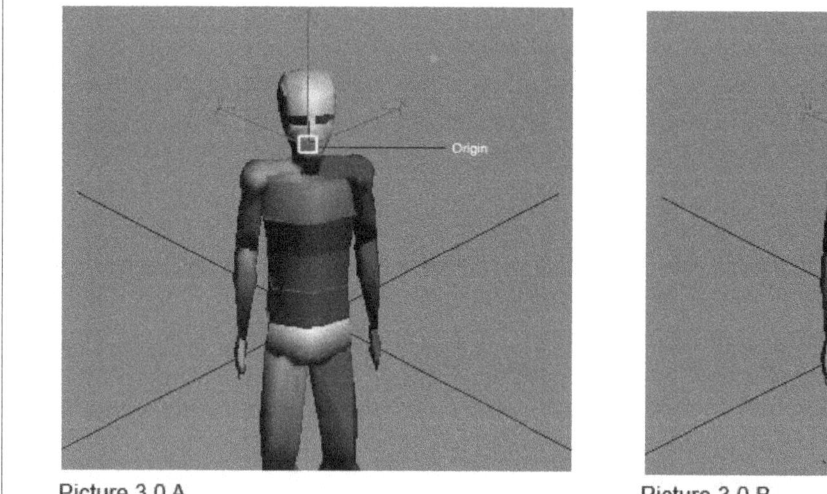

Picture 3.0 A

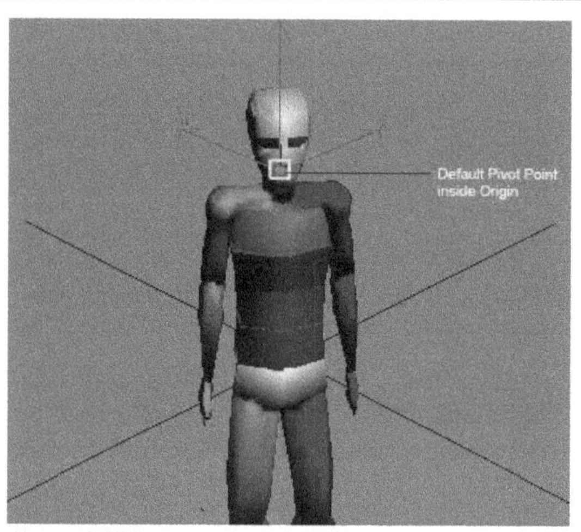

Picture 3.0 B

3. Press the **Insert key** to display the pivot point on the selected object. The picture 3.0 B shows the default pivot point.

4. Click the **axis** you want to activate, and then **drag** the axis to move the pivot point to a new position. Press the **Insert key** again, or select any of the transform tools in the Tool Box to exit from the pivot point mode. It is essential because in the pivot point mode, the transformation affects the pivot point not the object.

Working with Camera Views

When you open a viewport in Maya, it opens with a full-screen perspective view which is a camera view and expresses the real-world depth through the simulation of perspective. What it means is that whenever you view any scene in Maya, you look through a camera. In the viewport, you can see the 3D objects that you create and move around it in real-time to get an idea about the proportion and depth. Your field of view is restricted to what you can see through the camera lens. By default, Maya has four views (cameras): one perspective and three orthographic (side, front, and top). An orthographic view can be defined using a parallel plane and a direction; while a perspective view can be defined using an eye point, a look at a point, and a focal length. Cameras are of primary concern in the creation of effective animation. You can use cameras to take wide, medium, and close-up shots of characters in an animation. And you can even create additional cameras to manipulate the views of a scene. When you navigate between the different views, you can view scenes from various angles. You can view an object from front, top, and side. To switch between different views, you can just press the <u>Spacebar key</u> or use the Panel menu. To change the active perspective view to another view, you can select Panels> Orthographic and select front, side, or top views.

In Maya, you can also use various preset layouts as they save time during the modeling process by allowing you to use some of the Maya UIs, such as Hypergraph, Trax, and Outliner, as one of the view. The preset layout options are Single Perspective View, Four View, Persp/Hypergraph, Persp/Outliner, and Persp/Graph. In order to access preset layouts, you can go to Panels> Saved Layouts.

Lesson 7
Exploring Views

In some scenes, there may be a few hidden objects that you can not see clearly in the camera view. At that time you can manipulate the camera view to see the hidden objects. You can also manipulate views to view scenes from different angles, by rotating the camera view or zooming in or out of the camera view. The methods that allow you to manipulate the camera are: Dollying, Tracking, and Tumbling.

Dollying in a Camera View

Using Dolly Tool, you can view objects in a scene either from close up or far shot in both perspective and orthogonal views. For this, hold Alt key down and press right-button of mouse. Click and drag the mouse-pointer downward to zoom in and upward to zoom out the active view. You need to follow these steps for practice:

1. Open a scene and select **View> Camera Tools> Dolly Tool** from the panel menu, or use Alt + right mouse button. It changes the cursor inside the viewport.

2. **Drag** the Dolly Tool cursor upward and downward as it will allow you to zoom in and zoom out the active view.
You can also reset the camera to its default setting by selecting View> Default View from the panel menu. You can also press the [(left bracket key) to move to the previous view and the] (right bracket key) to move to the next view.

Tracking in a Camera View

Tracking also known as panning is the state of moving a camera view upwards, downwards, or sideways. While tracking, the position of the objects doesn't change, instead the grid moves with object. Suppose, you need to show a portion of an object that is not visible in the view, you can move the camera to display the object. To do this, you can select View> Camera Tools> Track Tool. You can also use the shortcut Alt + middle mouse button, and drag the mouse to left, right, up, or down to track in the view.

Tumbling in a Camera View

Tumbling means rotating the camera view around a center of interest to change the position or an angle from where the camera views the scene. You can tumble a camera view by dragging the mouse in any direction – right, left, up, or down. Tumbling also helps you in viewing a scene from different angles. Tumble Tool allows you to rotate the active camera view. To do this, you can select View> Camera Tools> Tumble Tool. You can also press the Alt + left mouse button, and drag the Tumble Tool cursor to rotate the view.

Using Viewport Modes

Maya allows you to view a 3D object either in wireframe mode or in shaded mode. In wireframe mode, objects appear as the wired outlines (transparent) that indicates their position and general shape. In shaded mode, objects are displayed in an opaque dark gray color (solid). Shaded mode gives you a better idea of the 3D volume of the model as well as the surface details of the object. The wireframe mode is the fastest mode, because it makes fewer processing demands on the computer. However, the shaded modes can work quickly, depending on the graphics card and system processor of your computer. By the way, Maya 2013 works with latest system configuration, so you don't need to worry about it.

Now what can be surprising to you is that you can display the object as shaded in the perspective view and set the orthographic views to display objects in wireframe mode. That means, you can control the display mode of an object in each viewport separately. You can also set the viewport display to show both in shaded and wireframe mode. To display in shaded and wireframe simultaneously, you can select Shading> Wireframe on Shaded from the panel menu. In addition, there are few other modes, such as Textured, Shadows, High quality, and Use all lights. The picture 3.1 shows Panel Toolbar Icons for all modes and their shortcut (hotkeys) with functions.

Panel Toolbar Icon	Hotkey	Function
	4	Toggles into Wireframe mode
	5	Toggles into Shaded mode
		Toggles into Wireframe on shaded mode
	6	Toggles into Textured mode
	7	Toggles into Use all lights mode
		Toggles into Shadows mode
		Toggles into High quality mode

Picture 3.1

Textured mode displays the image textures that have been applied to the object as long as the Hardware Texturing option is enabled. The Hardware Texturing option displays Maya's hardware textured rendered results in the active viewport. You can enable this option by selecting Shading> Hardware Texturing from the panel menu. The Shading menu displays all options that you can use to display objects in the viewport. You can go ahead and create some objects selecting Create tab from the main menu bar, and change the view mode. For changing view modes, you can use either hotkeys or select Shading and click any option from the panel menu. Before moving ahead to the next lesson, make sure you have done proper practice till now.

Lesson 8
Transforming Objects in Maya 2013

Transforming an object means changing its position, shape, and orientation. Maya gives you several options to move, rotate, and scale objects around a scene, and many shortcuts to perform these common tasks known as transformation. There are different methods of transformation that you need to learn. The first method is using the manipulation tools such as Move Tool and Scale Tool available in Tool Box. And the second is typing new coordinates or values in Channel Box.

There is one tool called Universal Manipulator to perform all transformation operations simultaneously. You can use this tool when an object requires all three transformations. Each tool including Universal Manipulator has a gizmo that consists of three axes. The gizmo helps you to transform an object by moving, rotating, or scaling along a particular axis or all three axes. To constrain the transformation to a particular axis, you can click and drag the axis along which you want to perform the transformation. The three axes coincide with the three colors of the red, green, blue (RGB) color mode. X-axis represents red, the Y-axis represents green, and the Z axis represents blue.

Moving an Object

The Move Tool is used to move or reposition objects in the viewport as required. For that, you need to select Move Tool from Tool Box or press W key, click the object that you want to move, and then drag in the desired axis. For free movement of the object, click and drag the center of the move manipulator (gizmo), or use the Universal Manipulator.

Rotating an Object

When you rotate objects, you can view them from different angles. You can change the view of the objects towards the camera by rotating them, and the camera can also be rotated to change the view. The Rotate Tool is selected from Tool Box by clicking on it or pressing E key. The rotate manipulator has arcs that represent three axes. Red arc is for the X-axis, green arc is for the Y-axis, and blue arc is for the Z-axis. The outer yellow ring rotates about the view axis. When you rotate an object, a gray pie slice appears that indicates the degree of rotation of the object. You can also see the transformation in the Channel Box. If you want to rotate the object freely without constraining the movement to a particular axis, you can click in the center of the rotate manipulator and drag the mouse.

Scaling an Object

Doing scale up or scale down, you can change the shape of an object. The Scale Tool is selected by clicking on it or pressing R key. Using this, you can click the object and drag in the axis you want to scale. You can also use Universal Manipulator to scale objects. The scale manipulator is used to scale an object proportionally or along a single axis. The small cubes of different colors represent the axes on which you want to scale the object.

Using Universal Manipulator

Universal Manipulator allows you to simultaneously perform all types of transformation on the selected object in the viewport. It combines the functionalities of three transformation tools: Move Tool, Rotate Tool, and Scale Tool. This tool also allows you to type precise values to transform the object directly in the viewport providing real-time information about the transformation. But using Universal Manipulator, you cannot transform object component such as vertices and faces.

When you select this tool from the Tool Box and click on an object in the viewport, the Universal Manipulator gizmo (or interface) appears on the object. When you can click on any translation axis, it turns yellow and a text box appears on the Universal Manipulator gizmo. By default, the value appears as 0.000. Type a new value in the text box (for example: 15) and press enter to apply the new value. The selected object moves in the viewport by the specified value.

Similarly, you can rotate and scale any object by selecting the respective axis in the Universal Manipulator gizmo. When you move or rotate an object using this tool, the length of the movement or degree of the rotation is displayed near the Universal Manipulator gizmo. This gizmo appears as a bounding box with several rotation and move arrows. Dragging the Move Tool arrows translate the object. If you select any of the curved arrows in the middle of the edges of the Manipulator box, it rotates the selected object in that axis. In addition, dragging the cyan boxes in the corners of the Manipulator box scales the polygon cone. Holding down the Ctrl key while you drag the mouse scales the object in one axis. The professional animators like to use Universal Manipulator tool for all kind of transformation works in the viewport.

Using Channel Box
Channel Box functions in such a way that you can edit the attributes of a selected object using it. The attributes are edited to transform the object. In case the Channel Box is not visible in your screen, select Display> UI Element> Channel Box/Layer Editor from the main menu bar. When an object is selected, its attributes are listed with their current values. To transform an object, type the desired value in the respective text box. For instance, to move an object in X-axis, type a value in the Translate X text box. Similarly, to scale an object in Y-axis, type a value in the Scale Y text box. For uniform scaling, type the same value for all three axes. Perform the following steps to transform an object using Channel Box:

1. **Select** the object in the viewport that you want to transform. The picture 3.2 shows the pyramid object with the Channel box on the right side.

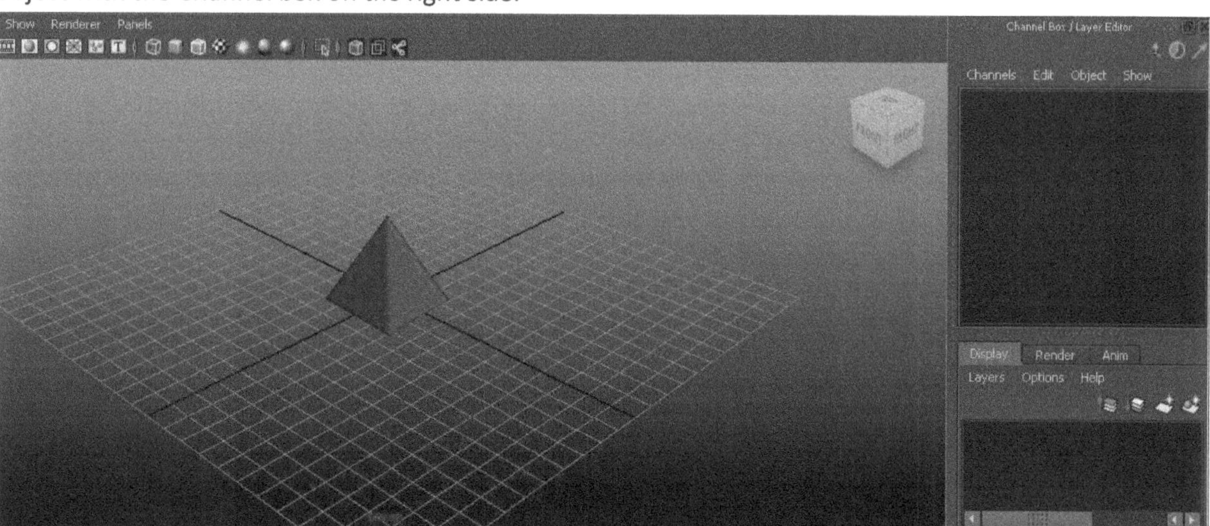

Picture 3.2

2. **Click** the text box (in Channel Box) next to the attribute that you want to change and type a value to move in that axis. In our case, we select the **Translate Y** text box and type **10**. Press enter to move the object in the Y-axis, as shown in picture 3.3.

Like this, the values of other attributes, such as Rotate and Scale can also be changed to transform the selected object. You are also allowed to type a negative value in the text boxes. Moreover, you can select multiple attributes simultaneously and type a value that affects all the attributes.

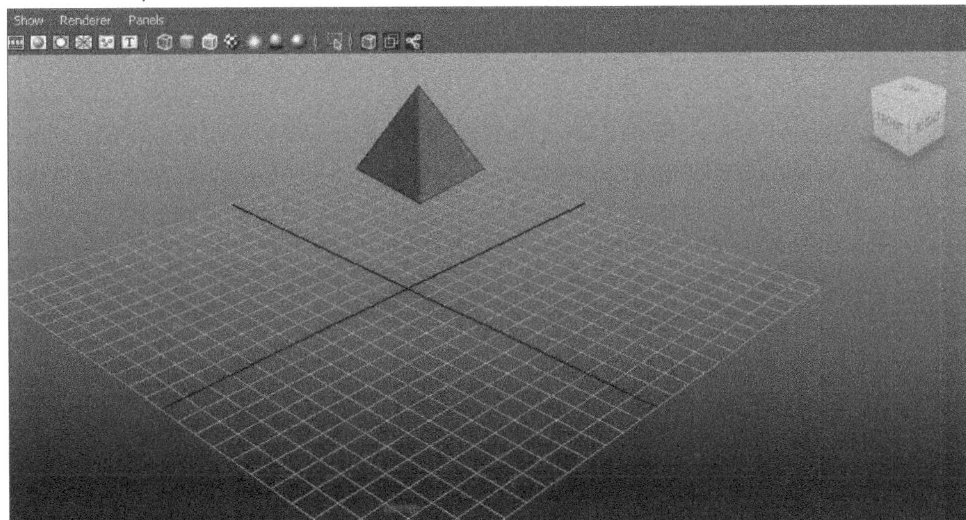

Picture 3.3

Using Attribute Editor

In the previous section of the lesson you learnt about transforming an object using Channel Box. The Attribute Editor also allows you to do the same listing the attributes of the selected object and lets you edit those attributes. Similar to Channel Box, you can type the new value of an attribute on the respective text box and then press the enter key to apply the new value. This tool gives you a graphical control and a more detailed display of attributes for the selected object. You can perform all transformation, such as move, rotate, and scale without selecting their respective tools. Perform these steps to understand Attribute Editor more clearly:

1. **Select** the object (pyramid) you want to transform using Attribute Editor, and go to **Display> UI Elements> Attribute Editor** from the main menu bar.

The Attribute Editor appears in the place of Channel Box with the pPyramidShape1 tab selected by default. This tab is referred to as the shape node. The attributes in the shape node control the geometric shape, when the object was first created. The shape node also includes other types of attributes such as object display attributes. Unlike Channel Box, various attributes of the selected object appear under various tabs.

2. **Click** the first pPyramid1 tab in the Attribute Editor. The pPyramid1 tab is known as the transform node. The attributes in this tab control object transformation. **Type: 180** in the Rotate text box for the Z-axis in the Transform Attributes section, and **press enter**. The selected objected is rotated in Z-axis.

Every visible object in Maya including cameras and lights has a transform node. As you saw in Attribute Editor, the Rotate Order dropdown list box is selected as xyz, which determines the axes order for the Rotate transformation node. Similarly, you can translate, scale, and shear the selected object using the respective options in the Transform Attribute Editor section. You can also modify attributes for pivot point, object display, mental ray, or node behavior in their respective section in Attribute Editor.

Lesson 9
Duplicating Objects

In Maya, you can make a copy of an object, and the copy will have the same characteristics as that of the parent object. You get several tools and commands, such as Duplicate, Duplicate with Transform, and Duplicate Special.

Duplicate: Creates a copy of selected object. The copy object appears at same position as the original object, making the newly created object invisible at first. However, the duplicate copy is selected by default, so you can move it to a different location using Move Tool. The shortcut to it is Ctrl+D.

Duplicate with Transform: Creates an identical copy of the selected object and applies the last transformation that is performed using the current manipulator. The shortcut to it is Shift+D.

Duplicate Special: Allows you to create duplicate copies with transformations (move, rotate, and scale) applied optionally. You can use the Duplicate Special Options window to specify various settings. The shortcut key is Ctrl+Shift+D. You can perform the following steps for practice:

1. **Select** the object in the viewport that you want to duplicate. In our case, we select a polygon cube object that we want to duplicate to create stairs, as shown in picture 3.4.

Picture 3.4   Picture 3.5

2. Go to **Edit> Duplicate Special> (Rectangle Box)** from the main menu bar. The Rectangle box is the small box just on the right of the option. The Duplicate Special Options window appears where you can specify different attributes for the duplicate object. You can set transform attributes like: Geometry types, Group under, Translate, Rotate, Scale, and Number of copies.

3. Select the **Instance** radio button for the Geometry type option. The Instance option lets you redisplay the geometry being instanced. You do not create actual copies of the selected geometry.

4. Type **-6.3000** in the Translate text box for X-axis.
   Type **1.4000** in the Translate text box for Y-axis.
   Type **8** in the Number of copies text box.

5. Click the **Duplicate Special** button. The seven identical copies of the selected object appear in the viewport, similar to what is shown in picture 3.5. **Save** this scene for next section of the lesson.

Using Pre-selection Highlight Feature

The Pre-selection Highlight feature works only in case of polygon primitives. It provides a visual indication about the component that the mouse is pointing to. It highlights the appropriate components that will be selected, if the mouse is clicked. This feature allows you to highlight the component of an object with a different color. It is the enhanced selection workflow that increases the productivity for common tasks by reducing the number of clicks. This feature is selected in the Preferences windows by default, which you can disable by un-checking the Pre-selection Highlight option under the Modifiers section. To do the practice on this, open the same scene that you saved in previous section.

1. **Right-click** and **hold down** the mouse button on the object. It opens a marking menu in which you need to select **Face** option. It will enable Face component selection mode.

2. **Move** the cursor over the face component that you wish to select. Maya assist you by highlighting the face under the cursor. You'll see that non-selected components appear in the default color, while highlighted component appear in red. As other objects are instanced, it highlights the face in the other polygon cubes.

3. **Move** the cursor over other faces and see how they are highlighted. When a face is highlighted, you can click to select it. The Pre-selection Highlight feature can be used with all component selection modes, such as Vertex, UVs, Edge, or Multi. You can select any of these modes from the marking menu.

Using Reflection Feature

Reflection feature is used while modeling a character, when you make changes in the one-half of the character and you want those changes to be automatically applied on the other half. Whenever you select a component(s) from one half of the character, the Reflection feature of Maya highlights the symmetrical component(s) on the opposite side of the character using the white color. Such a phenomenon is called Color Feedback. Let's perform the following steps to manipulate components of an object using the Reflection feature:

1. **Draw** the object **Polygon head** by selecting it from Create menu. Do not draw Biped for this feature. You're going to change polygon head using Reflection feature.

2. When Polygon head is selected, go to **Modify> Transformation Tools> Move Tool> (Rectangle Box)** from the main menu bar. It opens Tool Settings window for Move Tool. You can also access the Tool Settings window for Move Tool by double-clicking Move Tool in the Tool Box.

3. **Scroll down** in the Tool Settings window and select the **Reflection** check box in the Reflection Settings group to enable Reflection mode.

4. **Right-click** the polygon human model in the viewport and select a component selection mode. In our case, we select the **Face** component selection mode from the marking menu which is shown in the picture 3.6.

5. **Move** the cursor over the face (polygonal part) of the model that you want to select and then **click** it to select. As you can see that the model is made of many polygonal objects (parts), so you need to select any one of them. In our case, we select a single face, as shown in picture 3.7.

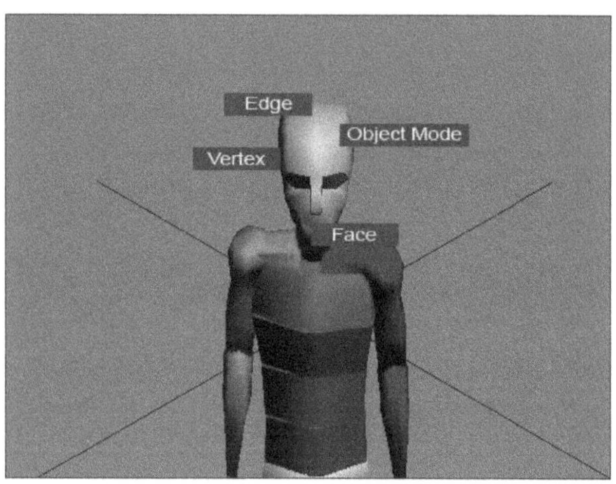

Picture 3.6

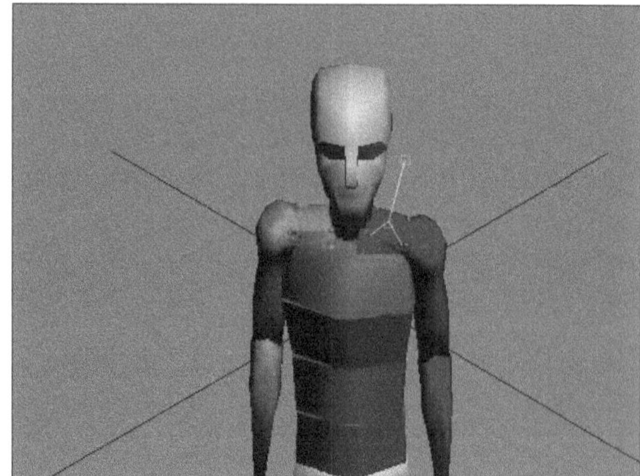

Picture 3.7

6. When you select a single face, the Reflection feature automatically selects the symmetrical vertices on the other side of the polygon human model. Now select **Move Tool** from the Tool Box. The move manipulator appears on the selected component.

7. **Drag** the selected face to move. You'll see that the corresponding highlighted component on the other side of the human model move to the same extent. However, the Reflection feature works in a different manner when the Soft Selection feature is turned on. You will learn about it in the coming lessons.

Understanding Construction History

As you build objects in creating a scene, Maya stores the information about the creation process in the memory. So in the Construction History, which refers to the history of actions performed to create a scene, nodes are created based on the actions performed on an object. This way we can say that a complete scene is the ultimate result of all nodes that are a part of Construction History. For example, you revolve a curve to make a new surface out of it and then again move it to another location, and finally change its shape to a cube. All this process constitutes Construction History of a cube created from a curve. That means the chain of nodes that lead to the construction of cube out a curve is called Construction History of the cube.

Although, Construction History is a part of the dependency graph (which is the graphical representation of the relationship between connected nodes); yet it can be called a set of actions that constitute a scene. Whereas, the dependency graph represents the connection between different types of nodes created as a result of any action that performed to create a scene. Construction History usually constitutes all inputs listed in Channel Box during the creation of any scene. In specific cases, you may want to delete the Construction History of an object, as the history state increases; Maya spends more time for calculating the nodes and slows down the system. To delete the Construction History, you can select the object whose history you want to delete, then go to Edit> Delete by Type> History.

In some situations, you may also want to delete the history of an entire scene. For that, you can select Edit> Delete All by Type> History. You can also turn off Construction History creation by clicking the Construction History on/off icon in Status Line.

Lesson 10
Working with NURBS

The modeling techniques that you can use in Maya are: Non-Uniform Rational B-Spline (NURBS), polygon, and subdivision. NURBS is one of the geometry types that is used to created 3D curves and surfaces, which are the building blocks of a NURBS object. Curves and surfaces provide greater flexibility over their polygon counterparts and most favorable for creating organic, smooth-flowing surfaces as well as industrial surfaces. You can control the curvature and smoothness of contours by easily manipulating the control points.

Non-Uniform refers to the process of defining the parameters required to draw Bezier curves. Using NURBS curves, you can add multiple knots, which is essential for Bezier curves. A knot or edit point joins two segments. Rational refers to the underlying mathematical representation to assign more weight to few knots in a shape than others. B-Splines (B stands for basis) are polynomial curves with parametric representation that lie outside the curve. NURBS use one common mathematical form for both, standard analytical shapes and free form shapes; provide precise control with fewer control points; and can be evaluated faster by numerically stable and accurate algorithms. After defining the profile using curves, the final surface can be produced using certain specific construction methods, such as lofting, revolving, or extruding.

Working with NURBS Curve

NURBS curves are referred just curves also. 3D artists extensively use these curves in modeling as these are main objects of NURBS. When you need to build the profile of a 3D object and apply a surface to add volume, you use curves at that time. Curves are the base for the underlying mathematical structure constituting a NURBS surface. They provide greater flexibility over their polygon counterparts, as you can create high-poly models using fewer control points. There are several components of NURBS curve: control vertices, edit points, and control points. You can modify a curve using the control vertices. You can use various tools, such as CV Curve and EP Curve to create a curve. For practice, select Edit> NURBS Curve in the main menu and draw some lines in the viewport. As you draw, you'll see some points and knots which are explained below.

Deconstructing a NURBS curve

NURBS curves are the base for the underlying mathematical structure constituting a NURBS surface. The foundation of a NURBS surface is a curve or web of interconnected curves. To define the basic contour of a 3D form, known as profile, you can construct a NURBS curve. You can position points on a curve and reshape the surface by moving control points that lie on the curve. A NURBS curve consists of control vertex (CV), edit point (EP), curve point, hulls, and degree. But curves are not renderable, as they do not appear in the final render.

Control Vertex

While using NURBS, lines and surfaces are not manipulated by moving vertices, edges, faces, or polygons; instead, they are manipulated by special control points known as control vertex. Each open NURBS curve (or curve) has a start and an end point known as CV. These are the most basic and important means to control the contour of a curve or a surface. CVs control the pulling of a curve or weight of the curve between edit points (EPs). They do not exist on the actual 3D surface with the exception of the start and end CVs, as shown in picture 3.8. As you can see in this picture, CVs use different icons to represent the start and end points of a curve. The start and end points determine the inner and outer sides of a NURBS surface. The first CV appears at the start of the curve as the hollow box. The second CV appears as the English alphabet U. All remaining CVs are drawn as small dots. The marking of CVs are made to show the increasing U (horizontal) dimension from the start point or the first CV. The first and second CVs are used to define the direction of the curve.

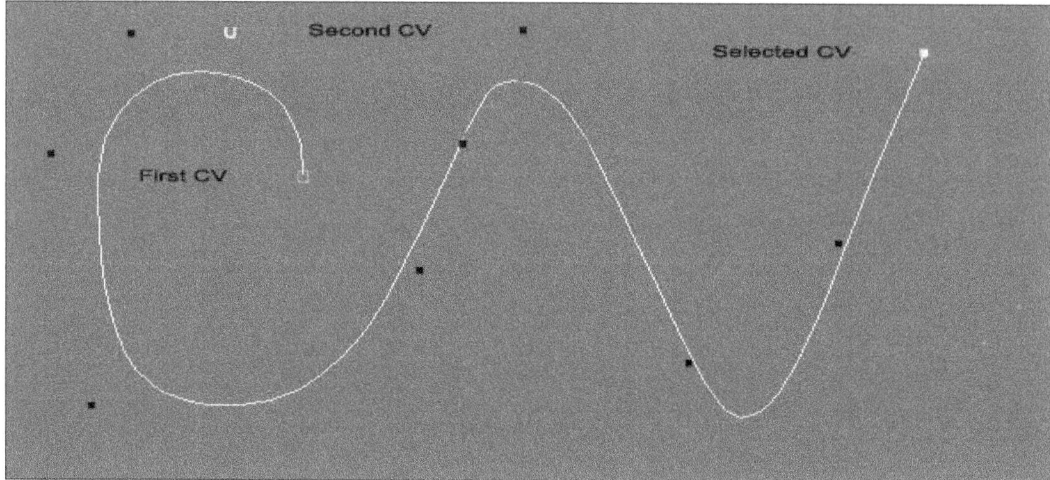

Picture 3.8

In Maya, you are not allowed to manually insert CVs directly into a curve. They are automatically inserted on inserting edit points. The number of CVs in a curve varies based on their degree. It is equal to the degree of the curve plus one. To increase the number of CVs, you must either increase the degree of the curve or the number of spans. Increasing the number of CVs in a curve facilitates easy manipulation of its shape. To access the Control Vertex component selection mode (or component type), right-click a NURBS curve and select Control Vertex from the making menu.

Other Editing Points
Edit Point: At the time of drawing a curve, the curve segments (also called spans) are drawn by joining points. These joining points are known as edit points or knots. And edit point appears as a small x on a curve. These points mark the connection point between two spans. You can directly insert edit points on a curve.

Curve Point: A curve is a line defined by points and a curve point is an arbitrary point on the curve. You can move curve points along the U direction of a curve. You can insert a knot in a curve by selecting the Curve Point component selection mode, and then click anywhere on the curve.

Hull: When you draw a curve in Maya, a straight line goes with the curve. This line is called hulls, which works as a visual aid to the location of the interconnected CVs. To maintain a consistent pattern and flow between CVs, hulls are drawn in between. These lines act as a bridge between two CVs. Hulls also help you to determine a complete row of control points in a curve.

Drawing a NURBS curve
The form of a NURBS curve affects the deformation of an object when Maya deformers, such as lattice or jiggle are applied to it. A NURBS curve can have a periodic, closed, or open form. The start and end edit points of an open curve are located in different positions. The tools to create NURBS curves are:
(1) CV Curve Tool (2) EP Curve Tool (3) Bezier Curve Tool (4) Pencil Curve Tool

Using CV Curve Tool

You select this tool by clicking Create> CV Curve Tool from the main menu bar. This is the most commonly used tool to create curves in Maya. With this tool, you can click in the grid to place CVs and define the shape of the curve. Edit points are created based on the location of CVs. The curve appears only after you place a certain number of CVs. The number of CVs that you need to place before the curve appears depends on the Curve degree setting. With the default Curve degree setting (3 Cubic), you must create minimum four CVs to show the curve. You can change the default degree in the CV Curve Settings group of the Tool Settings window. Higher Curve degree allows you to create smoother curves. A curve degree of 3 is sufficient for most modeling task. To open the Tool Settings window, you can select Create> CV Curve Tool> (Rectangle Box) from the main menu bar.

You can also specify settings for the curve, such as Knot spacing to assign U position values to edit points. The curve end edit points are superimposed on the end CVs if the Multiple end knots checkbox is selected. Let's perform the following steps to create a NURBS curve using CV Curve Tool:

1. **Enable** orthographic view in Maya and **select** top viewport. As the shortcut of it, you can press Spacebar key to display the four-viewport panel, and move the cursor over the top viewport and then press Spacebar again.

2. Select **Create**> **CV Curve Tool**, which will change the cursor to a cross-hair. If you want to hide the grid in the viewport, select grid icon in the panel tool bar. Then, move the cursor to the top viewport and **click** to place the first CV.

3. **Move** the cursor over any other location and **click** to place the second CV. Again, **move** the cursor over any other location and **click** to place the third CV. As you'll see that the hulls are created, but curve does appear. If the 3 Cubic radio button is selected, you must click four times to display the curve.

4. **Click** in the viewport to place the fourth CV. The curve appears in the viewport. You can continue placing new CVs until you get a preferred shape. At the end, you can press **enter** or **Q** key to exit the tool.

Always try to create the simplest curves that can describe the shape you want. Simpler curves help in simple, faster rendering of surfaces and better quality output. While inserting the CVs, you can press the delete or backspace key to delete the last inserted CVs.

Using EP Curve Tool

Using EP Curve Tool you can create NURBS curves by calculating the position based on the edit points position. In the Tool Settings window, you can modify the default settings for EP Curve Tool. The settings are similar to CV Curve Tool. To open the Tool Settings panel for EP Curve Tool, you can select Create> EP Curve Tool> (Rectangle Box). Follow these steps to create a NURBS curve using EP Curve Tool:

1. Go to **Create** and select **EP Curve Tool** which will change the cursor to cross-hair. Alternatively, you can click the EP Curve Tool icon in the Curves tab of Shelf.

2. Select your **top viewport**, move the cursor to any location, and click to place the first edit point in the viewport.

3. **Move** the cursor to any other location and **click to insert** the second edit point. The shape of the curve is drawn for each edit point after the first is placed.

4. **Move** the cursor to any other location and click to insert the third edit point. You can continue placing new edit points until you get a preferred shape. Press enter to exit the insertion mode and select the last used tool.

While inserting edit points or CVs, you can modify their position without exiting their respective tool, by pressing the Home or Insert key or holding the scroll wheel. Also, a manipulator appears on the previous point, which you can use to move the points.

Using Bezier Curve Tool

Bezier Curve Tool allows you to draw freehand parametric curves known as Bezier curve. Unlike polygonal lines, Bezier curve appear smooth at all scales and are subset of the NURBS curves. You can click and drag the Bezier Curve Tool cursor in the viewport to create straight and curved segments by adding anchor points. To create straight segment, click the Bezier Curve Tool cursor, and to create curved segment, click and drag the Bezier Curve Tool cursor in the viewport. Clicking and dragging creates smooth anchor points with tangents, which can be used to further adjust the curvature. You can drag the tangents individually to modify the shape of a curve. Using anchor points, you can manipulate a Bezier curve any time. There are some points that you need to consider while working with Bezier curves:

A. To remove an anchor point, press the Delete or Backspace key.
B. To add an anchor point, click anywhere on a curve to insert the new anchor point without altering the shape of a curve.
C. To display the tangents of an anchor point, move the cursor above that anchor point.
D. To close the curve, hold the Ctrl+Shift keys down and click the first anchor point.
E. To move an anchor point to a different location, select the anchor point and click with the middle mouse button to display the move manipulator by default.
F. To break (adjust one half) the tangent, keep the Ctrl key down while dragging it.
G. To go to the settings window of Bezier Curve Tool, you can click Create> Bezier Curve Tool> (Rectangle Box).

Now let us go ahead and perform the following steps carefully as we are going to create a NURBS curve using Bezier Curve Tool:

1. Go to **Create** and select **Bezier Curve Tool** which will change the cursor to cross-hair. Then, **click** in the viewport to insert a <u>corner anchor point</u>.

2. **Click and drag** to insert a smooth anchor point and create a curved segment.

You can see that the last anchor point appears selected with the tangents. Similarly, you can create multiple straight and curved segments to create any shape. You can also later modify the straight segments to create a curved segment.

3. Press **enter** to quit Bezier Curve Tool insertion mode. This is how you create a NURBS curve using Bezier Curve Tool.

It is important to know the options in tool settings of Bezier Curve Tool. In the Tool Settings window of Bezier Curve Tool, you can specify the following settings:

(1) <u>**Manip Mode**</u>: Determines the manipulator that appears on clicking the selected anchor point with the middle mouse button. There are two manipulators available – Translate (Move) and Scale.
a. <u>Translate</u>: Displays the translate manipulator, when selected.
b. <u>Scale</u>: Displays the scale manipulator, when selected.

(2) <u>**Select Mode**</u>: Determines manipulating the tangents of an anchor point.
a. <u>Normal Select</u>: Creates smooth and symmetrical curves. The tangent remains unbroken and scales both sides. This is known as even tangent weight manipulation.
b. <u>Weighted Select</u>: Creates smooth curves weighted to one side. The tangent remains unbroken, but scales only the select tangent. This is known as uneven tangent weight manipulation.
c. <u>Tangent Select</u>: Creates a sharp point by scaling the tangent on the selected side only. This is known as broken and unlinked tangent manipulation.

Using Pencil Curve Tool
Pencil Curve Tool helps you define freehand curves. Instead of defining a curve by placing CVs or edit points, you can drag the mouse-pointer to define the curve. This tool creates a curve with a large number of edit points that you can later simplify or smooth the curve by selecting Edit Curves> Rebuild Curve. By the way, the Edit Curves menu appears only when the Surfaces menu set is selected.

Importing Curves
As you've learnt so far creating curves using various tools, but you'll be pleased to know that you can import curves from external applications. You can import curves in EPS (Encapsulated PostScript) or AI (Adobe Illustrator) formats. However, you should not use the File> Import option to import EPS or AI files, as it does not allow proper importing of the content into Maya. The safe option for this is: Adobe (R) Illustrator (R) Object under Create menu. Perform the following steps to import a curve into Maya:

1. **Open** a scene in Maya and select **Create> Adobe (R) Illustrator (R) Object> (Rectangle Box)** from the main menu bar. The Adobe (R) Illustrator (R) Object Options dialog box appears, as shown in picture 3.9. As you can see, the Bevel radio button (on right side) is selected for the Type setting by default.

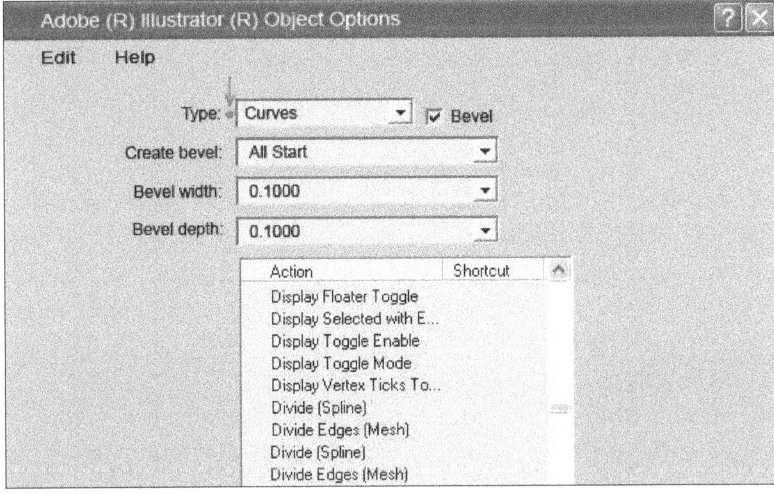

Picture 3.9

2. Select the **Curve** radio button for the <u>Type</u> setting which is shown in red in the picture. The setting disappears as you select the Curves radio button, and it opens <u>another dialog box</u>, (which we can name dialog box 2 for now).

3. Click the **Create** button at the bottom of the dialog box 2. It opens one more dialog box named **Open** (dialog box 3).

4. Select the file type in the **Files of type** dropdown list. You can browse and select the file that you want to import. And click **Open** button at the end. This way, a curve-made file created and saved in Illustrator 8 is opened in Maya.

Lesson 11
Editing a NURBS Curve

You can use NURBS curves to create the base of a 3D surface (model). These NURBS curves are edited to change the shape of curves as well as entire models. You can also attach and detach curves or open and close them. There are two forms of curves in Maya – open curves and close curves. Both curves help to understand object deformation in Maya. You can modify the shape of a NURBS curve using tools such as Curve Editing Tool, Rebuild Curve tool, or Move Tool. To further refine, you can insert more knots in the curve, attach two curves, and smoothen a curve.

Using Move Tool

Move Tool is commonly used for editing the shape of NURBS curves. You must select any component selection mode to use Move Tool and use to modify the curvature of a shape. After selecting the component, you can drag them to rearrange and modify a shape.

1. Select a **shape** that you want to edit and select **Move Tool** from the <u>Tool Box</u> which opens the move manipulator gizmo on the selected CVs.

2. **Right-click** and select **Control Vertex** component select mode from the marking menu. Here you can select one or more CVs by dragging a marquee. Alternatively, with a CV selected, you can press the Up-arrow or Down-arrow key to select the next/previous CV in the row.

3. **Drag** the move manipulator to move the selected CVs. This way, you can select and move individual CVs to edit the shape of a curve more precisely.

Using Curve Editing Tool

Curve Editing Tool shows a manipulator on a selected curve used to change the position and direction of a curve at arbitrary points. It can be used to edit only the curve created with the curve tool. This tool does not work on a curve that has a Construction History. In other words, Curve Editing Tool cannot edit a curve created in more than one step or has been used in other surface or object. When you select Curve Editing Tool, its manipulator appears with the elements like – the Parameter Position, Tangent Scale, Point Position, and Tangent Direction handles.

1. Select a **NURBS curve** whose shape you want to edit, and then, select the **Surface** menu set in the <u>Status Line</u>.

2. Select **Edit Curves> Curve Editing Tool** from the main menu bar. The Curve Editing Tool manipulator appears with different elements.

3. **Drag the Parameter Position** handle to move the manipulator along the curve to any position to edit the shape.

4. **Drag** the **Point Position** handle to edit the shape as required. This way, you can drag the Tangent Direction handle to change the direction of the curve at the point of the Tangent Direction handle. You can also click any one of the four dashed lines of the Tangent Direction handle to align the tangent along its axis.

Inserting a Knot on a Curve

Knots or edit points are inserted on a NURBS curve to increase the number of spans in a curve. You can insert an edit point at the selected curve point without affecting its shape. Adding an extra edit point gives more flexibility in reshaping a curve.

1. To insert a knot on a NURBS curve, select a curve in the viewport and **right-click** and select the **Curve Point** component selection mode.

2. Click anywhere on the curve to insert the new knot. A yellow dot appears indicating the selected curve point.

3. Select **Edit Curve> Insert Knot** from the main menu bar to insert a knot at the selected curve point. This exits from the Curve Point component selection mode and selects the Object Mode.

4. **Right-click** on the curve again, and select the **Edit Point** component selection mode from the marking menu. The new knot appears at the selected curve point. Like this, you can add knots at different positions. To add multiple knots simultaneously, select multiple curve points with the Curve Point component selection mode active.

Attaching Curve

Now you're going to learn about attaching or detaching two different curves into a single unit or vice versa. While working with NURBS curve, sometimes you need to join or split two different curves into a single unit. You can join curves either at the end that are closest or at a specific point. Joining two curves creates a single curve.

1. Select **two opens curves** that you want to attach, and choose **Edit Curves> Attach Curves** from the main menu bar. The Attach Curves Options dialog box appears.

2. Uncheck the **Keep originals** check box. If the Keep original check box is selected, copies of the original curves are created and joined to create a new curve. This keeps the original curves intact.

3. Click the **Attach** button at the bottom in the same dialog box. The two curves join together by blending two closest end points. Apart from joining two NURBS curves at their ends to create a single unified curve, you can also join curves at specific end. For this, select two curve points, one in each curve.

Closing and Opening Curves

If you need to create open and closed curves, or close an open curve and open a closed curve, this is what you have to learn. For that, select an open curve and choose Edit Curves> Open/Close Curves from the main menu bar. The two ends are joined to form a closed curve.

Making a Curve Smooth

Making a curve smooth means the process of removing the sharp edges and twists along a curve's surface. Using Pencil Curve Tool, you can create curves that are not smooth. You can smooth a curve selecting Edit Curve> Smooth Curve command. This command doesn't change the total number of CVs in the curve. However, Maya doesn't allow you to smooth a closed curve or curve-on-surface.

1. To smooth a NURBS curve, select a curve and choose **Edit Curve> Smooth Curve> (Rectangle Box)** from the main menu bar. It opens the Smooth Curve Options dialog box.

2. **Type** a value in the Smoothness text box. In our case, we type: **20**. Then, click the Smooth button at the bottom. It makes the selected curve smooth.

Lesson 12
Working with NURBS Surface

In Maya, a NURBS surface means a 3D objects with volume, not a NURBS curve. The NURBS surfaces can be formed using a series of curves. Similar to NURBS curve, NURBS surface is also parametric. The equations that define the shape of a surface depend on parameters that are specifically part of the geometry. Unlike to NURBS curve, a NURBS surface has two parametric directions – U and V instead of one. These two directions define its normals, which determine the front and back of a surface. These surface properties, such as surface normals and curve directions help to model and render scenes in Maya. Using NURBS surface components; you can create and modify different surface forms.

Deconstructing a NURBS Surface

In this section, you're going to learn about creating NURBS surfaces. Similar to NURBS curves, NURBS surfaces consist of several components, such as isoparm, CV, hull, surface patch, surface point, surface UV and normal. As you have already learnt about CV and hull components, now we'll discuss remaining components beginning with isoparm.

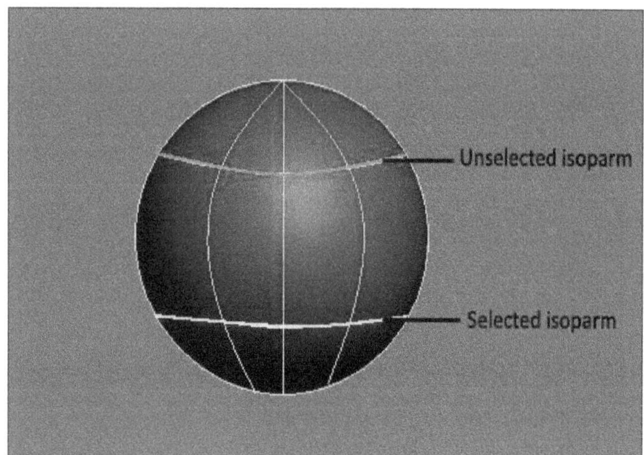

Picture 4.0

Isoparm

Isoparm (isoparametric curves) are curves that run on the entire width of a NURBS surface. These lines connect the points with constant U or V coordinate values. Isoparms represent the cross sections of a NURBS surface in the U or V directions. You need to increase isoparms to increase the number of surface edit points. You can select isoparms in the Isoparm component selection mode. The picture 4.0 displays both the selected (yellow) and unselected (cyan) isoparms on a NURBS sphere.

Maya lets you insert, remove or use an isoparm to create curves. The important distinction is that if you select an isoparm that is not a span or section, it is displayed with yellow dots. If you select an isoparm that is a span or section, it is displayed as a solid yellow line. At the time of extracting surfaces, you have to keep this distinction in mind.

Surface Patch

A surface patch in Maya is an enclosed span square. Another important component of a NURBS surface is a patch, an area enclosed by four adjacent isoparms. It is the smallest element of NURBS surface.

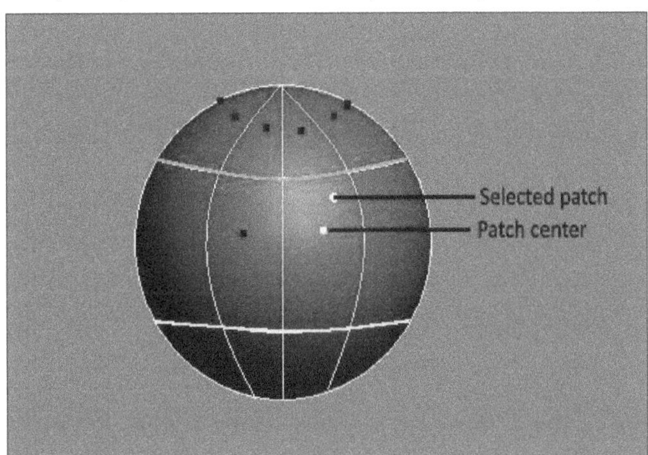

Picture 4.1

Several patches can be selected and duplicated to create individual NURBS surfaces. Each patch has a certain number of CVs controlled by the degree of a curve. You can insert extra isoparms into a surface or increase the degree of a surface to increase the number of CVs. NURBS surfaces are 4-sided patches; hence, all patches in a NURBS surface have four distinct edges and a center called surface patch center. You need to select the center to select the entire surface patch. The picture 4.1 shows a surface patch with patch center.

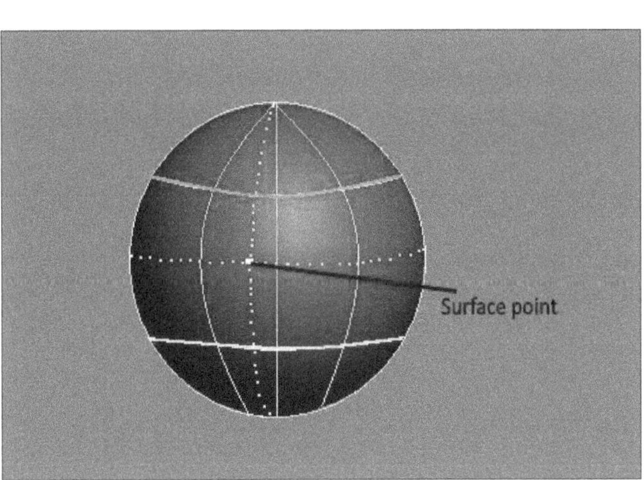

Picture 4.2

Surface Point

Now you are learning about surface points. Surface points are present on the surface of a NURBS object and are invisible on selecting Surface Points Component selection mode from the marking menu. You can use these points to edit a NURBS object. The values of these points depend on the parameterization of a surface. You need to click the surface of a NURBS object to display the surface points. The picture 4.2 on the left is showing a dotted line which is a surface point on a NURBS sphere.

Normals

Normals are imaginary lines perpendicular to each point on a curve or surface. Unlike the components of a polygon, a NURBS curve does not have normals, but only directions. However, NURBS surfaces have normals that are only displayed in the shaded mode. The direction of U and V on a surface determines the direction of the surface normals. By default, normals are not displayed on a surface. Unlike other components, you cannot display them using marking menu. To display the normals, you need to select Display> NURBS> Normals (Shaded Mode). It will show the object with a lot of lines helping you to edit and make any changes to the object.

Creating NURBS Surfaces

In order to do NURBS modeling, what you need to do first is creating a surface to work on it further. The starting point for the surface can be constructed from the pre-defined NURBS primitives available in Shelf or in the Create menu. You can also create a NURBS surface using NURBS curves, and then mold the surface into any character. You can also use the curves to create simple surfaces, which can be modified by manipulating CVs. There are two methods of creating NURBS surfaces: Using NURBS primitives, and Using NURBS curves.

Using NURBS primitives

Primitives are the predefined 3D geometric shapes. NURBS primitives are widely used to create NURBS surfaces. You can use NURBS primitives, such as NURBS spheres, NURBS cubes, and NURBS cylinders to create surfaces. Primitive objects in Maya are often used as the building blocks for complex shapes. For instance, the sphere primitive can be used as the foundation for a human head model. There are three distinct ways to create NURBS primitives, such as using the Create menu, using Shelf, and creating NURBS primitives interactively. All the NURBS primitives are listed in Create> NURBS Primitives submenus. The Interactive Creation option allows you to create NURBS primitives interactively by dragging in the viewport. You can perform the steps mentioned below to create a NURBS surface using NURBS primitives:

1. Select **Create> NURBS Primitives> Sphere** from the main menu bar, and click the **Smooth shade all** button on the panel toolbar which will display the sphere in shaded mode.

2. **Drag** the cursor in the viewport to create a NURBS sphere in the wireframe mode, as shown in picture 4.3 A. Holding Ctrl key down will allow you to constrain an object creation from the center, and Ctrl+Shift to create a cubic from the center.

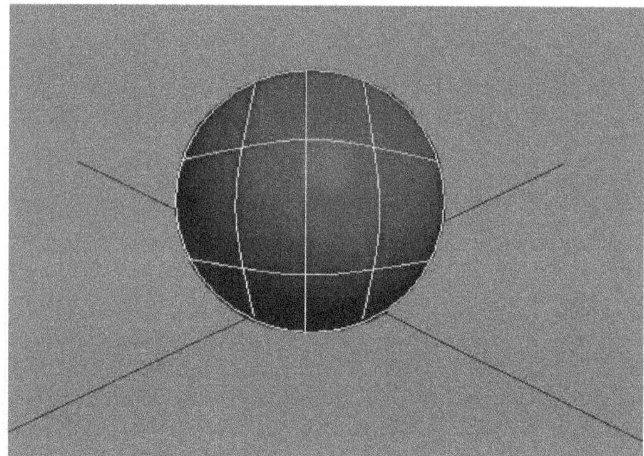
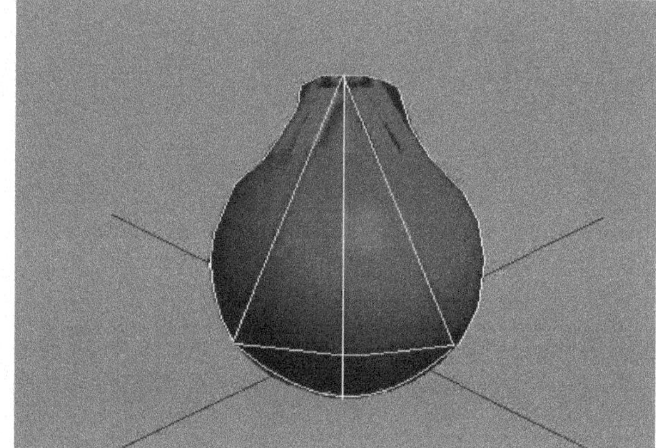

Picture 4.3 A   Picture 4.3 B

3. To start modeling by selecting the component selection modes, select **Move Tool** from the Tool Box, choose the **Control Vertex** component selection mode, and select the **CVs** in the right viewport.

4. **Drag** the CVs in any direction to modify the shape, as shown in picture 4.3 B. You can also scale and rotate it or apply various other commands, such as Extrude and Bevel.

While creating a 3D palace environment for a game or a move, you can use primitives directly in a scene without any or little modifications, as cylinder primitives can be used for pillars in the palace.

Using NURBS Curve

Though primitive objects are the base models to start modeling in a 3D program, but they are limited, and so, you need other base models. In Maya, you can create more complicated surfaces using NURBS curves. You can use curves in several ways such as revolving, extruding, and lofting to create surfaces. You can create a surface using these methods: **(A)** Revolving a NURBS curve **(B)** Lofting a NURBS curve.

(A) <u>Revolving a NURBS Curve to Create a NURBS Surface</u>

Using the Revolve command, you can create a surface by revolving a profile curve around a pivot point. Revolving changes the attributes of curves transforming to create a NURBS surface. You need to curve representing the cross-section of the surface that you want to create. Perform these steps to revolve a curve to create a NURBS surface:

1. **Draw a curve** representing the cross-section for the NURBS surface. In our case, we have created the cross-section of a <u>wine glass</u> in the <u>front viewport</u>, as shown in picture 4.4.

2. Select the **Surfaces** menu set if not selected (shown as <u>Step 2</u> in picture 4.4). This menu set is in the Animation dropdown at the top left corner just below <u>Main menu bar</u> (as explained in lesson 2). When you select Surfaces menu set, the <u>Main menu bar</u> changes to **Specific menus** (as explained in lesson 2).

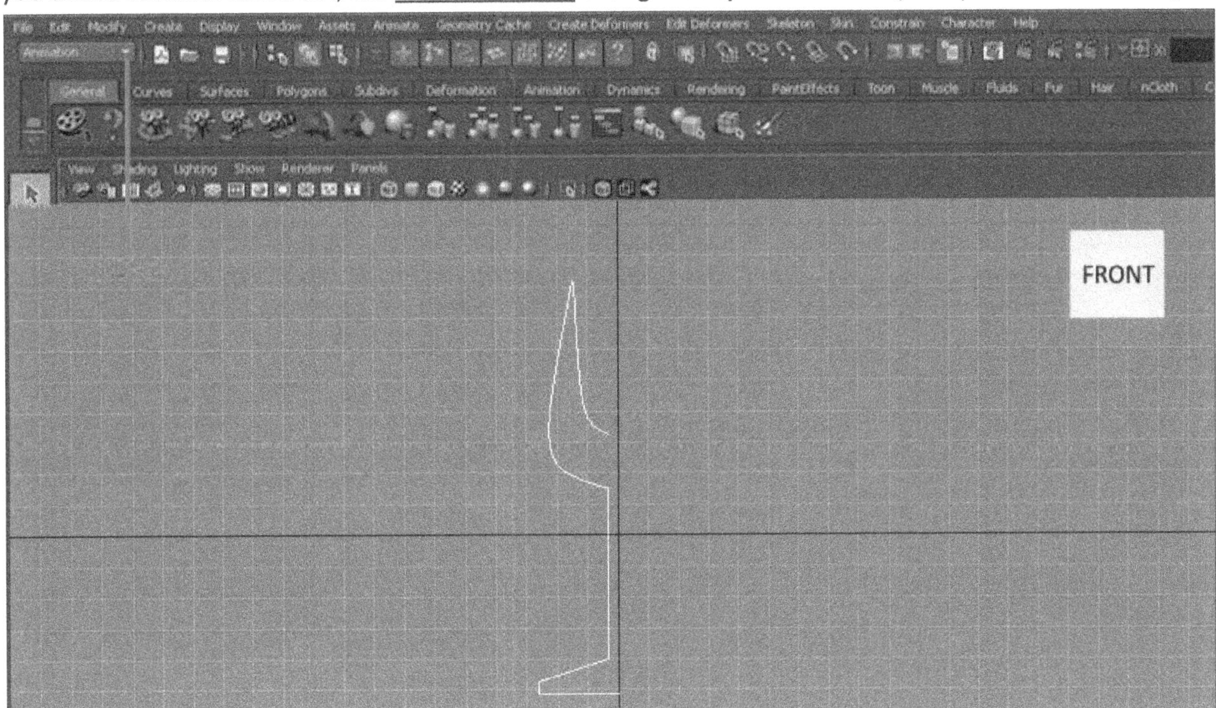

Picture 4.4

3. As the Main menu bar at the top is changed to Specific menus, now you can select **Surfaces> Revolve> (Rectangle Box)** from the <u>main menu bar</u>. It opens <u>Revolve Options</u> dialog box, as shown in picture 4.5.

4. Type: **10** in the <u>Segments</u> text box and click **Revolve** button at the bottom (shown in picture 4.5). It will create a wine glass in the viewport. The picture 4.6 shows a similar view of the final wine glass. Save this file to use in the next lesson.

If you look at this dialog box on your computer screen, you'll see some other options that will allow you to set values for Surface degree, Start sweep angle, End sweep angle. The Surface degree option determines whether the V parameter direction of the surface should be linear (with flat faces) or cubic (smooth). The Cubic radio button (degree 3) is selected, by default. You can also select the axis about which you want the profile curve to revolve. Using the Output geometry option, you can create a new surface as NURBS (default), Polygon, Subdiv, and Bezier. You can click Edit> Reset Settings in the Revolve Options dialog box to reset any previous changes to the default settings.

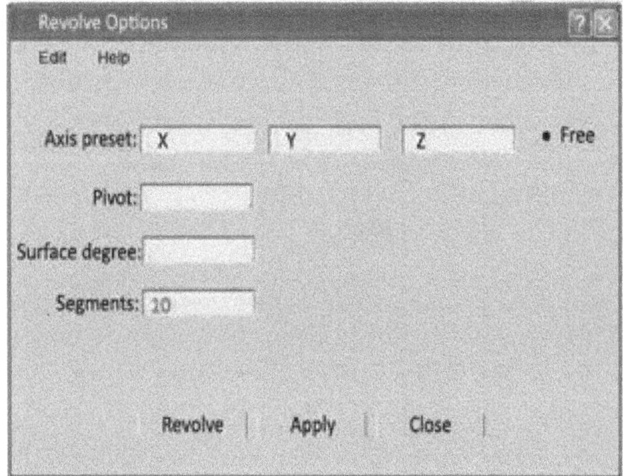

Picture 4.5

Picture 4.6

(B) Lofting a NURBS Curve to Create a NURBS Surface
The lofting feature is used to create a NURBS surface with a series of cross-section or profile curves. And a series of curves that define the shape of an object can be lofted to form a surface. Profile curves can be normal 3D curves that are created using the different curve creation tools, such as CV Curve Tool, EP Curve Tool, Bezier Curve Tool, and Pencil Curve Tool. Profile curves can also be created using surface isoparms or edges, or trimmed edges. Let's do these steps to use the Loft command:

1. Open a new scene in Maya and create a **profile curve** in the front viewport. The picture 4.7 shows a profile curve created of a flyover.

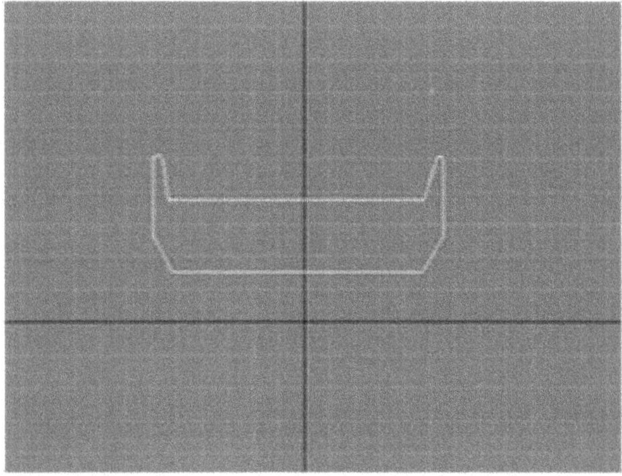

Picture 4.7

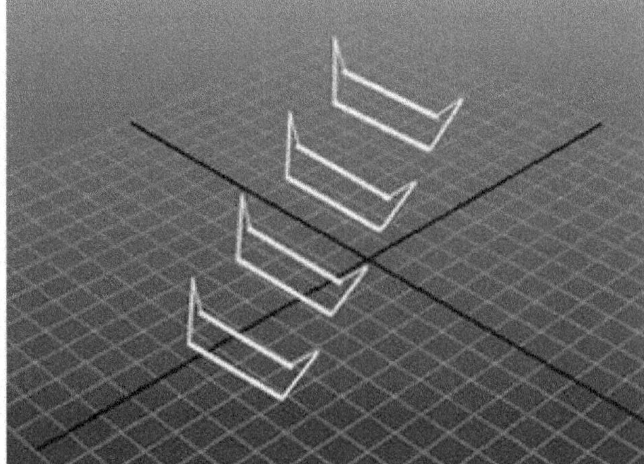

Picture 4.8

2. **Create** duplicate copies of the curve using the **Duplicate** command and place them as sown in the picture 4.8. If you have all the curves of similar parameters, they'll work well with lofting.

3. Click the **Smooth shade all** button the panel toolbar, and select **Edit**> **Select All** from the main menu bar to select all the curves. When multiple objects are selected in the viewport, the last selected object appears in green and all other objects appear in white.

4. Select **Surface**> **Loft** from the main menu bar. It creates a flyover in the perspective viewport connecting all the curves. Save this file to use in the next lesson.

Editing a NURBS Surface

Maya has many commands to modify a surface. The commands are: Attach Surfaces, Detach Surfaces, Extend and Trim Surfaces, and Insert Isoparms. While editing NURBS surfaces, you can add realism to the shape of a model, and you can insert isoparms into a surface, attach and detach a surface, and open/close surfaces. You can also use the Sculpting feature to edit NURBS surfaces. Now you're going to learn about inserting isoparms in an existing NURBS surface.

Inserting Isoparms in a NURBS Surface

You have already learnt that each NURBS surface is composed of a large number of patches, and each patch is enclosed by four adjacent isoparms. An isoparm is inserted into a surface while modeling. Inserting isoparms into a surface increases the number of CVs in the surface. These CVs can be used to further modify the shape of a NURBS surface introducing greater sharpness and flexibilities which are required for advanced modeling in Maya. You can perform the following simple steps that will insert isoparms in a surface:

1. **Select** the surface to insert an isoparm. For now, you can select the flyover surface you created in the previous section.

2. **Right-click** the selected surface and select **Isoparm** component selection mode from the marking menu. Then, **click** and **drag** an isoparm to any location which will show a dotted and a solid line.

3. Select **Edit NURBS**> **Insert Isoparms** from the main menu bar. It inserts a new isoparm at the selected location and the Object Mode becomes active.

Like this, you can add multiple isoparms into a surface. In the Insert Isoparms Options dialog box, you can add multiple isoparms between two selected isoparms, by selecting the Between selections radio button. By default, the At selection radio button is selected, which allows you to add isoparms at selected locations.

Splitting and Attaching NURBS surfaces

As you learnt attaching NURBS curves in the previous lesson, in the same way you can attach two or more NURBS surfaces together to create a single surface, or detach a single surface into two or more surfaces and work on each surface separately. You can use the commands, such as Attach Surfaces and Detach Surfaces for this purpose. This section of the lesson is categorized as **(A)** Splitting a NURBS Surface **(B)** Attaching NURBS Surfaces.

(A) <u>Splitting a NURBS Surface</u>

Maya allows you to attach and detach a surface and split it into multiple surfaces. Using Detach Surfaces under the Edit NURBS menu, you can split a surface. You can also detach a single surface, a group of surfaces, or a surface at the selected isoparm. The steps to split a NURBS surface are:

1. **Select** a surface that you want to split. For now, you can select the Wine glass surface in the perspective viewport.

2. **Right-click** on the surface and select the **Isoparm** component selection mode from the marking menu. Then, **select** the isoparm where you want to split the wine glass surface.

3. Select **Edit NURBS> Detach Surfaces** from the main menu bar. This detaches the surface at the selected isoparm and you have to manually **move** them to separate using <u>Move Tool</u>.

(B) <u>Attaching NURBS Surfaces</u>

Attaching refers to joining multiple surfaces to make them a single unified unit. The gap between two separate NURBS surfaces can be filled by attaching these surfaces together. To fill this gap, a new surface is created between the two unattached surfaces. Perform the following steps to attach two NURBS surfaces:

1. First you need to **select** both of the isoparms that you separated of the wine glass. And to select the two isoparms, select the first surface, right-click on it and select the Isoparm component selection mode, and then, click an isoparm to select it. Now hold the Shift key down and click the other surface.

2. Select **Edit NURBS> Attach Surfaces>** (**Rectangle Box**) from the main menu bar which will open the **Attach Surfaces Options** window.

3. **Uncheck** the <u>Keep originals</u> check box and click the <u>Attach</u> button at the bottom. The two separate surfaces are joined with new surfaces. These surfaces are blended as the Blend radio button for the Attach method option is selected in the Attach Surfaces Options window.

Extending a NURBS Surface

Extending a NURBS surface refers to increasing the size of a surface, by making changes in its U and V directions. For this, you don't have to remodel the entire surface, but just select the isoparm from where you want to extend the surface. You can perform the following simple steps to extend a NURBS surface:

1. **Select** the surface that you wan to extend, and then **select an isoparm** in the <u>Isoparm component</u> selection mode from where you want to extend.

2. Select **Edit NURBS> Extend Surfaces** (**Rectangle Box**) from the main menu bar which opens Extend Surface Options window.

3. Type: **9.0000** in the <u>Distance</u> text box to set the length of the extension, and then click the **Extend** button at the bottom to extend the curve. The surface is extended by 9 units.

Projecting a Curve on a Surface

You can cut the surface with a user-defined curve in Maya. For that, you need to project a curve onto a surface using the Project Curve on the Surface command. This command is mostly used to define regions on a NURBS surface for trimming. To create a curve on a NURBS surface, first activate the surface, and then draw a curve using any of the curve creation tools. In Maya, there are several techniques for creating curves on a surface. You can also use text as curves to project them on a surface. Now you're going to learn about projecting a user-defined curve onto a surface:

1. **Create** the surface on which you want to project a curve. In our case, we've created a NURBS cube primitive object (picture 4.9 A).

2. **Draw** a curve that you want to project onto the surface of the NURBS cube in the front viewport and **position** it as shown in picture 4.9 A: step 2.

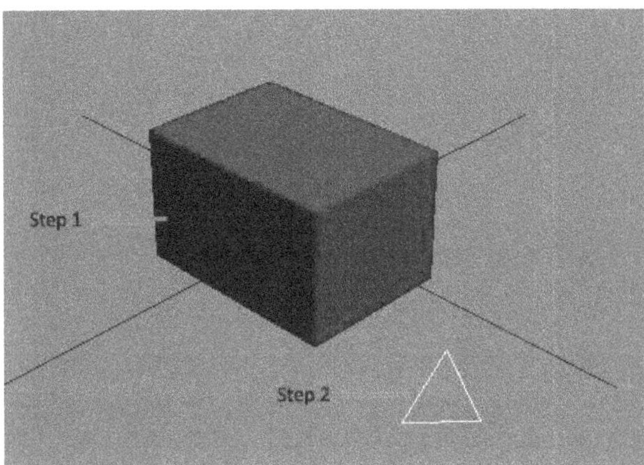

Picture 4.9 A

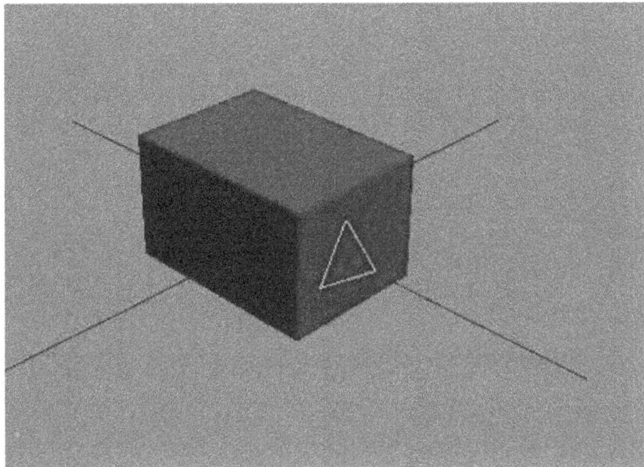

Picture 4.9 B

3. **Press** the **Spacebar** key to move the viewport to the four-view, and then **select** both the surfaces (NURBS cube and the curve) in the front viewport.
You need to select the viewport in the direction in which you want to project it. We want to project the curve along the Y-axis, so we selected the curve in the front viewport.

4. Select **Edit NURBS> Project Curve on Surface** from the main menu bar. It will make the curve projected on the surface in the perspective viewport, as shown in picture 4.9 B. Save this file to use for the next section of the lesson.

Trimming a Surface

Trimming refers to the process of cutting or dividing a surface using a curve. This is used to create complex edges and holes on a NURBS surface. Trim tool helps you to make a region on a surface invisible instead of deleting it. The trimmed region can be easily recovered using Untrim Tool. For trimming, you need to create curves-on-surface before you can trim the surface. Perform these steps to trim the area defined by the curve on a surface:

1. **Open** the same file that you saved in previous section in which you projected a curve on a surface (picture 4.9 B).

2. **Click** the projected region in the <u>perspective viewport</u> to select it, and select **Edit NURBS> Trim Tool> (Rectangle Box)** from the main tool bar. It opens the <u>Tool Settings</u> window for Trim Tool and a trim grid on the surface.

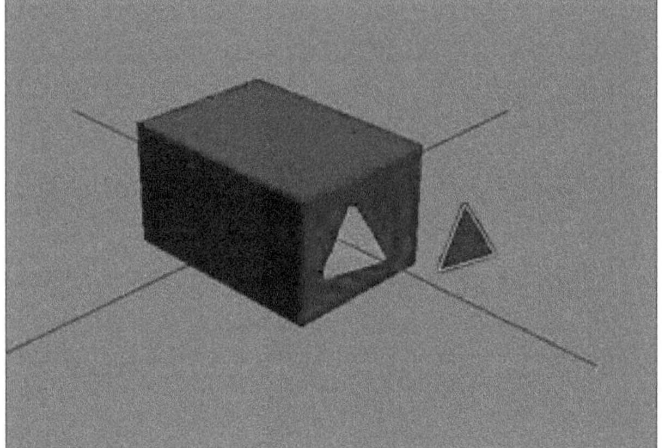

Picture 5.0

3. Select the **Discard** radio button for the <u>Selected state</u> setting in Trim Tool window. The Discard option removes the region you trim.

4. **Click** twice inside the area defined by the curve. A yellow diamond shape appears inside the area. Press **enter** key to trim the area defined by the curve. The area defined by the curve is deleted, creating a hole in the shape of the curve, as shown in picture 5.0.

Lesson 13
Working with Booleans

Booleans allow you to easily cut holes in a mesh using geometric operation. They represent actions performed on two solid surfaces to create the appearance of a union, intersection, or subtraction. You can create complex shapes easily using the Boolean operation, which is difficult to create in a normal modeling process. However, Boolean operations can be problematic because you may not get the intended result and the entire mesh might disappear. In such cases you can undo the operation. Booleans operation can be used to create the first surface of a model using almost every object available in Maya, such as polygonal primitives, NURBS primitives, or curves. There are three ways to perform Booleans:

<u>Union</u>: Creates a new shape by adding two shapes together.
<u>Difference</u>: Creates a new shape by removing one shape from another.
<u>Intersection</u>: Creates a new shape by intersecting two shapes.

Performing the Union Boolean Operation

The starting point of the Union Boolean operation is two overlapping 3D primitives or objects. These objects are combined and the overlapped geometry inside the objects is removed. This operation trims the surface, so that they appear to be merged. The material of the first object that you select during the Union Boolean operation inherits the material of the second object you select. You can use the Union Tool under the Booleans submenu to merge two objects. Follow these steps to merge two NURBS surfaces using the Union Boolean operation:

1. **Create** a scene with overlapping objects. In our case, we have created a **NURBS sphere** and a **NURBS torus** and placed them overlapping each other, as shown in picture 5.1 A.

2. Select **Edit NURBS> Booleans> Union Tool** from the main menu bar to activate Union Tool.

3. **Move** the cursor over the perspective viewport and **press Spacebar** key. Then, **click** the <u>first surface</u>, which is the NURBS sphere and **press enter** key.

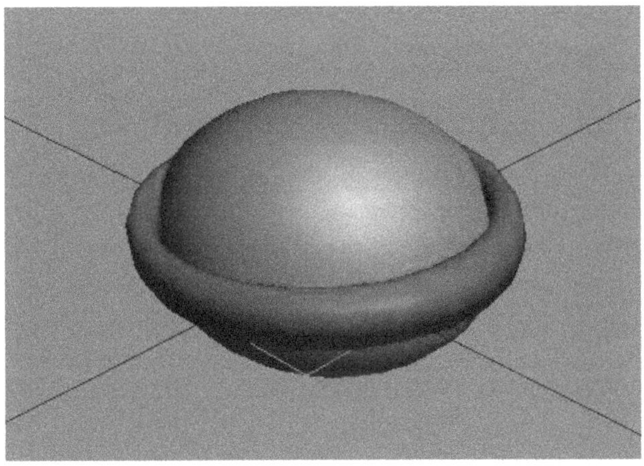

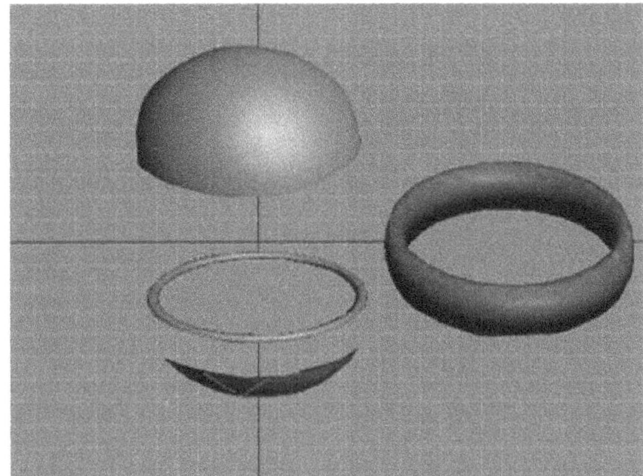

Picture 5.1 A   **Picture 5.1 B**

4. **Click** the other surface, which is the NURBS torus. Now the surfaces appear merged with the sphere surface material.

5. Use **Move Tool** to separate the surfaces, (picture 5.1 B). The order in which you click the surfaces is critical for Difference Tool, as the second surface that you click from the first surface is subtracted. You can learn to subtract one surface from another using Difference Tool in the next section of the lesson.

Performing the Difference Boolean Operation
Difference Tool allows you to subtract one surface from another. Similar to the Union Boolean operation, the starting point of Difference Boolean operation is two overlapping 3D objects. To select the Difference Tool, you can click Edit NURBS> Booleans> Difference Tool from the main menu bar. Difference Boolean operation trims the surfaces so that the volume of the second surface appears to be subtracted from the first. There can be two types of subtraction:

Subtraction (A-B): Object A is subtracted from object B.
Subtraction (B-A): Object B is subtracted from object A.

The steps that you can perform to subtract one surface from another using the Difference Boolean operation are as follow. (1) Create two NURBS surfaces and place them overlapping each other. (2) Select Edit NURBS> Booleans> Difference Tool. (3) Click the first surface in the viewport and press enter. (4) Click the second surface and press enter key again to subtract it from the first surface.

Difference Tool remains active even after the Boolean operation, which allows you to execute another Boolean operation, but you can disable it by selecting Exit on completion check box in the NURBS Boolean Difference Operations window.

Performing the Intersection Boolean Operation
Similar to the previous two Boolean operations, you need overlapping objects to execute the Intersect Boolean operation which intersects the overlapping objects. Intersection trims the surfaces to retain only their shared volume. The steps for this are as follow. (1) Create two NURBS surfaces and place them overlapping each other. (2) Select Edit NURBS> Booleans> Intersection Tool. (3) Click the first surface in the viewport and press enter, and then click the second surface and press enter to interest.

Lesson 14
Working with Polygons

There are numerous modeling techniques in terms of geometry types, such as NURBS, polygon, and subdivision. We can say that polygons are the most popular type used for modeling because of its ability to create models having low polygon count. A low-poly model is preferred for real-time simulations in games, Web applications, and virtual realities. The modeling process using polygon object types is known as polygonal modeling. You create polygon geometry or polygon mesh by inter-connecting three or more flat surfaces called faces. By selecting various components including vertex, edge, and face, you can modify a mesh. Moreover, you can also modify a mesh using various tools and commands to create new polygon meshes and modify existing polygon meshes. These tools include Interactive Split Tool, Bridge, Wedge Face, Bevel, Extrude, Cut Faces Tool, Mirror Cut, and Smooth. You can also project curves onto polygon surfaces and use those projected curves to split or cut apart those polygons.

Planning for a Model

Before you start development process in Maya, you need to understand the requirement of the scene. It is compulsory to select a modeling method in order to model a character. For instance, if you want to model a character for a game, you need to consider the polygon count of the final model, as you need a low-poly model for games. In games, for real-time simulation, low-poly models are preferred. Based on the task, you must select a modeling technique, such as polygon modeling, NURBS modeling, or subdivision modeling.

In planning, you also need to understand the construction of the model. The act of dissecting an object to model it into primitive object, help you to translate and recreate it in three dimensional forms. You can create various elements of the model separately and join them together to form an object. For instance, you can dissect a human character into basic primitive objects, such as sphere, cube, and cylinder. The head can be simplified to a basic shape sphere or box, the torso can be simplified into a box or cube, and the hands and legs can be represented by cylinders. It is sensible to collect most information about an object that you want to model, and record the size and dimensions. You also need to determine the position of the model in a computer graphics (CG) screen. For instance, if an object is shown, away from the camera (for shot); you can make it a low poly-model. If it is shown in a close-up shot, you can make a model with higher level of details. Thus, you can keep the total polygon count of a scene minimal and reduce the rendering time. It is important to plan a model in accordance with the level of detail required. If you are not certain about the level of detail, it is always better to create a high-poly model. Later, if you need a low-poly model, you can reduce the total polygon count of the high-poly model. You can increase the detail of a model during the texturing phase of production. You can achieve good and high quality output with simple geometries with well-painted texture maps. Another important aspect before deciding the level of detail of the model is the hardware configuration of the system. A high detail model requires a lot of memory, which may increase the rendering time considerably. All these things are important factors of creating a model in Maya.

Deconstructing a Polygon Mesh

You have understood how important planning is before stating the development process. Now you need to know about polygon mesh. A polygon mesh is an object that is created by combining polygon faces. It can be either a simple shape as a polygon primitive or a complex shape as an alien creature. Maya primitives are prebuilt 3D geometric shapes that include sphere, cube, cylinder, cone, and plane. You can also create a polygon mesh using other different techniques.

A face is primarily a two dimensional (2D) geometrical shape enclosed by three or more straight line segments. Polygon meshes are made up of several components such as vertices, edges, faces, and normals. The order of vertices around the face determines its direction (whether, a polygon side is the front or back). A polygon front face is graphically represented using a vector described as normal. The number of polygons differs from one model to another. However, every polygon mesh is considered to have few basic components, such as Vertex, Edge, Face, UV, and Normal. Now let's see what these components are.

Vertex
A vertex defines the outline of a polygon face. It is a point in space, in combination with other vertices. In a polygon mesh, the corners at the intersection of two lines segments are known as the vertices of that polygon. The vertices of one polygon face coincide with the vertices of the adjacent polygon mesh resulting in a 3D surface. They appear on the surface mesh as solid squares as shown in picture 5.2.

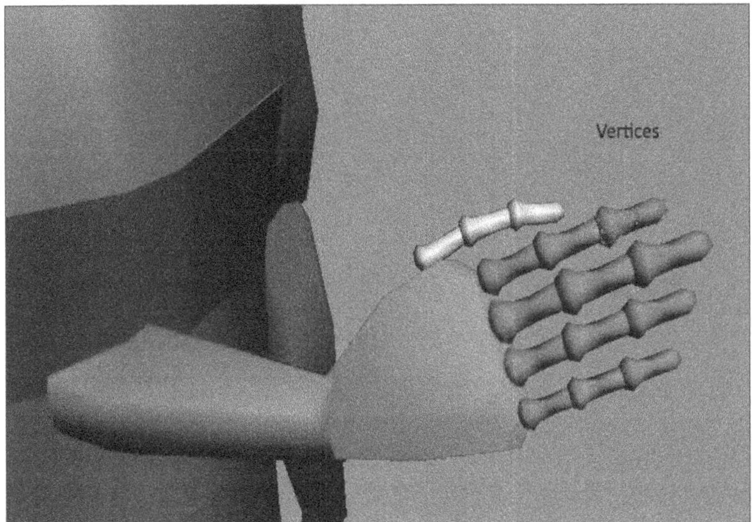

When you select the vertices they turn yellow in color. To select a vertex, click on it or drag a marquee around it. To select multiple vertices, hold the Shift key down and click the vertices that you want to add to the selection. To deselect a vertex, click a selected vertex with Ctrl key down. After selecting vertices, you can move them as required to modify the shape of the polygon mesh.

Picture 5.2

When you need to select vertices of a polygon mesh, select the Vertex component selection mode. You can also control the size of the vertices display in the viewport which is 3.0 by default. To increase or decrease the size of the vertices, you can go to Display> Polygon> Vertex Size from the main menu bar.

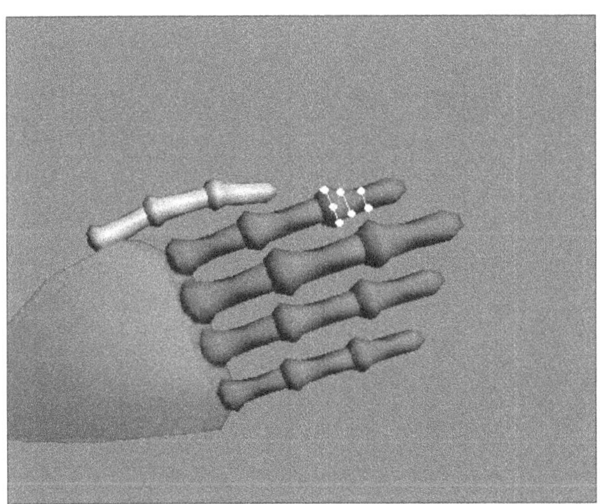

Edge
If you look at your computer screen, you'll see a straight line connecting a vertex to another. This line is called an edge. The length of an edge depends on the distance between two consecutive vertices. Depending on the position of the vertices in a polygon, the length of the edges can be of varied lengths. You can select one or more edges and use them to modify a polygon mesh using the transform tools. Edges are useful when connecting separate polygonal meshes. You can merge the edges of the disconnected meshes together to connect them. To select the edges, select the Edge component selection mode.

Picture 5.3

But in a polygon mesh, two continuous polygons share their vertices implying that the edges between those vertices are also shared. The edges that appear on the border of the polygon mesh are called border edges. By default, the border edges of a polygon mesh are not visible; you can display them by selecting Display> Polygons> Border Edges from the main menu bar.

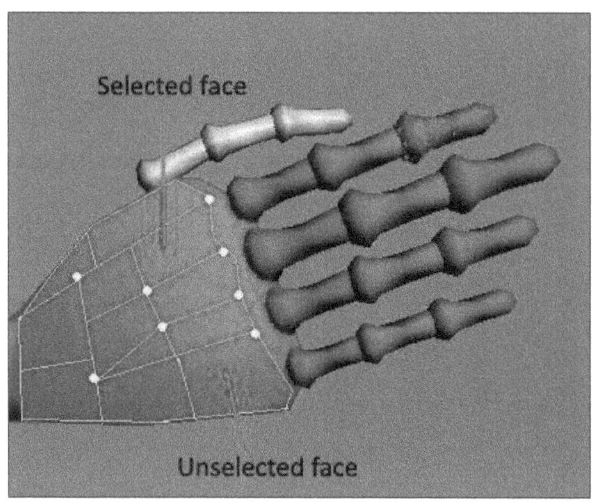

Picture 5.4

Face

According to Maya, a face can be defined as a solid unit bounded by edges and vertices. Every polygon mesh consists of one or more faces. The shape and structure of a face is determined by the position and the number of vertices in the polygon. For instance, if there are four vertices in a polygon, the face of the polygon is quadrilateral. You can extrude, bevel, or combine faces to modify a polygon mesh. You can also project textures onto selected faces and use the mapping manipulator to adjust the textures as required. The picture 5.4 helps you understand a polygon mesh with quadrilateral faces.

The face of a polygon mesh can be planar or non-planar. A planar face exists in a single plane; all vertices defining the face appear in the same plane. A polygon mesh with non-planar faces might render incorrectly in the final output. The face center provides the visual indication of the center of a face, while using certain features such as Bevel. By default, face centers are not displayed; to display them, select Display> Polygons> Face Centers from the main menu bar.

UV

UVs are 2D texture coordinates and exist with the vertices of a polygonal mesh in the shape of lines, as shown in picture 5.5. They define a 2D texture coordinate system known as the UV texture space. This

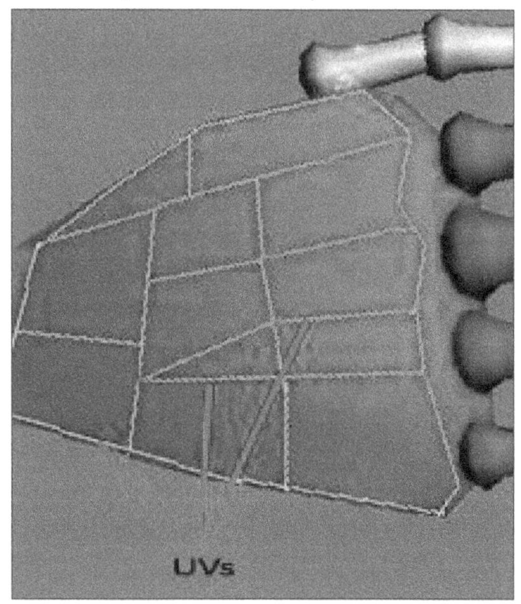

Picture 5.5

space uses the coordinate (denoted by U and V alphabets) values along 2D coordinate system for width and height. The UV value helps to place image texture maps on a 3D surface. The U and V values range from 0 to 1. Polygonal UV coordinates represent the projections onto the XY-plane in Maya and are created optionally. Unlike vertices, edges, or faces, you can create objects without UVs, by setting the Texture option to Off or None while creating primitives. UVs can either be generated automatically by the application, manually by the artist, or by a combination of both. The UVs in a polygon mesh appear in the same location as the vertices of that mesh. The U and V dimensions represent a plane (U for the width and V for the height). A texture map is always defined by U for the horizontal component and V for the vertical component. UVs define how you can map the image texture onto the surface mesh.

When you select the UVs, they appear in green. You need to ensure that there are UVs on an object; otherwise you cannot see the mapped textures in the viewport. This happens when you accidently create an object without UVs or import a model without UVs. By default, UVs are created for many primitives types; however, you need to rearrange them to accurately place an image map.

Normal
A vector displayed as a fine line perpendicular to the faces of a polygon mesh is called Normal. It is used to indicate the orientation of a face. You can always change the orientation by changing the normals. The orientation of the vertices in a polygon mesh determines the front of the face. While creating a polygon, if the vertices are placed in a clockwise direction, the front of the face is away from you. Else, if the vertices are placed in an anti-clockwise direction, the front faces you.

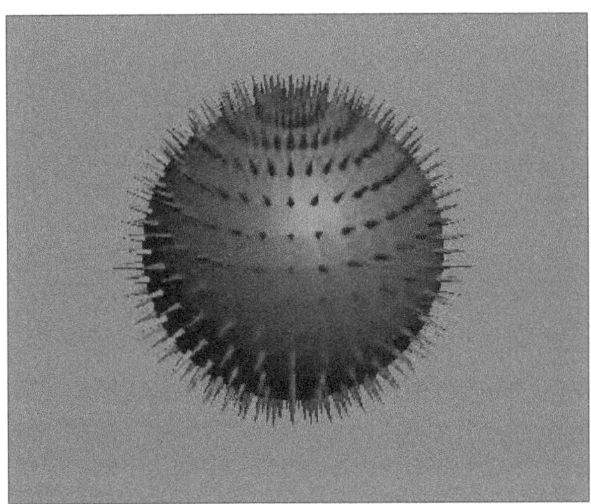

You will find two types of normal: face and vertex. A face normal is a perpendicular line that protrudes from the center of a face of a polygon mesh to indicate its direction. By default, the face normals of a polygon mesh are not visible in the viewport. To display face normal, you can select Display> Polygon> Face Normals or Vertex Normals from the main menu bar. And you should also know that face normals are visible only in the object mode and not in the component mode. If you still cannot see the face normals, you have to select the Normals check box in the Preferences window where you can also change the size of the normals using the Normal size option. Picture 5.6 shows the face normal.

Picture 5.6

Vertex normals also look similar to face normals. A vertex normal is defined by averaging the surrounding face normals that share the vertex point. It simulates smoother surfaces during lighting calculations, while rendering. If you can't see the vertex normals or you want to change the length of them, you can go to Display> Polygons> Custom Polygon Display from the main menu bar.

Lesson 15
Making Component Selections in Maya
It is important to know how to select objects and their components in Maya workflow. There are different methods of selection, but the most common method is using Select Tool. To select one component, you click on it using Select Tool, and to select more than one component, hold the Shift key down and click the components. You can also use Paint Selection Tool to paint the components that you want to select, and the Soft Selection feature to select components using the falloff value. Let's go in detail about it.

Using Paint Selection Tool
Using Paint Selection Tool you can select components of a polygon mesh by painting them with the brush or the stylus. This helps to select those components that are not easily selectable using the bounding box. By default, Paint Selection Tool selects vertices when you click and drag the brush over a polygonal mesh. You can also select faces and edges by switching the component selection mode to

Face or Edge. The Paint Selection Tool cursor appears as a circular brush. The Tool Settings window of it enables you to change the brush radius, brush profile, or painting operations. To access the Tool Settings of it, you can double-click the Paint Selection Tool icon in Tool Box. Let's do these steps to select components using Paint Selection Tool:

1. **Select** a polygon mesh in the viewport, and then double-click **Paint Selection Tool** in Tool box. It opens the Tool Settings window and activates the Vertex component selection mode, by default.

2. Type a radius value: **1.5000** in the Radius (U) text box in the Brush group. Press enter key after the value is entered.

3. **Move** the Paint Selection Tool cursor over the polygon mesh. You can **click** and **drag over** the area you want to select.

You'll see that the brush-tip appears as a circle with S+. The Plus (+) sign indicates that when you drag the brush tip over vertices, the selected vertices are added to the current selection. The S alphabet indicates that the tool is in Select mode. You can also choose Unselect and Toggle modes in the Paint Operations group. We can discuss here the available modes in the Paint Operations group.

Select: Selects components when you paint. When this option is selected, you can press Ctrl key and drag over the selected components to deselect them.
Unselect: Deselects the selected component when you paint.
Toggle: Selects unselected components and deselects selected components when painted.
Add to current selection: Allows you to add components to the existing selection. This option does not require the Shift key pressed to add a component to the selection.
Select All: Selects all components of an active polygon mesh.
Unselect All: Unselects all components of an active polygon mesh.
Toggle All: Selects all unselected components and unselects all selected components.

In the brush group, the default brush type or profile is selected as Soft Brush. You can also select other options for profile, such as Gaussian brush, Solid Brush, and Square brush. By the way, Paint Selection Tool only selects components of the polygon mesh that faces the camera.

Using the Soft Selection Feature
This is also one of the features to select components. It uses a falloff value to define the area surrounding the selected components. The effect of the tool gradually weakens when you move from the center to the edges. For instance, when you transform a component; the area closer to the selected component is affected the most and the area farther is less affected. Transforming components with the Soft Selection Feature enabled lets you perform a smooth transformation. This feature is frequently used during organic modeling including human characters, where a smooth transformation is required. You can use this feature to select components on polygon meshes or NURBS surfaces. In Maya, the falloff is represented with a color gradient. The color gradient appears on vertices and edges regardless of the selected component selection mode. Let's do these steps to use the Soft Selection Feature:

1. **Select** a mesh object, **right-click** on the polygon mesh and select the Vertex component selection mode from the marking menu.

2. Double-click **Select Tool** in the <u>Tool Box</u> to open the Tool Settings. And then, select **Soft Select** check box in <u>Soft Selection</u> group. By default, Soft Selection feature is turned off. All options are now enabled.

3. Select the **vertex** or vertices that you want to transform. The selected vertex will appear in <u>yellow</u> and will be affected the most when you transform the object.

The effect of transform decreases gradually towards black. You can also see that the Falloff color gradient is set from black to yellow by default, which is also reflected on the selection in the perspective view. To increase or decrease the affected area, increase or decrease the Falloff radius value respectively, which is 5.00 by default.

4. Type a new value: **2.00** for the <u>Falloff radius</u> text box. And then, click **Move Tool** in Tool Box to <u>transform</u> the selected vertex by moving it.

The Tools Settings window displays options for Move Tool. Curve presets are predefined shapes for the Falloff curve option and used to quickly set it. The shape of the Falloff curve can be manually adjusted by dragging the existing points on it. You can add additional points by clicking the graph.

5. **Drag Z-axis** (or any) to move the selected vertex in perspective view and create the shape you want.

Creating a Polygon Mesh

You have learnt in the previous lessons that a polygon mesh is made up of a number of faces, which are connected together by vertices and edges to create a network of faces called a polygon mesh. The details of a polygon mesh surface are defined by subdivisions representing the number of rows and columns of faces that run up, down, and across. You can create a complex polygon mesh from a single face, which is used for character animations. There are two ways to create a polygon mesh: **(A)** Using Polygon primitives **(B)** Using Create Polygon Tool. By the way, polygon meshes can also be created by converting existing NURBS or subdivision surfaces using the Convert command under the Modify menu.

Using a Polygon Primitives

Maya has all the primitives as built-in 3D shapes to be used for creating objects. Polygon primitives can be used as the starting point for more complex objects or models. To create complex meshes, you can modify the attributes of a basic primitive object. For instance, you can modify number of divisions as required. You can also modify a primitive object by splitting, extruding, merging, or deleting various components. The built-in primitive objects in Maya are: sphere, cube, cylinder, cone, plane, torus, prism, pyramid, pipe, helix, soccer ball, and platonic solids. To create any of these primitives, you just select Create> Polygon Primitives from the main menu bar and select a primitive object. The list below is giving a brief description of most of the 3D polygon primitives:

<u>Sphere</u>: Refers to an object in which all the points on the surface are equidistant from its center. It is like the 3D equivalent of a circle.
<u>Cube</u>: It is bounded by six square faces and each face shares an edge with four other faces.
<u>Cylinder</u>: It has two equal circular faces parallel to each other and a curved surface along the circumference of the circular faces. The circular faces appear at the top and bottom of curved surface.
<u>Cone</u>: This object has a circular face (base) at the bottom and a curved surface from the circumference of the face to a point above the face.
<u>Plane</u>: It is a flat 2D surface. <u>Torus</u>: It is like a thick ring having a circular hole in the center.

<u>Prism</u>: Refers to the object with two horizontal triangular faces at the top and bottom and rectangular faces on its sides. The number of rectangular face is same as the number of edges in the horizontal polygon faces. The triangular sides of the prism are parallel to each other.

<u>Pyramid</u>: Refers to the object that has a polygonal base and triangular faces that converge at a point above the base. The number of triangular faces is same as the number of edges in the polygonal base.

<u>Pipe</u>: It contains two concentric cylinders, one inside the other.

<u>Helix</u>: Refers to a spiral-like object. <u>Soccer Ball</u>: It has a total of 32 pentagonal and hexagonal faces.

<u>Platonic Solids</u>: Refers to tetrahedron and octahedron objects, in which all the edges have the same length, the faces have the same shape, and the angles have the same measure.

Instead of selecting Create tab in the main menu bar, you can click on icons in the Polygon tab of Shelf to create these primitives. Though Shelf shows only eight icons out of twelve, but you can add remaining icons into Shelf by holding the Ctrl+Shift keys down and then selecting the primitive object from the Create> Polygon Primitives submenu. The following simple steps can help you create a polygon mesh using a polygon primitive: (1) Select **Create> Polygon Primitives> Soccer Ball**. (2) Click the **Smooth shade all** button in the panel menu to display the polygon cocker ball in the shaded (not default wireframe) view. (3)**Drag** in the grid (perspective viewport) to create a ball. In the shaded view, Maya applies the default shading material (like color and map) to an object that you can change later on the polygon mesh surface. You will learn about it next lessons.

When you selected the option from Polygon Primitives submenu (like Soccer Ball), you would notice that there appears an instruction saying: 'Drag on the grid' in the gird of the perspective viewport. Different objects take different number of clicks (one click, two, or three clicks) to be created in the viewport. You can create them with any dimensions and at any location. After creating, you can also change its dimensions in Channel Box. You can also set the dimensions of primitive objects before creating them using the Options window. Once created, you can modify it using extrude, bridge, or cut commands to create a complex polygon mesh features on its components. Now we can see how a polygon mesh is created using Create Polygon Tool.

Using Create Polygon Tool

Create Polygon Tool helps you create individual polygons of a polygon mesh. You can also place vertices anywhere in the viewport. The edges and the faces of polygons are automatically created in the process. After creating a polygon face, you can split or extrude it to create additional polygon faces that are attached to the original polygon face. This technique can be used while creating an exact copy of a particular object. Let's perform the following steps to create a polygon mesh using Create Polygon Tool:

1. Select **Polygons menu set** from the menu selector drop-down list in <u>Status Line</u>, shown as step 1 in the picture 5.7.

Picture 5.7

2. When <u>Polygons menu set</u> is selected, the menus specific to working with polygons, such as Select, Mesh, Edit Mesh, Proxy, or Normals appear. Now **click** the **Smooth shade all** button in the <u>panel menu</u> to display the polygon mesh in the shaded view (shown as step 2 in picture 5.7).

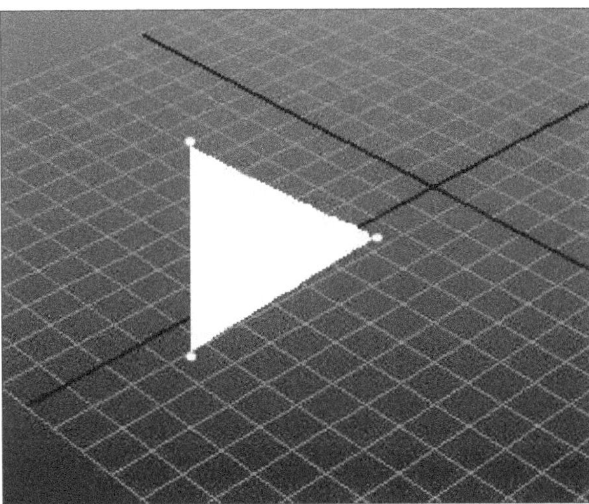

Picture 5.8

3. Select **Mesh> Create Polygon Tool** from the main menu bar. The Create Polygon Tool cursor appears as a cross-hair and an instruction appears in the active viewport.

4. **Move** the cursor anywhere in the viewport and **click** to place the <u>first vertex</u> of the polygon mesh. Then, move the cursor elsewhere and **click** to place the <u>second</u>, and then the <u>third</u> vertex, as shown in picture 5.8.

After placing the third vertex, you'll see that the area bounded by these vertices appear in the shaded mode.

5. Press **enter** to complete the polygon mesh and exit Create Polygon Tool. This new polygon mesh will appear in the default gray shading material.

Using the <u>Tool Settings</u> window for Create Polygon Tool, you can specify various settings for the tool before you create a polygon. For instance, you can specify the number of vertices added per edge and specify the minimum number of vertices required to create a new polygon. Using the option 'Limit the number of points' in the Tool Settings; you can specify the minimum number of vertices for a polygon. This setting is disabled by default. The Divisions text box is enabled only when the Limit the number of points option is disabled. If you want to remove a vertex while creating a mesh, press the Delete key.

Using <u>Create Polygon Tool</u>, you can create simple as well as intricate faces of a polygon mesh. The faces can be planar and non-planar. In addition, you to create any number of faces that you want, and then extrude, merge, or divide these faces to form a polygon mesh that you'll learn in the next sections.

Modifying a Polygon Mesh
The animators want their creation to resemble the real-world, and for that, you need to modify, edit, and accurately model the polygon meshes. As modifying a polygon mesh is the most challenging for polygon modeling, so Maya has various tools and command for it. Some of these tools work on a single polygon mesh, while others affect multiple polygon meshes. And a few tools and commands influence the entire polygon mesh; whereas, others affect only the individual components of the polygon mesh. There are following ways to give your creation a look of real-world: (A) Adding a polygon to mesh (B) Subdividing a polygon mesh (C) Extruding polygon components (D) Beveling an edge of a polygon mesh (E) Combining and bridging polygon meshes (F) Smoothening a polygon mesh (G) Using the Subdiv Proxy feature (H) Using Project Curve on Mesh feature. The subsequent sections are giving you the detailed information about these ways.

(A) Adding a Polygon to Mesh

At the time of modeling, sometimes you need to add polygons to an existing polygon mesh. You can only add polygons to a non-boundary face or at border edges. This helps to create a polygon to close a hole in a polygon mesh. The new polygon becomes the part of the existing polygon mesh. To do this, you use the Append to Polygon Tool command, which adds new polygons at the border edge. It creates the new polygons using an edge as a starting point. Here are the simple steps for it:

1. Select a **polygon mesh** with border edges, and choose **Edit Mesh> Append to Polygon Tool** from the main menu bar. The cursor changes and an instruction "Click a boundary edge and then click to place new vertices" appears in the grid.

2. **Click** any one of the border edges. You'll see arrows appearing on the border edges indicating the directions of the edge.

3. **Click** the next border edge in the direction of the arrows point. It displays a triangular face. Now **click** the next border edge in the direction arrow. The number of clicks required to create the polygon depends on the number of border edges. You may need to click four-five times to close the open end. At the end, press **enter** to exit the creation mode.

The new polygon appears in the similar material as the existing polygon mesh and it closes the open end of the polygon mesh.

(B) Subdividing a polygon to mesh

When you subdivide a polygon mesh, it adds details on the mesh wherever required. Subdividing the faces creates extra edges and vertices in a polygon mesh, which gives more flexibility to edit and create high-poly models. In many cases, at the time of modeling basic primitive objects like sphere or cube gradually adding details to it, you can subdivide or split faces of a polygon mesh into multiple faces using commands, such as Interactive Split Tool, Cut Face Tool, Insert Edge Loop Tool, and Add Divisions. There are four commands that allow you to split a polygon face into multiple faces: 1. Interactive Split Tool 2. Cut Faces Tool 3. Insert Edge Loop Tool 4. Add Divisions feature. Now we can see how these tool and commands are used to subdivide a polygon face.

Using the Interactive Split Tool Command

Interactive Split Tool splits one or move faces on a polygon mesh into multiple faces interactively; after you specify the split location on the polygon mesh. This tool allows you to draw lines across the faces that indicate the location for the split operation. You can also subdivide a face into multiple faces using this tool. Follow these simple steps to split a polygon cube using Interactive Split Tool:

1. **Select** a polygon mesh in the perspective view that you want to split, and **ensure** that Polygons option is selected in the menu selector drop-down list at the top left corner of Maya screen (just below File tab).

2. Select **Edit Mesh> Interactive Split Tool** from the main menu bar. Then, **move** the cursor over the edge of the polygon face, and **click** the edge to add a vertex. It displays a dot indicating the point of split.

3. **Move** the cursor over the second edge which shows a connecting line between the inserted vertex and the highlighted point.

4. **Click** the edge to add the second vertex. This way, you can click other edges to split the polygon face. At the end, press **enter** to end the splitting process. This process adds new edges and vertices to the polygon mesh.

Using the Cut Faces Tool Command

You can use this Cut Faces Tool command to split a face or multiple faces of a polygon mesh along a line. When you click a polygon mesh with the Cut Faces Tool command selected, a cut line appears indicating the location of the split. Depending on the option selected in the Cut Faces Tool Options window, a portion on a side of the cut line is deleted or extracted by an offset distance specified in the Extract offset option. New edges are created in the polygon mesh dividing the original polygon. Apart from creating new faces and edges, the Cut Faces Tool command can also be used to extract and remove polygon faces from the polygon mesh. Perform these simple steps on your system to subdivide a polygon mesh using the Cut Faces Tool command:

1. **Open** orthographic viewport for better result, **select** a polygon mesh in the right viewport, and choose **Edit Mesh> Cut Faces Tool> (Rectangle Box)** from the main menu bar.

It opens the Cut Faces Tool Options window where you can specify the way in which you want the split or cut the polygon mesh. The faces can be cut either interactively or suing the YZ, ZX, or XY plane. By default, the Interactive (click for cut line) option is selected. You can always select Edit> Reset from the Cut Faces Tool Options window to reset the previously made changes to its default settings. In case you want to remove faces, select 'Delete cut faces' check box in the Cut Faces Tool Options window.

2. **Select** the Extract cut faces check box for now. It will extract the portion of the polygon mesh by the distance specified in the Extract offset text boxes below. You can specify the coordinate values for X, Y, and Z axes in their respective text boxes to move the faces after the cut operation.

3. Type: **1.0000** in the 'Y' text box for the Extract offset option, and **click** the **Enter Cut Tool And Close** button. It displays an instruction (Click-drag to cut) on the polygon mesh.

4. **Click and drag** to cut the polygon mesh interactively. The cut line appears across the viewport indicating the location for the cut operation. Then, **release** the mouse button. The polygon mesh splits into two separate meshes.

Using the Insert Edge Loop Tool Command

Professional animators use this tool extensively for character modeling. An edge loop is a line or path of edges that are connected in sequence by their shared vertices. This is quite useful when you want to insert edges along a user-defined path. You can insert one or more edge loops across the edge ring on a polygonal mesh using the Insert Edge Loop Tool command. Do the following simple steps on your system to insert an edge loop:

1. **Select** a polygon mesh in the perspective view and choose **Edit Mesh> Insert Edge Loop Tool** from the main menu bar. It displays an instruction stating 'Click and drag' to insert edge loops.

2. **Move** the cursor on the edge where you want edge loop to appear. Then, **click** the edge and drag to insert an edge loop in the polygon mesh.

It shows the Edge Loop Preview Locator in the viewport. Once the Insert Edge Loop Tool command is active, you can click multiple times to insert multiple edge loops in the selected polygon mesh.

3. **Click** outside the mesh. The edge loop appears on the mesh and the Edge component selection mode is selected.

Using the Add Divisions Command

This tool allows you to subdivide selected polygon faces into smaller three-sided (triangles) or four-sided (quadrangles) faces. Using this, you can add details to an existing polygon mesh. You can also subdivide the edge components. The steps for subdividing faces of a polygon using Add Divisions command are:

1. **Right-click** on a selected polygon mesh and **select** the Face component selection mode from the marking menu.

2. **Select** the face or faces that you want to subdivide. Then, choose **Edit Mesh> Add Divisions** (**Rectangle Box**) from the main menu bar. It opens the Add Divisions to Face Options window.

3. Select the **Linearly** radio button for the Add divisions option. This option is used to subdivide the face based on the width and height separately.

You can specify the number of divisions that occur along U and V for the face, which represent the names of the axes of the face (2D plane), since X, Y and Z are used for the coordinates in the 3D space. For instance, when the Divisions in U and Divisions in V options are set to four each, the polygon face would be divided into 16 smaller faces.

4. Type: **4** in the Divisions in U text box, and type: **4** in the Divisions in V text box. Then, **click** the **Add Divisions** button at the bottom.

You'll see that each selected face subdivides into smaller faces. Using the default option for Add Divisions, you can divide a face into four equal faces, if the level of division is set to 1.

(C) Extruding Polygon Components

This command adds more polygon faces to an existing polygon mesh. For example, you can extrude a polygon face from the torso to create a hand. You can extrude faces, edges, or vertices of a polygon mesh by pulling them out or pushing them in. the Extrude command allows you to extrude selected components. Let's extrude a face of a polygon mesh following these steps:

1. **Right-click** a selected polygon mesh and **select** the Face component selection mode from the marking menu that appears.

2. **Select** the faces that you want to extrude. For now, you can select a single face, as shown in picture 5.9 A. Then, go to **Edit Mesh> Extrude** from the main menu bar. If you want to select multiple faces, you can click them while holding Shift key down.

This creates an extrude node and activates Show Manipulator Tool, which appears only when Construction History is on. Three sliders for Thickness, Offset, and Divisions appear with their default values in the manipulator. You can drag the name of the controls to modify their values.

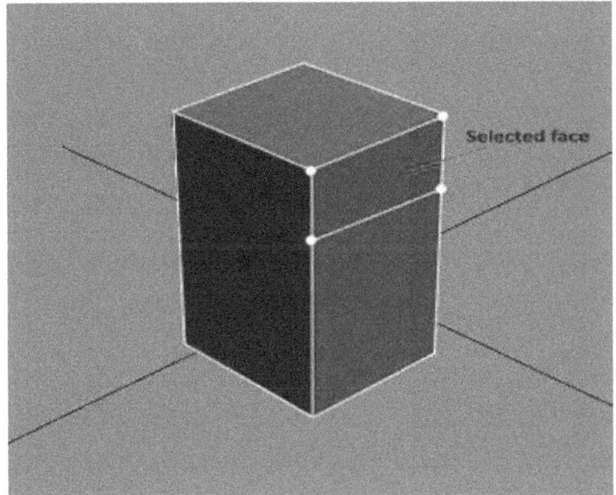

Picture 5.9 A

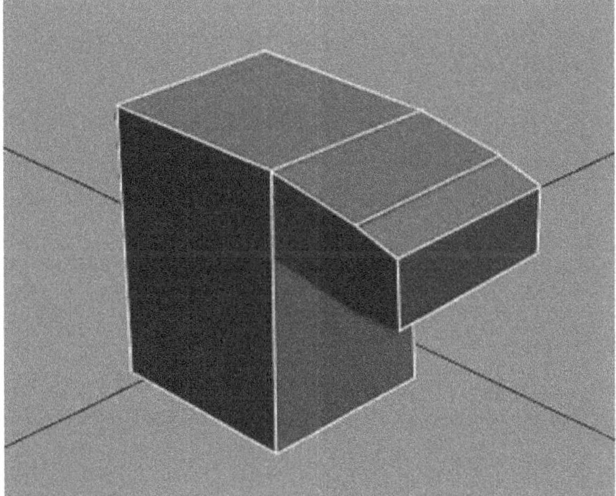

Picture 5.9 B

3. **Click** and **drag** on the Thickness to set a new value to 2.8. **Set** the Offset value to **0.3** and Divisions value to **2**. Alternatively, you can click the numeric value to activate a text box, enter a value, and press enter to apply the new value. The result will show similar to the picture 5.9 B.

You can also move, rotate, or scale the selected faces using the Show Manipulator Tool. For extruding multiple faces simultaneously, you can extrude them as an individual face or separate faces using the Keep Faces Together option. You can access this option at the top of the Edit Mesh menu; it helps to keep the newly created faces together during the extrusion. This option is selected by default. You can toggle this option by selecting Edit Mesh> Keep Faces Together from the main menu bar.

(D) Beveling Polygon Components
In beveling, what you do is that you expand the edges and vertices of a polygon mesh to create new faces. You can also bevel sharp edges of a polygon mesh to create smooth edges using the Bevel command. You are also allowed to position the newly created faces at an offset from the original edge using the Bevel Options window. The UV assignment options in this window allow you to specify the method by which UVs are created for the beveled object. When you use the Bevel command to create new faces, it automatically creates UV texture coordinates. You can perform these simple steps to bevel the edges of a polygon mesh:

1. **Select** a polygon mesh, **right-click** on it, and **select** Edge component selection mode from the marking menu.

2. **Select** all edges of the polygon mesh by dragging a marquee covering the whole mesh. Then select **Edit Mesh> Bevel> (Rectangle Box)** from the main menu bar. It opens Bevel Options window.

3. **Set** the Width value to **0.7000**, and Segments to **3**. Then, click the **Bevel** button at the bottom to see the beveled polygon mesh in the viewport. **Exit** the component selection mode by selecting the Object Mode at the end.

(E) Combining and Bridging Polygon Meshes

Using the Combine command, you can assemble multiple meshes into one polygon mesh. When the Combine command is performed to create a single polygon mesh, a new polygon mesh node is created for it. The Bridge command creates new faces between two selected border edges. The newly created faces are merged into the original mesh. The Bridge command is useful when you need to connect two separate meshes together with additional faces. The Bridge command doesn't work on two separate polygon meshes. In this case, you need to combine multiple meshes into one mesh. You can combine multiple meshes by first selecting them, and then, selecting Mesh> Combine from the main menu bar. You can perform these simple steps to combine two polygon meshes and merge them:

1. **Select** two separate polygon meshes with border edges, and choose **Mesh> Combine** from the main menu bar. This command combines the two separate meshes. Now you can bridge them using the border edges.

2. Go to **Select> Select Border Edge Tool** from the main menu bar. Then, **double-click** the border edges that you want to select. For now, you can select two border edges holding Shift key down. A single-click selects a single edge, while double-click selects the whole border edge.

3. Go to **Edit Mesh> Bridge** from the main menu bar. It will connect the two border edges. The divisions in the newly created polygon mesh depend on the Divisions option in the Bridge Options window.

In the window, the default division level is set to 5 for the Divisions option. If required, the several other options such as Twist, Taper, Smoothing angle, and Bridge can be set for the bridge operation. You can open the Bridge Options window by selecting Edit Mesh> Bridge> (Rectangle Box) from the main menu bar.

(F) Making a Polygon Mesh Smooth

Maya lets you use several commands, such as Smooth and Subdiv Proxy to smoothen a polygon mesh. The Smooth command which you can apply selecting Mesh> Smooth, evenly subdivides a polygon mesh or selected faces and add divisions to the existing faces of the mesh. This command also helps to increase the polygon count of a polygon mesh. Here are the steps to follow:

1. **Select** a polygon mesh in the perspective view to smooth, and choose **Mesh> Smooth> (Rectangle Box)** from the main menu bar. It opens the Smooth Options window.

2. Type: **2** in the Division levels text box. Then, **click** the Smooth button to smooth the selected mesh. It will make the polygon mesh look more real than geometrical. This command is extensively used in Maya.

(G) Using the Subdiv Proxy Command

Unlike the Smooth command, the Subdiv Proxy command actually creates a second smooth mesh and places it inside the original mesh. Any changes to the original mesh are reflected on the smooth version beneath. This command links the original and the high resolution smooth versions using Construction History. You can modify and animate the original mesh and see the output on the smooth version or proxy of the polygon mesh. The subdiv proxy version of the mesh is renderable and can be skinned and weighted for animation similar to any other mesh. Here are the steps to smoothen a polygon mesh using the Subdiv Proxy command:

1. **Select** a polygon mesh in the perspective view, and choose **Proxy> Subdiv Proxy> (Rectangle Box)** from the main menu bar. The Subdiv Proxy Options window appears.

2. Type: **4** in the Division Levels text box and **click** Smooth button. The original mesh appears with a transparent material covering the smooth version, which appears inside it.

You can toggle the display to show either high resolution or low resolution, by pressing Ctrl+~ keys together. The Toggle Proxy Display (Ctrl+`) and the Both Proxy and Subdiv Display (~) options are available under the Proxy menu.

(H) Projecting a Curve on a Mesh

Using Project Curve on mesh command, you can project a curve onto a polygon surface. The projected curve appears on the polygon surface, and simultaneously moves when you move the original curve. You can perform these steps to project a curve on a polygon surface:

1. **Create** a polygon mesh and **draw** a curve in a scene, similar to the picture 6.0 A. The red angle is the curve in the picture.

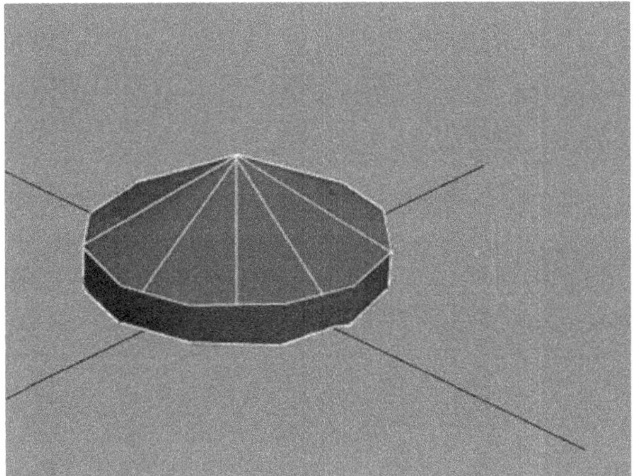

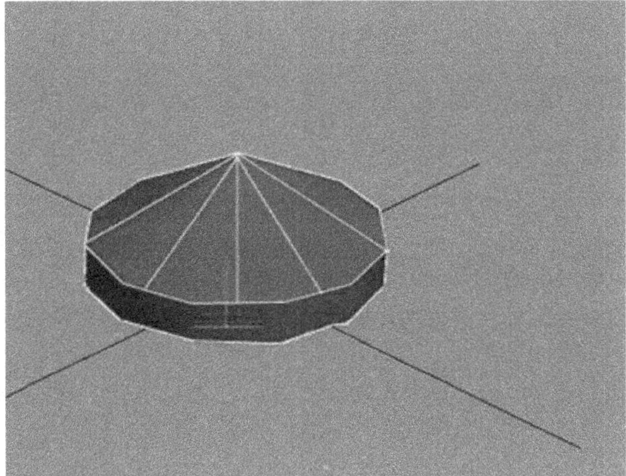

Picture 6.0 A   Picture 6.0 B

2. **Place** the curve in front of the polygon mesh in the front viewport. Then, choose **Edit> Select All** to select both the polygon mesh and the curve.

3. Select **Edit Mesh> Project Curve on mesh** from the main menu bar. The curve appears on the polygon mesh, as shown in picture 6.0 B.

Lesson 16
Creating Symmetrical Polygon Meshes

You need to use the symmetry feature to create a model that is exactly same across the dividing line or axis. It is advantageous in saving time and efforts. For example, when modeling a car, you can divide it into two halves. In such case, you can create one half (left side) of the car and use the symmetry feature to create the other half (right side). When a polygon mesh is identical, it is also symmetrical along that axis or plane. It other words, you can consider a symmetrical polygon mesh to be divided into two halves such that both are mirror images of each other. There are different types of symmetry. The most common types are bilateral symmetry (axis of symmetry is a plane, mostly a vertical plane) and radial symmetry (symmetrical around either a central point or an axis). You will learn different methods to create a symmetrical polygon mesh, such as Mirror Geometry, Mirror Cut, Subdiv Proxy, and Duplicate Special.

Using the Mirror Geometry Command

This command allows you to create a duplicate copy of an existing polygon mesh along a particular axis. For example, if you're creating a human character, you can create the left half of a character and mirror it to create the right half using the Mirror Geometry command. The original half of the human character is duplicated across an axis of symmetry based on its bounding box or pivot point. You can also merge the duplicated mesh (right half) with the original mesh (left half) to create a single polygon mesh. Let's perform these steps to create a symmetrical mesh using the Mirror Geometry command:

1. **Select** a polygon mesh, and choose **Mesh> Mirror Geometry> (Rectangle Box)** from the main menu bar. It opens the <u>Mirror Options</u> window.

2. Select **–X** radio button for the <u>Mirror Direction</u> option. Then, select the **Connect border edges** radio button. This option fills any gap between the original and mirror copy of the mesh.

3. Click **Mirror** button at the end. It creates the symmetry and merges with the original by default.

While performing the steps mentioned above, you saw the various options available in the Mirror Options window. We can discuss here in detail about them:

<u>Mirror Direction:</u> Defines the direction in which the selected polygon mesh is mirrored. By default, the +X is selected in the Mirror Direction option.

<u>Merge with the original:</u> Selects options to merge polygons. By default, this option is turned on. When selected, the original mesh is duplicated, flipped, and merged with the original mesh to create a single object.

<u>Merge vertices:</u> Merges adjacent vertices to create a single polygon mesh object.

<u>Connect border edges:</u> Connects the original polygon mesh with the mirrored polygon mesh at the border edges and fills in the gap with new faces to create a closed shape.

With the Mirror Geometry command, you can only create a duplicate of an existing polygon mesh along a predefined axis of symmetry. If you want to create a polygon mesh that is symmetrical along a particular plane, use the Mirror Cut command explained in the next section of this lesson.

Using the Mirror Cut Command

Using this command, you can create a polygon mesh and copy it along a user defined axis. You can also merge the duplicated polygon mesh with the original mesh to create a single polygon mesh. This command also lets you create interesting symmetry results depending on the location of the axis of symmetry using the Mirror Cut command. You can reposition the symmetry plane using the manipulator. Perform these steps to create a symmetrical polygon mesh using the Mirror Cut command:

1. **Select** a polygon mesh, and choose **Mesh> Mirror Cut> (Rectangle Box)** from the main menu bar. It opens the Mirror Cut Options window.

2. Click the **Mirror Cut** button with default settings. It will open Show Manipulator Tool on the selected polygon mesh. You can use the manipulators to edit the selected mesh. By default, the Move manipulator is active.

3. **Drag** the manipulator in the X-axis. The newly created symmetry mesh reflects any changes made in the original polygon mesh, if the Merge with the original option is unselected in the Mirror Cut Options window.

By the way, the plane of symmetry is still visible in a scene. If you don't want the plane of symmetry to be visible, assign the value off for the Visibility channel in the Channel Box. Now you can know in detail about the options available in the Mirror Cut Options window:

Cut along: Specifies a pair of axes, such as YZ plane (default), XZ plane, and XY plane to mirror the mesh object.
Merge with the original: Combines both the original and the mirrored polygon mesh into a single polygon mesh. So any changes made to the original mesh subsequently are not updated on the mirrored object. By default, this option is selected.
Merge vertex threshold: Merges vertices with each other based on the distance specified. This option is active only when the Merge with original option is turned on.

Lesson 17
Animating in Maya 2013
Animation can be defined as an art of creating movement using images that are slightly different. By animating an object, you add virtual life to it. Maya provides a set to tools to make the animation process easier. You can animate an object by changing its position in the virtual 3D space, by rotating it, or modifying its shape over a period of time. Every object has a set of attributes that you can animate over time. Further, the animation time can be tweaked to make it more realistic. In the context of three-dimension (3D) animation, time is the fourth dimension and an integral part of animation. In Maya and all other animation software, time is represented using frames, which are static images of a scene at a given point in time. Besides frames, keyframes that correspond to a particular state of an object is used at a given time. Keyframes store the object attribute in a particular time. The position or state of an object is automatically calculated for in-between frames. This is known as Keyframe animation and is a popular method used by most of the animators. In Maya, there are several user interface elements, such as Time Slider, Range Slider, and Graph Editor to create and modify keyframes. You can also preview an animation before rendering it using Playback Controls, or other methods, such as motion trail, ghosting, and playblast.

Exploring Types of Animation
With the evolution of 3D animation software such as Maya, animation has become simple and fascinating. Using the wide range of animation techniques, you can animate the objects and characters in a scene. According to the need to animate an object, you can use one of the following animation techniques: Keyframe animation, Path animation, Non-linear animation, Driven key animation, Motion capture animation, Layered animation, Dynamic animation, and Expressions.

Keyframe Animation

Using this simple and easy animation technique, the transformational changes of objects can be captured by setting special keys also called keyframes. A keyframe refers to a unique state or condition of an object captured at a particular time. In other words, every keyframe signifies a change in one or more attributes of an animated object. For instance, to create a bouncing ball animation, you can define the initial position of the ball in the air at the first frame. Then, select another frame and position the ball (on the ground) from where it bounces back and set a new keyframe there. Now, select the end frame of the animation and position the ball back in the air and again set a keyframe. In this case, you have defined three keyframes at different frames. Maya automatically interpolates the position of the ball in the remaining frames of the animation. When you need to add a sense of reality to the animation, Maya allows you to add slow-in and slow-out and stretch and squash effects animating various attributes of the object. For example, if you want to add the stretch and squash effect, you can animate the Scale attribute of an object. The picture 6.1 shows keyframe locations in a bouncing ball animation.

The actual number of frames per second of an animation depends on the output format and the required quality. For standard quality web animations, you can use 12 frames per second and for high quality web animations, 15 frames per second. Generally, 24 frames per second is used to create animation for televisions; 30 frames for high quality cinematic animations. The number of frames per second also varies based on the video standards, such as National Television Standard Committee (NTSC) and Phase Alternate Line (PAL). In the animation film industry, 48p is a format and is currently in trial. Higher frame rate reduces motion blur and flicker in films to make it more realistic.

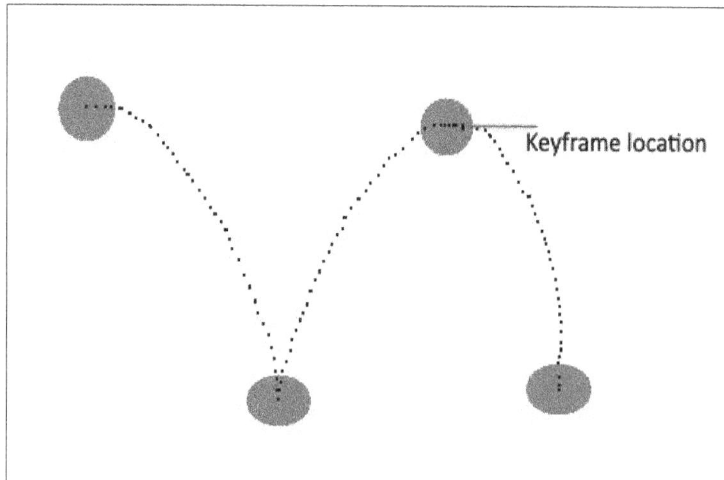

Picture 6.1

Path Animation

This is a process of animating an object to navigate a curve or path. You can use NURBS as the path in an animation. This curve is attached to the object, which you want to animate and known as the motion path. Then, the object automatically turns and blends following the path of the curve. The shape and direction of the curve determines the trajectory of the object. Note that only the transition and rotation attributes of the object are changed during the path animation. You can use this technique to show an object, such as bus or train moving.

Non-linear Animation

As an animator, you may require to animate a character in a scene to keep it moving in a loop. If you do it repeatedly, it might be tedious to you. In this case, you can use the non-linear animation technique, which involves manipulating animation clips by splitting, duplicating, and blending the clips to obtain the final motion of a character. An animation clip refers to a small portion of an existing animation sequence that can be produced using other animation techniques mentioned before, such as keyframe animation and path animation.

There are two types of clips in Maya – source and regular. Source clips store the original animation curves of a character and not used to animate characters. Instead, you can use the copies or instances of source clips, which are called regular clips to animate characters. You can work with animation clips through an animation window known as Trax Editor. You can edit the clips by arranging, splitting, merging, duplicating, and grouping them in Trax Editor. You can also loop the clips to repeatedly play the same animation sequence. In addition, the clips can be overlapped with one another. Non-linear animation is ideal to experiment and test an animation sequence, as the changes made on clips do not affect the original animation sequence (source clip) on which the clips are based. This implies that you can use the same clips multiple times to build animation sequences.

Driven Key Animation

Maya has a special type of key called a driven key that links one attribute value of an object to the attribute of another. The animation in which driven key is used, is called driven key animation, which allows you to animate two objects by establishing a connection between the appropriate attributes of those two objects. You need to specify a driver attribute value and a driven attribute value (attributes affected by the driver attribute value) for creating a driven key. These two values are inter-dependent. Any change in one attribute value changes the other attribute value. For instance, you can set driven key to open a door when a person walks in. this way, multiple attributes can drive a single attribute. Attribute values are keyed to frames in the standard animation keys, but for a driven key, attribute values are keyed to the value of a driving attribute.

Motion Capture Animation

Using this technique, you can capture the motion or physical actions of a real entity such as a person and apply it to a character in a 3D scene. There are several motion capture devices such as the Maya Motion Capture Developer's Tool Kit to perform motion capture animation. At the time of capturing motion, you need to rehearse by enacting the motions several times, and then, apply them on a character. This technique has prime significance in developing games and movies. For instance, in sports-based video games, motion capture animation is used to capture the motion or actions or a sportsperson, which is then applied to a player in the game. Similarly, you can use motion capture animation to record the movements of a person or actor, and then, apply it on a character in an animated movie.

Layered Animation

This animation allows you to create and blend animations on separate layers, similar to the layer system of two-dimensional (2D) image editing program such as Adobe Photoshop. For instance, you can animate one part or section of a body simultaneously using the layered animation. First, you can animate the up/down movement of the hips in a layer, and then, animate the torso of the body in another layer. Similarly, you can also animate feet, arms, and wrists in separate layers. All these layers combine to form one cohesive walk with the different parts of the body being driven, pushed, pulled, and rotated by other parts of the body. Animation layers are displayed in the Animation Layer Editor, where you can also hide or show animation layers as required.

Dynamic Animation

This technique can use the rules of physics to create realistic animations and simulations. For instance, you can simulate natural forces such as gravity using these rules. You can use this animation to create effects such as tea pouring from a teapot or snow falling from the sky. You can also create dynamic objects such as particle objects, soft bodies, and rigid bodies. You can typically animate the motion of dynamic objects using emitters to generate particles for effects such as steam, fire, rain, fireworks, and explosions. The emitter acts as the source of particles and its location in 3D space that determines where they are generated. Maya calculates dynamics from every frame. The position of an object in each frame is derived from the position of an object in the previous frame. This differs from keyframe animation, where the position of an object at any frame is derived from key values set at different frames in the animation.

Using Expressions

Expressions are series of instructions to control attributes of an object over a period of time. It can be interpreted by Maya to perform different tasks. Each instruction in an expression, which is also called a statement, ends with a semicolon (;). An example of an instruction is:

Ball.translateX = Cube.translateX + 4;

You can use Expression Editor of Maya to type expressions. Expressions are ideal for attributes that change incrementally, randomly, or steadily over time. They are also used to link attributes of different objects, where they are inter-dependent. For instance, you can make the car stop on pressing the brake, this represents inter-dependency. Expressions provide a simple way of animation compared to more challenging keyframe animation technique.

Exploring Animation Controls

In the main screen of Maya, there are several user interface elements, such as Time Slider, Range Slider, and Playback controls that help you to set number of frames for an animation, keyframes, and preview the animation. Both Time Slider and Range Slider help you to animate objects and control the animation by setting time constraints. Using playback controls buttons; you can monitor and control an animation. These user interface elements appear below the viewport panel. Let us see in detail about these interface elements.

Time Slider

Time Slider is a long horizontal bar that appears just below the viewport. It allows you to work with the fourth dimension of a 3D animation represented by time. Time Slider shows you the time range defined by Range Slider, the current time, and the keys for the selected objects or characters. You can also use Time Slider to scrub through an animation; you can drag the Current Time Indicator (CTI) to move forward and backward in an animation. Time Slider also allows you to view the playback range (the duration for which the animation played), set keyframes, and playback an animation. The picture 6.2 shows Time Slider of Maya 2013 with the CTI and Key Ticks.

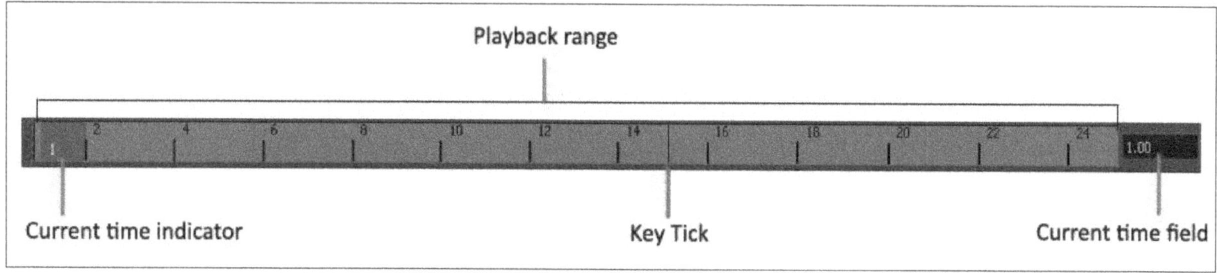

Picture 6.2

Time Slider is a long bar with a playback range which is also known as the timeline. It is divided into equally-spaced numerical markings. These markings represent different points of time or frame in an animation. Viewing an animation containing multiple frames in rapid succession gives the impression of a motion. The speed at which the frames move is measured in frames per second (fps). This is known as the frame rate and is used to set the timing of an animation. The frame rate is required depending on the output format of the animation.

You can also use frame rate to synchronize the animation with sound and live-action footage. By default, Time Slider provides 24 frames that are shown by even-numbered markings (2 to 24) on the playback range, which displays a gray block known as the CTI. As the time or frame advances, the CTI also moves to the right. The current time field indicates the frame at which the CTI is currently placed. You can also use the current time field to move to a specific frame or time duration. To move to a specific frame, enter the frame number in the text box and press enter key. As a result, the objects are displayed in the scene as they appear in that frame. By default, Key Ticks in the Time Slider represent the keyframes you set for the selected object.

Range Slider
Using this slider you can control the playback range of an animation. It is divided into various parts, such as Animation Start Time, playback range, the Range Slider bar, Playback End Time, and Animation End Time, which represent the editable fields. The picture 6.3 shows the different parts of Range Slider.

Picture 6.3

Using these fields, you can control different functions of the playback range, such as setting time during an animation start and end or animation-related preferences. Now we can discuss in detail about the components of Range Slider:

Animation Start Time: Allows you to view or type the start time of an animation, which is the first frame.
Animation End Time: Allows you to view or type the end time of an animation, which is the last frame.
Playback Start Time: Allows you to view or type the start time of a playback, the frame at which playback starts. If you type a value smaller than the current start time of an animation, this value automatically becomes the start time of the animation.
Playback End Time: Allows you to view or type the end time of a playback, the frame at which playback stops. If you type a value greater than the current end time of an animation, this value automatically becomes the end time of the animation.
Range Slider bar: Allows you to view and edit the playback range of an animation. You can drag the Range Slider bar to change the start time and end time of the playback range.

You have already learnt that there are only 24 frames in Maya, by default. These 24 frames are played in one second, which is the standard frame rate for motion picture films. You can increase or decrease the number of frames by changing the playback range, which signifies the range of frames for which the animation is played. The changes in the playback range are reflected in Time Slider. You can perform either of the following tasks to change the playback range of an animation.

1. Enter any value for the playback start and end time in the Playback Start Time and Playback End Time field, respectively.
2. Drag the Range Slider bar towards the right to adjust the playback range.

Playback Controls

The set of 8 buttons in the Playback Controls allow you control the playback of an animation. Using these buttons, you can play an animation and go to the previous frame, start of the playback range, or end of the playback range. Playback Controls appear on the extreme right of Time Slider, as shown in picture 6.4. The list below describes the functions of all the 8 buttons starting from left side.

Picture 6.4

Go to start of playback range: Moves the CTI to the start of the playback range.
Step back one frame: Moves back one frame; the CTI moves to the frame that immediately precedes the current frame.
Step back one key: Moves back one key; the CTI moves to the key that immediately precedes the current key.
Play backwards: Plays an animation in the reverse sequence; from the last frame to the first frame.
Play forwards: Plays an animation in a sequence; from the first frame to the last frame.
Step forward one key: Moves forward one key; the CTI moves to the key that immediately follows the current key.
Step forward one frame: Moves forward one frame; the CTI moves to the frame that immediately follows the current frame.
Go to end of playback range: Moves the CTI to the end of the playback range.
Stop button: It stops playing an animation. This button appears in place of the Play forwards or Play backwards button.

Lesson 18
Working with Keyframe Animation

The most common method to animate an object is using keyframes. This method allows you to rearrange, delete and duplicate a key or sequences of keys in the timeline. For example, you can copy the animated attributes of one object and paste those attributes onto another object. You can also stretch a piece of animation over a longer period of time without animating it from the start. In Keyframes Animation, when you set a keyframe for an object, its attribute values are recorded for that frame. So, when you select that frame, the object always appears with the same attributes that it was set. Now we can see the functions of Keyframes Animation.

Setting Animation Duration

Before stating an animation, you need to decide the duration of the animation or the number of frames required for it. The default scene in Maya has 48 frames in a scene. With more number of frames, the duration of the animation becomes longer. For instance, if you want the animation for 4 seconds, at 24 fps, you need to set the total duration to 96 frames (24x4). Using the 'Set the end time' of the animation text box of Range Slider, you can set the total duration of an animation. However, it doesn't change the playback end time. So, you need to manually set the playback end time. In case you change the playback end time more than the current animation end time, only the animation end time automatically changes to the new playback end time. Using this method, you can quickly set the end time of playback animation. Perform these steps to understand practically about setting an animation end time:

1. **Start** Maya 2013, and type: **96** in the <u>Set the end time of the playback range</u> text box in <u>Range Slider</u>. This point is shown in the picture 6.3 mentioning 'Playback End Time'.

2. Press **enter** after you type the number. It changes the <u>playback range</u> and the <u>Animation End Time</u> simultaneously. The playback range in Time Slider will grow longer showing 96 frames.

Setting Keyframes Manually

Now you are going to start animation. When we speak about setting keyframes manually, it means we set the keyframes to animate an object. To set a keyframe, move the CTI to any frame where you want the keyframe to appear, change the values for the attributes as required, and then, select Animate> Set Key from the main menu bar. You can also press the S key on the keyboard to add a keyframe at the current frame. The Animate menu appears only on selecting the Animation menu set. You can create any number of keyframes using this method. For animating, you first create an object, and then, set keys for the attributes that change during an animation. You can either enter attribute values in the Channel Box or transform the object in a viewport to record the attribute values for the keyframe. Perform the following steps to set the keyframes in an animation:

1. **Open** new scene in Maya. In the previous section of this lesson, you have set the <u>animation end time</u> to **96**, so let it be as it is.

2. Select **Animation** menu set from the menu selector drop-down list in <u>Status Line</u>, which is at the top left of Maya screen (below File tab). After this menu set is selected, it opens Animation-specific menus (Animate, Geometry Cache, Create Deformers, Skeleton, Skin, and Character) in the main menu bar.

3. **Create** and **place** an object that you want to animate using keyframes. For now, you can create a NURBS sphere in the perspective viewport similar to what is shown in picture 6.5. Then, **place** the object anywhere in the viewport. For placing the object precisely, you can use Channel Box.

4. **Click** the first frame in the <u>playback range</u> from which you will start the animation. Playback range is shown in picture 6.2.

5. Select **Animate> Set Key** from the main menu bar or press the S key to add a new keyframe at the first frame. This way, you add a keyframe at the current frame which looks like a red line also known as Key Tick.

Picture 6.5

The Key Tick indicates that the changes in the attributes of the selected object have been keyed (recorded) to the current frame. You also see that the attribute values of the object appear highlighted in Channel Box. The highlighted attributes indicate that the values have been recorded in the first keyframe.

6. **Click** the **45th** frame in the playback range to make it the next frame. Alternatively, you can drag the CTI to the 45th frame. You can also enter the frame number in the Set the current frame text box that appears next to the playback range in Time Slider.

7. **Select** <u>Move Tool</u> from Tool Box, and **move** the sphere object to any other location. Then, select **Animate> Set Key** from the main menu bar to add a keyframe at the 45th frame.

8. **Click** the <u>Play forward</u> button to play the animation. You will see the object (ball) moving on the screen. The frames are automatically interpolated between the keyframes.

The animation plays in a loop, by default. To stop the animation, click the Stop playback button, which appears in place of the Play forward button, or press Esc key. The animation is played continuously because the Continuous radio button is selected against the Looping option in the Preference window. This looping option can also be set to Once or Oscillate. The Oscillate option plays an animation forward and then backward or vice versa. To open the Preference window, click the Animation preference button located on the right of Range Slider. It opens the preferences settings for the Time Slider subcategory. You can also open the Preferences window by selecting Window> Settings/Preferences> Preferences from the main menu bar.

As you play the animation, you can see that the movements between two frames are automatically generated. Like this, you can add any number of keyframes at any frames. In certain cases, you may want to set a keyframe only for a particular attribute of an object. For instance, to show a train moving on the tracks in one direction, you can animate the train by setting a keyframe for a specific translation attribute. To set a keyframe only for a specific attribute:

A. Right-click an attribute to set a keyframe in Channel Box.
B. Select the Key Selected option from the context menu.

A keyframe is set for the selected attribute in the selected frame. This only affects the selected attribute, which is highlighted and the remaining attributes are not affected. You can also set multiple keyframes for an attribute. Similarly, to set a keyframe for multiple attributes in Channel Box, click the attributes holding the Ctrl key down.

Adding Keyframes Automatically
Maya allows you to automatically set keyframes whenever you move to another frame and change an attribute value of an object. By default, automatic keyframing is disabled; to enable it, select the Auto keyframe toggle button in Range Slider. Though it allows you to add keyframes automatically, you must specify the initial keyframe of an animation, the subsequent keyframes are automatically added as you advance to the next frame and change the attribute values. You can automatically add keyframes for a specific attribute of an object. Perform these steps to automatically add keyframes for an object:

1. **Open** new scene in Maya, and **click** the <u>Smooth shade all</u> button in the panel toolbar. Then, **create** an object and **position** it at a place in the perspective viewport.

2. Type: **120** in the <u>Set the end time of the playback range</u> text box, and press **enter** key to change the total number of frames for the animation to 120.

3. **Select** the <u>first frame</u> as the initial keyframe for the object in Time Slider. You can select any frame to make it initial (first) frame of the animation by moving the **CTI** to any frame in Time Slider.

4. **Click** the <u>Auto keyframe toggle</u> button in Range Slider. The Auto keyframe toggle button turns red indicating that the automatic keyframing is enabled. Then, select **Animate> Set Key** from the main menu bar to add the first keyframe at the first frame. It shows a Key Tick at the first frame.

5. Select **50**th frame as the next frame and **move** the object in the viewport to another location. A Key Tick is added at 50th frame as you release the mouse button. Similarly, you can select other frames to transform the object, keyframes are automatically added.

6. Select **110**th frame as the next frame, **move** the object again to another location, and **click** the <u>Auto keyframe toggle</u> button again to deactivate the automatic keyframing. Then, **click** the <u>Play forwards</u> button to preview the animation. You can save this animation for next section.

Adding a Breakdown

While animating objects in Maya, keyframes must be placed appropriately to give realistic result. You may need to often fine tune an animation by modifying the keyframe timing. To fine tune animation timing, you can add Breakdowns and Inbetweens in the existing animation. You can convert any frame between two keyframes to a Breakdown or Inbetween. Breakdowns are special keys with a similar to keyframes in its functioning; they represent a recorded set of attribute values at a given time. However, Breakdowns retain proportional time relationship with keyframes closest to them. If a Breakdown is set between two keyframes and either of them is repositioned at any other frame, the Breakdown between them is automatically moved to another frame maintaining the original proportion in time. You can perform these steps to understand it practically:

1. **Open** the scene with animated object that you created in the previous section or you can create one. Then, **select** the <u>animated object</u> to set a Breakdown.

2. **Select** any frame such as **30**th frame between two keyframes in <u>Time Slider</u>. Then, select **Animate> Set Breakdown** from the main menu bar.

A Breakdown is inserted at the selected frame. Unlike keyframes, Breakdown is represented by a green tick in Time Slider. Now, if you reposition any of the two keyframes between the two frames, the Breakdown between them is automatically moved to another frame maintaining the original proportion in time.

Adding an Inbetween

Maya allows you to manipulate the timing of an animation using Inbetweens. You can add an Inbetween at any frame in Time Slider. Inbetween shifts the keyframes at the current frame and the subsequent frames by one frame. Keyframes before the Inbetween remain unaffected. For instance, if you have a keyframe at frames 5, 10, and 12; you set an Inbetween at frame 10, the keyframe at frame 5 remain unchanged. However, keyframes at frame 10 and 12 are now placed at frames 11 and 13, respectively. You can perform the following simple steps for this:

1. **Select** an animated object for which you want to set an Inbetween. Then, **select** the **40**th frame in Time Slider.

2. **Right-click** the selected frame and select **Keys> Add Inbetween** from the context menu. An Inbetween is added at the current frame.

When the Inbetween is added, the keyframes available after the current frame are advanced by one frame. Using the Remove Inbetween option in the context menu, you can remove an Inbetween, which in turn decreases the space between the keys.

Editing a Keyframe

After setting keyframes and previewing an animation, if you want to change the attributes recorded at a specific keyframe, select the corresponding frame, change the attributes accordingly, and set the keyframe again. You can also set additional keyframes between the existing ones to refine an animation. At times, you may want to edit, copy, paste, or delete keyframes from an animation, to edit the values. For this, you can select the keyframe and change its values using Channel Box or manually in the viewport. You can delete unnecessary keyframes while animating an object. Perform the following steps to modify a keyframe of an animated object:

1. **Select** the same object of the animated scene you created before. It will show the keyframes of the object in Time Slider.

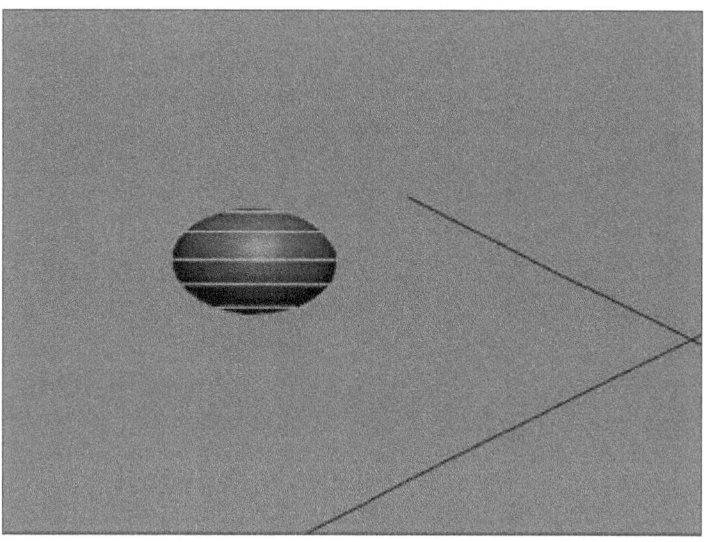

2. **Click** the 45th frame to select. Now, to create the squash effect as object (ball) bounces, select **Scale Tool** from the Tool Box and **drag** the object in the Y-axis to scale down and create the squash effect, as shown in picture 6.6. You can also see the change for Scale Y attribute in Channel Box. If required, move the object down to touch the surface using Move Tool.

3. Click to select **Animate> Set Key** from the main menu bar to record the change in attribute value in the selected keyframe.

Picture 6.6

4. **Click** the Go to start of playback range button to move to start. And then, **click** the Play forwards button to preview the animation.

You can see that the sphere object squashes gradually from the 1st frame to the 45the frame, and then, it shapes back to normal.

Copying and Pasting a Keyframe

In some cases, you may want to replicate a keyframe of one frame for another frame. You may also want to replicate a keyframe of one object for another object. For this, you can copy the existing keyframe and paste onto a frame for the same or different object. When you copy and paste a keyframe, the values of the attributes set for the keyframe are also copied and pasted. Perform the following steps to do it practically:

1. **Select** the animated ball object in the viewport. When the keyframes appear for the selected object in Time Slider, **select** the <u>keyframe</u> that you want to copy. For now, you can select the **45th** frame.

2. **Right-click** the selected frame, and select the **Copy** option from the <u>context menu</u>. This option copies the keyframe onto the clipboard. By the way, Maya allows you to copy multiple keyframes in a sequence by dragging the mouse over the respective frames in Time Slider, while pressing the Shift key.

3. **Create** a <u>cylinder</u> object in the viewport. Then **select** the cylinder and **select** the **50th** frame to paste the keyframe of the ball.

4. **Right-click** the selected frame (50th), and then, select **Paste> Paste** from the context menu. A keyframe appears at the 50th frame for the cylinder object.

You can also see that the attributes of the ball object at the 45th frame are also copied to 50th frame for the cylinder object. Similarly, if you want to reposition an existing keyframe onto another frame, right-click the corresponding frame and select the Cut option from the context menu. Then, paste the keyframe at any position using the Paste option from the context menu. This method also allows you to delete any unnecessary keyframes, for which, you can select the keyframe and click Delete option from the context menu.

Lesson 19
Creating a Turntable Animation

Using turntable animation, you can review or evaluate 3D models during the modeling process. By creating a turntable animation, you can create an effect of rotating object at 360 degrees. The object in your view is known as target object. To create a turntable animation, you need to add a turntable camera. The turntable animation is automatically generated, as turntable cameras are animated by default. The animation is generated for the number of frames you specify in the Number of Frames text box of the Animation Turntable Options window. To add a turntable camera into a scene, you can select Animate> Turntable from the main menu bar. By default, the turntable camera is locked; you cannot dolly, tumble, or track it. Perform these steps to create a turntable animation:

1. **Open** the Maya scene with the model that you want to review. Then, **select** <u>single or multiple objects</u> for which you want to create turntable animation.

2. Select **Animate> Turntable> (Rectangle Box)** from the main menu bar. New keyframes appear in the Time Slider and the Animation Turntable Options window also opens.

3. Type: **240** in the <u>Number of Frames</u> text box, and **click** the **Turntable** button to create the turntable animation.

4. **Click** the <u>Play forward</u> button to preview the animation. You will see the camera rotating around the objects in the animation.

You can notice that the name of the viewport changes to turnTableCamera1. And when you play this animation, the camera rotates around the objects to create the illusion of object rotation.

Working with Graph Editor

Graph Editor is one of the most important windows for animation in Maya. It displays the animated attributes for which keyframes are set in the entire animation. The animated attributes are represented by curves called animation curves. Using Graph Editor, you can easily set, copy, paste, delete, and move keyframes. To modify an animation, you can edit the animation curves in Graph Editor using tools, such as Add Keys Tool and Move Nearest Picked Key Tool. You can also view the Inbetween motion and edit curve tangents and move the keys and edit their values in Graph Editor. To display the Graph Editor, you can select Window> Animation Editors> Graph Editor from the main menu bar. When you select this option, you will see that the Graph Editor has a menu bar and toolbar using which you can access the tools and features required to work with keyframes. Graph Editor in Maya is divided into two main portions – Graph Editor Outliner and graph view. Graph Editor Outliner is similar to Outliner of Maya and displays the selected animated objects and their attributes for which keyframes have been set. Depending on the axis, the attributes appear in different colors.

If you look at your computer screen, you'll see several selected objects in Graph Editor Outliner and their animation curves in the graph view. Specifically, Graph Editor Outliner displays the attributes of the selected transform node. The gray area at the center of Graph Editor is the main work area with curves in various colors, which correspond to the attributes on Graph Editor Outliner. If you select a specific attribute, its curve is displayed in the graph view. You can see the frame numbers along the bottom of Graph Editor. The Graph view is split into a vertical axis on the left and a horizontal axis at the bottom. The vertical axis represents the values of attributes with set keyframes, while the horizontal axis represents specific points in time. Each axis has several numerical marking indicating the actual values of attributes or time. By default, the graph view displays 24 frames, but you can zoom out to display more frames. You can view animation curves and keyframes for an object in Graph Editor only when the object is selected in the viewport.

The animation curves drawn are similar to NURBS curves. Each curve exhibits the change in the value of an attribute over an entire animation. Animation curves are displayed in a similar color of their attributes. The black dots that appear on the animation curves indicate keyframes. When you click a keyframe, a dark brown straight line known as tangent appears; it turns yellow when selected. A tangent is a line that meets an animation curve at one point. The tangents determine the curvature at keyframes; they control the bending of animation curve around keyframes. The tangents at the keyframes are split into two line segments – in tangent and out tangent that appear on either side of a keyframe. The in tangent is the segment on the left of a keyframe on an animation curve, while the out tangent is the line segment on the right of a keyframe. Both line segments have a dot known as a tangent handle at their ends. You can move the tangent handles to modify the curvature of an animation curve at a keyframe. There are several types of tangents that you can use to control the curvature of an animation curve at different keyframes. The list below is describing all the tangents in detail:

Spline: Creates a smooth curvature at a keyframe, by making the curve round at the keyframe. The in and out tangents are placed on the same line.
Linear: Creates a jagged curvature at a keyframe, by making the curve as straight lines. The in and out tangent may not be on the same line; they may form an angle with each other.
Clamped: Creates a smooth curvature at a keyframe unless the neighboring keyframes have the same values, in which case, the curvature is flat. The Clamped tangents combine the features of Spline and Linear tangents. This is the default tangent type in Maya.

<u>Stepped:</u> Creates a flat curvature after a keyframe; the out tangent is horizontal. The curve after a keyframe remains flat up to the frame where the next keyframe is set, and then, dropsvertically or rises to the next keyframe.

<u>Stepped Next:</u> Creates an upright curvature after the keyframe; the out tangent is vertical. The curve after the keyframe remains vertical up to the attribute value of the next keyframe, and then, advances horizontally to the next keyframe.

<u>Flat:</u> Creates a horizontal curvature at the keyframe by making the curve around the keyframe flat. The in and out tangents are placed on the same horizontal line.

<u>Fixed:</u> Makes the in and out tangents of a keyframe fixed. The direction of the tangents remains unaffected even when you modify the keyframe.

<u>Plateau:</u> Creates an even and flat curvature at a keyframe. The in and out tangents are placed horizontally on the same line. Plateau tangents are similar to the Flat tangents; however, Plateau tangents restrict the curve to the highest and lowest values of keyframes.

Adding a Keyframe on an Animation Curve

In the previous lessons you learnt that to add keyframes, you select Animate> Set Key from the main menu bar. Now it is important to know that you can use Graph Editor to add keyframes to an animation. Additional keyframes are used to fine tune an animation. In Graph Editor, you can add new keyframes using Insert Keys Tool from the toolbar or the Add Key Tool command in Keys menu. You can perform the following steps to add a keyframe using the Add Keys Tool:

1. **Open** an <u>animation scene</u>, and select **Window> Animation Editors> Graph Editor** from the main menu bar.

2. On left side in the Graph Editor Outliner pane, **select** an <u>attribute</u> to add a keyframe. You may find an attribute such as <u>Translate Z</u> in the pane that you need to select.

If you look at your computer screen at this moment, only the animation curve for the Translate Z attribute is displayed in graph view. The animation curve appears as a straight line indicating that there is no animated keys for the Translate Z attribute.

3. **Click** the <u>animation curve</u> in the graph view, which turns the animation curve white with all the keyframes selected. You can also see a small white square that appears before the Translate Z attribute in Graph Editor Outliner.

4. **Click** <u>Insert Keys Tool</u> in the Graph Editor toolbar. Then, **move** the cursor <u>over the animation curve</u> where you want to insert the new keyframe.

5. **Click** the <u>animation curve</u> with the middle mouse button to add a keyframe, which appears with two tangents. Similarly, you can add any number of keyframes.

Modifying a Keyframe on an Animation Curve

If you find that a keyframe set at a particular frame can enhance the animation quality if moved to any another frame, you can delete it from the current frame and set it again at the new frame. However, this might consume time; hence, instead of deleting and setting the keyframe, you can reposition the keyframe in Graph Editor. With Graph Editor, you can easily and quickly reposition the keyframe by moving it on the animation curve. Perform these steps to do it practically:

1. **Select** an animated object in the viewport, and **open** Graph Editor. Then, **select** an attribute to view the animation curve in Graph Editor Outliner. For now, you can select Translate Z attribute.

2. **Select** the keyframe that you want to move, and then, **select** Move Nearest Picked Key Tool in the Graph Editor Toolbar.

3. **Drag** the keyframe on the curve to any other frame to position it using middle mouse button. For now, you can move the selected keyframe upward.

4. **Release** the mouse button, and then, **click** the Play forward button in the Playback Controls to preview the modified animation.

Working with Animation Layers

Using animation layer you can create and blend multiple animations in a single scene. Each layer contains animation curves representing the attributes used in animating a scene. Animation layers are arranged in the form of a stack in Animation Layer Editor. These layers are blended by changing the values of the X, Y, and Z attributes of the curves contained in the layers, which finally results in a complete animation. Animation Layer Editor provides a variety of tools and options to create and manipulate animation layers. Now you need to understand how you can add an object to an animation layer and set the mode of an animation layer.

Adding an Object to an Animation Layer

In Animation Layer Editor, animation layers are stacked in the order of their creation. The new layers appear on the top of the stack. As said earlier, you can create several animation layers and add them in a scene. There are two ways to add attributes of an object to an animation layer:

A. Create a layer for the selected object and add its attributes to the layer automatically. While creating an animation layer, you can create a layer from the selected objects in a scene or copy an existing layer using the options in the Layers menu. When you copy a layer, the keyframes are also copied to the new layer. The animation layer for the selected objects automatically incorporates all attributes of the objects.

B. Create an empty layer first, and then, add attributes to it. In an empty animation layer the attributes are added after creating it.

Animation layers can be added using the Anim tab in Layer Editor. You can click the Anim tab to display the animation layers. By default, the Display tab appears in Layer Editor. Perform the following steps to add an object to an animation layer:

1. **Select** an animated object, and then, **click** the Anim tab in Layer Editor to display Animation Layer Editor.

2. Select **Layers> Create Layer from Selected** from Layers menu. Alternatively, click the Create Layer from Selected button in the Animation Layer Editor to create a new layer with a selected object. To create an empty animation layer, click the Create Empty Layer button in Animation Layer Editor.

This way, a new layer named AnimLayer1 is added into Animation Layer Editor. It shows a green circle for the layer indicating that the object is currently selected in the viewport. Using the Layers menu, you can also add on override layer, copy/paste layers, change the order of layers in the stack, add selected objects to and from a layer, and export a layer to a different scene. In addition, you can rename a layer in the Animation Layer Editor by double-clicking its name.

Setting the Mode of an Animation Layer

There are two modes that are used in Maya for adding animation layers. First is Additive mode and second is Override mode. In the Additive mode, an animation layer adds its animation to the layers preceding this layer in the stack in Animation Layer Editor. For instance, if two animation layers: AnimLayer1 and AnimLayer2 contain the Rotate X attribute for a cone, the resultant Rotate X value for the cone is the sum of Rotate X values from both the layers. However, in the Override mode, an animation layer overrides the animation of any layer with the same attributes. For instance, if there are two animation layers (AnimLayer1 and AnimLayer2) and the Scale X attribute value for a cylinder on AnimLayer1 is 10 and the same attribute has the value of 15 on AnimLayer2, the resultant animation has the Scale X attribute value of 15. This is because the second layer overrides the layer preceding it in the stack in Animation Layer Editor. When an animation layer is in the Override mode, the name of the layer is displayed in bold. You can do these simple steps to understand it practically:

1. **Select** and **right-click** a layer to set the mode in Animation Layer Editor. It displays the context menu on the screen.

2. Select **Layer Mode> Override** from the context menu. Then, **right-click** the layer and **select** the Select Layer Node option from the context menu.

The attributes for the Select Layer Node option appear in Channel Box. The animation in this layer now overrides the animation affecting the same attributes on layers above it in the stack. When the animation layer is in the Override mode, you can also turn on the Passthrough option, which lets you turn the opacity of Override layers on and off.

Previewing an Animation

You need to preview an animation to ensure accuracy of the movements of an animation before sending it for final rendering. You can identify the precision in the animation and correct it by previewing. One of the easiest and quickest ways to preview an animation in Maya is to play it back using Playback Controls. You must balance the quality of the graphics with playback performance to save time while previewing. You can create motion trail to preview an animation and directly edit keys on the trail in the scene. In addition, you can turn on display options, such as ghosting and playblast to visualize the flow of an object motion. Now we can discuss the motion techniques available in Maya:

Using Motion Trails

At the time of animating, what you normally do is that you move the object to different positions in a scene. You may want to display and adjust the path followed by an object on animating it. In such a case, you can create a motion trail of the animated object with the keyframe animation. Motion trail of an animated object refers to the trajectory or trail on which the object moves. Motion trails provide a visual representation of keys of the selected object. Motion trail displays keys for the object's Translate X, Translate Y, and Translate Z curves only. Using the Create Editable Motion trail feature, you can preview and interactively adjust keyframes in the viewport. You can also display and adjust timing beads on a motion trail to control the ease-in and ease-out of animations at each keyframe. Each bead represents one frame in time. You can adjust the spacing of timing beads on either side of a key to slow or speed up the movement of an object as it approaches and moves away from the key. Stretching out the timing beads slows the movement of an object into or out of the key, while compressing the beads speeds the movement. Perform these steps on your system to preview and edit a motion trail:

1. **Select** an animated object in a scene and choose **Animate> Create Editable Motion Trail** (**Rectangle Box**) from the main menu bar which opens the <u>Motion Trail Options</u> window. The picture 6.7 shows a Hedra object selected in the scene.

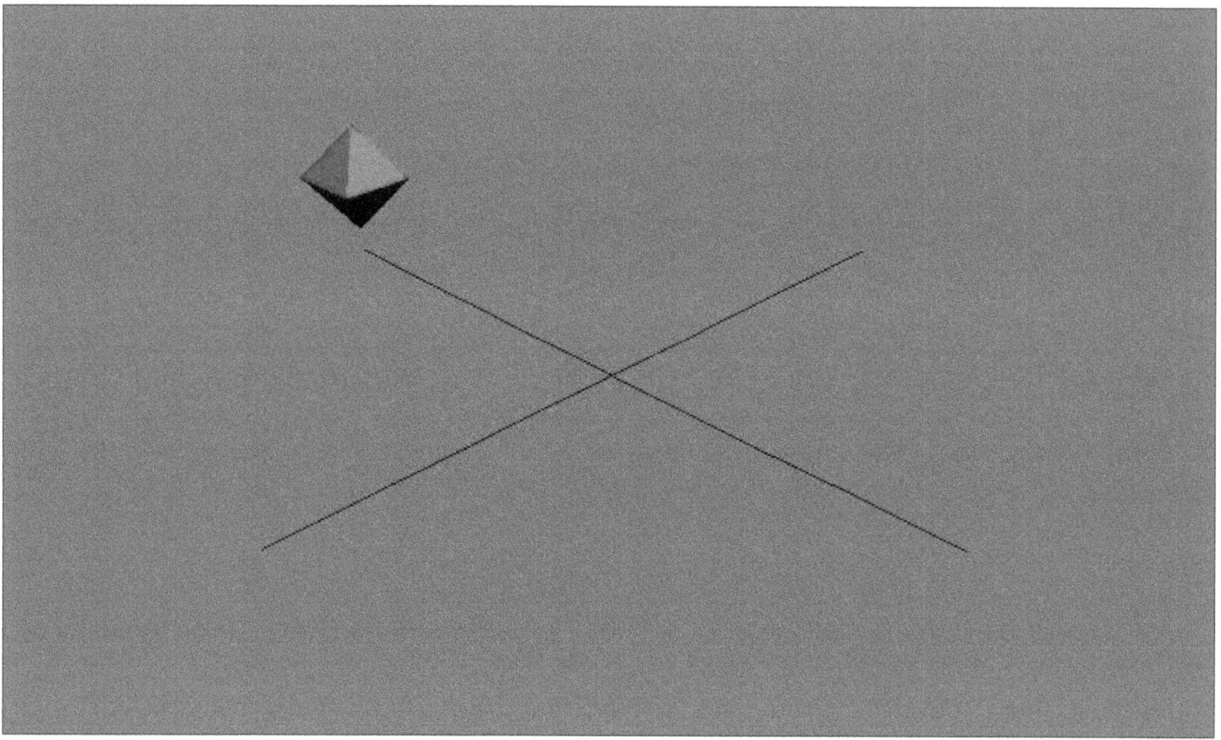

Picture 6.7

2. Type: **5.0000** in the <u>Increment</u> text box and press enter. Setting the Increment to 5 samples draws a motion trail point every five frames. If a motion trail key falls on a sample point, it is drawn on the trail.

3. **Select** the <u>Show frame numbers</u> check box to toggle the display of frame numbers at each keyframe on the motion trail.

You can also specify the frame numbers in the Start time and End time text boxes to make the motion trail to play a specific range (number) of frames. In addition, select the Start/End radio button for the Time range option to specify the start and end time in the Start time and End time text boxes. For now, you can select the default Time Slider option, which takes the total number of frames in the Time Slider and previews it.

4. **Click** the <u>Create Motion Trail</u> button. The motion trail appears for the selected object in the active viewport.

You can see in the picture 6.8 that the motion trail path indicates the movement of the animated object. Now we can try to adjust the motion trail path to modify the animation.

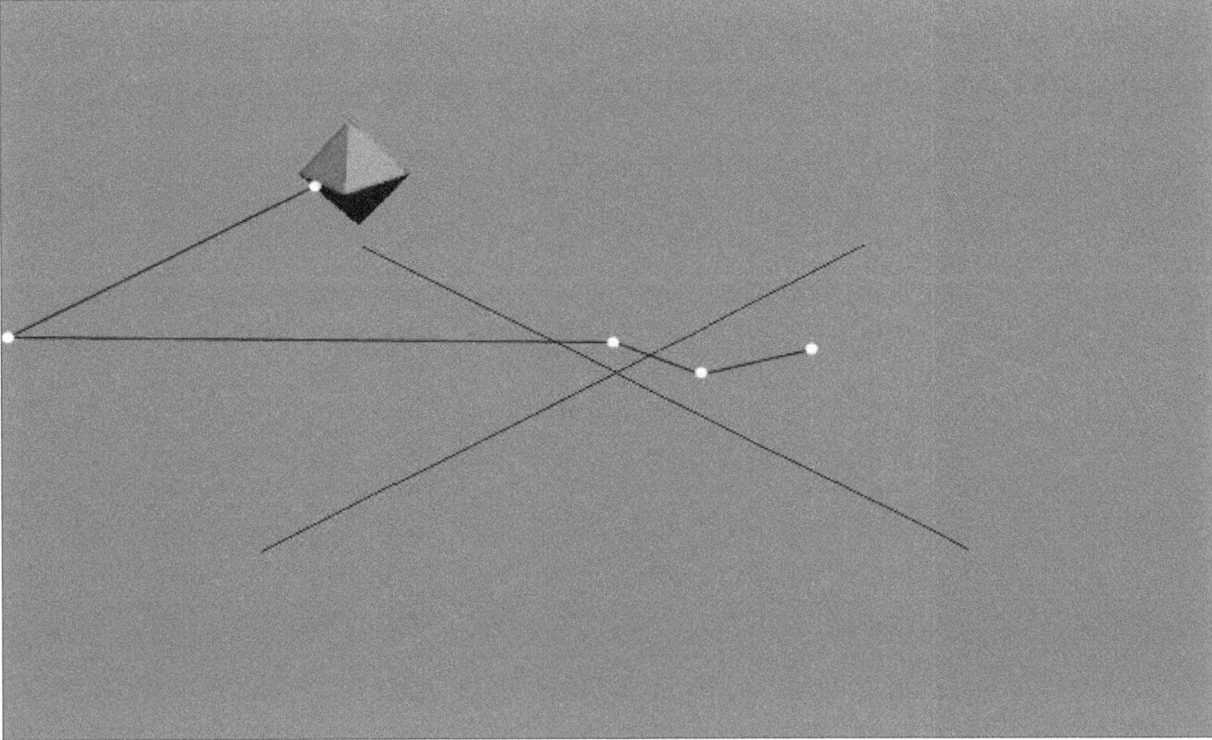

Picture 6.8

5. **Right-click** the <u>motion trail path</u> and **select** the <u>Modify Keys</u> option from the marking menu. This sets the motion trail to Modify Keys mode, where you can adjust keyframes directly on the motion trail.

You can adjust the keyframes in the following ways: (A) To insert keyframes, click anywhere on the motion trail path to insert. (B) To move keyframes along the motion trail, hold the Shift key down, and click and drag the keyframe with the middle mouse button or Move Tool. (C) To delete keyframes, hold the Shift key down and click the keyframe.

6. **Click** the <u>motion trail path</u> to insert a keyframe. For now, you can insert a keyframe at the 26th frame and you'll see two new keyframes appearing in the playback range of Time Slider.

7. **Select** <u>Move Tool</u> from Tool Box, **click** the <u>keyframe</u> to select it and drag it to move. For now, you can move the 26th frame. Then, **click** <u>Play forwards</u> in Playback Controls to preview the modified animation.

8. **Right-click** the <u>motion trail path</u> and **select** the <u>Modify Keys</u> option again to disable it. Similarly, you can add multiple keyframes into the motion path and edit them to modify the final animation.

Using Ghosts

Similar to the motion trail feature, the ghosting feature also helps in visualizing the path of an animation and attributes of objects at different frames. Ghosting refers to the process of generating positions of an animated object, a few frames before and after its current position. The 3D images generated are transitory and known as ghosts. When you ghost an object, you can view its position at different time durations during an animation. Here are the steps to create ghosts for an animated object:

1. **Select** an animated object and choose **Animate**> **Ghost Selected**> (**Rectangle Box**) from the main menu bar. The Ghost Options window appears.

2. **Select** the Custom frames option in the Type of ghosting drop-down. Then, you need to type the numbers for the frames where you want to see the ghosts in the Frames to display text box. For now, you need to **type: 1, 10, 20, 30, 40, 50**.

3. **Click** the **Ghost** button to apply these settings on the selected object. The picture 6.9 shows a similar view of the ghost effect. You can also unghost a selected object using the Unghost Selected option under the Animate menu.

Picture 6.9

Playblasting an Animation
When you play an animation using Playback Controls, the speed of the animation, especially for a complex animation is slower as compared to the final output. In Maya, playblasting is a better and quicker alternative to preview an animation. A screenshot of each frame in an animation is captured and assembled together in a sequence, which is then viewed using any movie player, such as Windows Media Player. You can save this sequence of screen grabs or playblast images as a movie file. Note that the playblast images are created from the frames in the current camera view (perspective, top, front, and side) of the screen. You can perform these simple steps to preview an animation as a movie:

1. **Open** a scene with an animation and select **Window**> **Playblast**> (**Rectangle Box**) from the main menu bar. The Playblast Options window appears where you can specify the output format (by default, avi), quality, size, and location.

2. **Set** the output quality to **100** in the Quality text box, and **select** the Save to file check box to save the output file in the hard drive. Then, **click** the Playblast button at the end.

It calculates each frame automatically and the scene is rendered in the viewport. It saves the output file in the default location and the animation is played in default media player. You can also specify if you want to create the playblast images for the entire Time Slider or for a particular range of frames using the Time range option in the Playblast Options window.

Adding Sound to Animation

At the time of animating objects, you focus on their movements and not on the sound that they generate. However, sound is very important an animation. In Maya, you can synchronize the movements of an object to the beats of the sound by importing a sound clip into a scene. You must synchronize the intensity and duration of the sound with the movements of an object. For instance, if you want to animate a bell, you need to synchronize the movements of the bell with its ringing sound. You can perform these simple steps to add sound to an animation:

1. **Open** an animation scene and choose **File> Import** from the main menu bar to import an audio file into the scene. It opens the Import dialog box.

2. **Browse** and **select** an audio file from the hard drive and **click** the Import button. The supported audio file formats in Maya are wav, aif, and aiff.

The selected audio file is now loaded in the current scene. In case you are unable to view the audio file in Time Slider, right-click in Time Slider and select Sound> (Name of the audio file) from the context menu. You can now animate the object based on the sound loaded into the scene. You can also control the speed of the sound playback. Right-click Time Slider and place the cursor over the Playback Speed option in the context menu, and then, select the appropriate playback speed option. You also delete the imported file from the scene by selecting Edit> Delete by Type > Sounds from the main menu bar.

Lesson 20
Shading Materials and Lights

The appearance of an object's surface depends on the position and attributes of lights in a scene. In Maya, geometry is used to define the shape of an object, while the material or shader is used to define the appearance of its surface. A shading material is a collection of attributes, such as color, transparency, shine, and texture. You can modify the attributes of a material, as required and apply it to the surface of an object. The process of manipulating the attributes of a material and applying to a surface is known as shading. It allows you to define the appearance of the surface, when illuminated. Using the shading materials such as Lambert and Blinn, you can control the appearance of the surface after the final render. Lambert is the default material used to create matte surfaces, while Blinn is used to create shiny surfaces. You can also apply texture maps that are images to modify the appearance of a surface. For instance, you can apply labels and a logo on a surface as texture maps. Texture mapping is the process in which you apply and accurately position images onto the surfaces. If we discuss about the light in Maya, we have to say that a light is a type of object that creates visibility of objects in a scene. It plays a key role in creating a realistic environment and follows the law of reflection and refraction while reacting to the various objects in a scene. For instance, a shiny surface reflects the light, but a matte or a diffused surface absorbs the light. Using the attributes of light, you can control the interaction between light and objects. Maya also allows you to create a wide range of effects including realistic shadows, lens flare, glow, or fog.

Understanding Maya Materials

When light hits the surface, it creates a gradation that gradually changes from light to dark which makes the surface 3D qualities apparent. When you create an object in Maya, a default shading material called Lambert is assigned to it. The default lights are used to light up objects if there are no other lights in a scene. Maya shading materials are a set of nodes with every node comprising a set of attributes that define it. Each shading material comprises a large number of material nodes, which contain all rendering information of an object material. You can use wide varieties of materials which are selected in different ways. You can either use the Hypershade window or select Lighting/Shading> Assign New Material from the main menu bar to assign materials to a selected object. The Assign New Material window appears

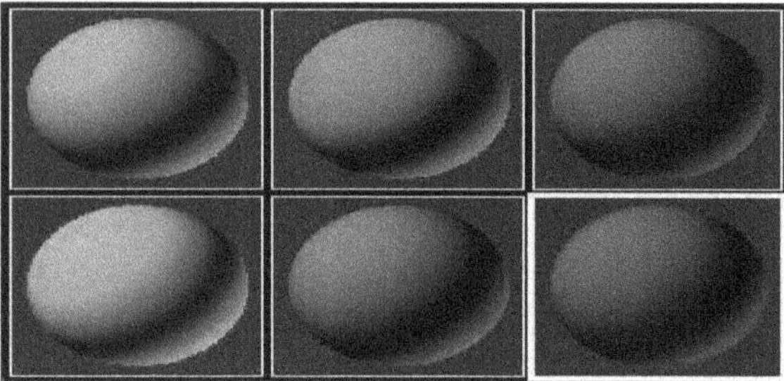

with all the materials, as shown in picture 7.0. The materials include: Anisotropic, Blinn, Hair Tube Shader, Lambert, Layered Shader, Ocean Shader, Phong, Phong E, Ramp Shader, Shading Map, Surface Shader, Use Background, Env Fog, Fluid Shape, Light Fog, Particle Cloud, Volume Fog, and Volume Shader. Now we can discuss about some of these frequently used materials.

Picture 7.0

Anisotropic: This material stretches highlights, which is the area on the surface where light reflects most and rotates them based on the relative position of a viewer. It creates uneven specular highlights, which are bright spots of light that appear on a shiny object when it is illuminated. They are used for deformed surfaces including: warped plastic or foil wrapper. Anisotropic surfaces reflect lights to create an irregular shaped specular highlight. These specular highlights are ideal to represent surfaces of brushed metals, such as compact discs.

Blinn: It creates accurate specular lighting and is effective on surfaces with metallic and shiny finish. This type of material is ideal for metallic surfaces with soft highlights, such as brass or aluminum. Blinn surfaces reflect light similar to Phong surfaces, but it creates a hot spot with a specular highlight that diffuses more gradually than in Phong surfaces.

Hair Tube Shader: It simulates a small thin tube highlights that are spread across the entire tube width. You can create this material by converting the Paint Effects hair system to polygons. On conversion, the color attributes for the Paint Effects hair system are automatically converted into Hair Tube Shader. Later, you can change the attributes using the Hair Tube Shader material. In terms of the specularity control, the attributes of the Hair Tube Shader material are similar to the Anisotropic material.

Lambert: It diffuses light evenly along the entire surfaces to give smoothness without any highlights. Lambert is a flat material found in almost all dull or matte surfaces. For instance, a sheet of paper is a perfect example of a Lambert surface. This is the default material in Maya and assigned to the newly created objects.

Layered Shader: You can use this material to combines multiple materials, so that, you can create a more complex material. For instance, to place chrome polka dots on a wood surface, you can use a polka dot mask in a Layered Shader material, and then, import the existing chrome and wood materials into Maya. You can use the transparency maps to control transparency. A transparency map defines the areas with respect to layers it shows.

Ocean Shader: This material allows you to simulate water wave patterns or pure fabric. The Ocean Shader material is designed to be used as a displacement map, which is mostly used on objects that need high polygon counts. It is also used for additional control for color changes with light and view angle. The Ocean Shader material has several attributes that control the behavior of the material over time, and it has graphs to add details to the base material. The attributes include Wave Speed, Wave Height, and Wave Turbulence.

Phong: It uses the surface curvature, amount of light, and camera angle to get accurate shading and highlights. Phong is named after its developer Bui Tuong-Phong. The mathematical calculations performed by Phong help you to create highlights. It is excellent for polished shiny surfaces, such as plastic, porcelain, metal, and glazed ceramic. Phong surfaces reflect light and create a sharp hot spot and a specular highlight that drops off sharply. The professional animators extensively use this material in their animation.

Phong E: This material provides additional features along with the Phong material for more control over the specular highlight. It creates a Phong surface with a specular highlight that drops off more gradually, and yet remains sharper than what is possible in Blinn material. Phong E also provides control over colors and has additional options with regard to metallic reflections. This material is similar to the Phong material, but provides more control over specular settings that allow you to adjust the glossiness of a surface.

Ramp Shader: When you want to create and control a cel (2D cartoon-like) surface, Ramp Shader makes the things easy for you. It is one of the most important materials and contains all colors that are useful for editing surfaces and objects in a scene. Ramp Shader is a self-contained shader node that has several ramp textures attached to its attributes, such as color, transparency, incandescence, specular color, and reflectivity. All editing done through the Ramp Shader's own Attribute Editor.

Shading Map: Renders the bright areas (areas that are facing the light) with a color and the dark areas with the hue of the former color. It is an advances material which is primarily designed to create various non-photorealistic shading effects, such as cartoon-style materials or sci-fi characters and places. This material can be used for a flat 2D cartoonist look, rather than smoothly shaded surfaces. Shading Map, Surface Shader, and Use Background are the advanced materials in Maya which can create more realistic lighting on objects.

Surface Shader: Allows you to control the color, transparency, and glow of a material in Maya. For instance, you can link the color to the XYZ position of an object, and the material changes colors as the object moves around a scene.

Use Background: Allows you to merge computer generated (CG) objects with scanned images. At the time of animating a scene, you may want to merge a CG object with the still images that you have in your system. This is when you apply the Use Background material to bring desired effect. An object with the Use Background material applied on it appears transparent in a scene; therefore, you can just see the background images of a scene. This material can also be used to cut a hole in an alpha channel of an image. However, shadows can fall on the material, and if it is made shiny, it can reflect other CG graphics. This material helps to combine individual rendered images in a compositing program to create a final result. The professional animators extensively use this material to animate a 3D movie scene when transparency effect is needed.

Understanding Material Attributes

Before applying materials on an object, you need to understand their attributes. Materials are composed of material nodes similar to other objects in Maya. These nodes also contain different attributes, which define the appearance of materials and their reaction to light and other objects in a scene. The key attributes of a material include: Color, Transparency, Ambient Color, Incandescence, Diffuse, Translucence Depth, Translucence Focus, Specular color, Reflectivity, Roughness, Highlight Size, Whiteness, Eccentricity, Specular Rolloff, and Cosine Power. You can access these attributes for an object in the Common Materials Attributes group of Attribute Editor. Now we can discuss about the common materials attributes.

Color: Refers to the attributes that defines the color of an object surface. By default, all materials in Maya appear in gray color (Lambert); however, you can change the color of a material using the Color attribute. It addition, you can create different types of colors in Maya by combining the three primary RGB colors – Red, Green, and Blue. You can also type the color values for every color in the Numeric Input section based on Hue, Saturation, and Value (HSV). RGV and HSV values are important for defining the color of a material. You can select a color in the Color Choose window, which appears when you double-click a color swatch in Attribute Editor. The Color Choose window enables you to do the following. (1) Select colors using Color Wheel or Color Palette. (2) Import images and choose colors from them. (3) Blend colors together. (4) Save frequently used colors in the Color History group. (5) Create and save custom color palette.

When you want to increase or decrease the brightness of a color, you can drag the slider next to the color swatch. A render node can also be created by clicking the small checker next to the slider. You can also access a compact version of the Color Chooser window by clicking the swatch next to the Color attribute in Attribute Editor. The Color History section shows the current selected color and allows to quickly picking a color.

Transparency: Controls the amount of light that passes through an object material. Increasing the value of the Transparency attribute of an object decreases its visibility and becomes more transparent. Generally, transparency of objects is represented in a black to white gradient, with black being opaque and white being translucent. For instance, if the transparency value is 0 or black, the surface is completely opaque. If the transparency value is 1 or white, the surface is completely transparent.

Ambient Color: Adds extra color to the surfaces in a scene. This attribute makes objects appear flat as the color is evenly spread over them. By default, the Ambient Color attribute is set to black. The appearance of the areas depends on the intensity of the ambient color. The lighter the ambient color, the lighter the areas appear and vice versa. Ambient color is also influenced by the number of Ambient Lights in a scene.

Incandescence: Refers to the ability of an object to self-illuminate. Incandescence, neither lights objects around it in regular renders, nor creates a glow. However, if flattens the object's color into a pure flat color. The Incandescence attribute helps in lighting a scene in Final Gather rendering using mental ray.

Diffuse: Determines the amount of light absorbed and scattered by a surface. This attribute measures the dispersion of light as it strikes the surface of an object and illuminates the surface. A higher diffuse value implies that the amount of light being absorbed is less, resulting in better diffusion of light. Similarly, a lower diffuse value implies greater absorption of light. For instance, metals have a very low diffuse value as they reflect most of the light compared to wood or plastic.

Translucence: Refers to the transmission of light through a medium. In CG, this attribute allows you to light up both sides of a surface. Using this attribute, you can create materials such as wax, paper, milk, and leaves. The default Translucence attribute value is 0. A translucence value of 1 implies that the light passes through an object at its peak value; whereas, a translucence value of 0 implies that no light is passing through a surface.

Translucence Depth: Determines the amount of light penetrating a surface. It helps to transmit light from the surface of an object. You can see this phenomenon by placing a piece of paper before the light.

Translucence Focus: Specifies the amount of light that is scattered depending on the direction of the light. Thin surfaces such as paper, have a higher translucence focus than thick surfaces such as metal or wood with a low translucence focus. You can lower the color value for very shiny objects that have a bright specular region on a surface for better result.

Specular Color: Refers to the color of the light of a specular reflection, which is a characteristic of light reflected from a shiny surface. The Specular Color attribute specifies the color of a highlight on a shiny surface. Note that the black color creates no specular; whereas, the white color creates a bright specular. The default color value of this attribute is 0.5. You can select a white color for the Specular Color attribute to shade glossy plastic surfaces. Similarly, for metallic surfaces, you can use a specular color similar to the surface color of an object.

Reflectivity: Refers to the amount of reflection that is visible on the surface of an object. A high value of reflection increases the rendering power of an object. The valid range of reflectivity is from 0 to infinity; however, in Maya, the range of Reflectivity attribute is 0 (which means no reflection) to 1 (which means clear reflections). The default value of the Reflectivity attribute is 0.5; however, values for common surface materials such as car paint, glass and mirror are 0.4, 0.7, and 1, respectively. It also increases the visibility of all true reflections occurring in a scene when objects are raytraced.

Roughness: Controls the specular highlights. It is available only for the Phong E material.

Highlight Size: Controls the amount of specular highlight.

Whiteness: Determines specular highlight color. White is the default color for this attribute. You can also use texture for this attribute. Additionally, Attribute Editor also includes the Raytrace Options group with attributes such as Refractive Index, Refraction Limit, Light Absorbance, and Surface Thickness that help you to set a material to enable raytracing. These attributes control the appearance of a surface only during raytracing calculations. If the Refractions checkbox is enabled, a refraction ray of a given color is cast with an index of refraction value specified in the Refraction Index attribute, and the result is merged with an input color. The indices of refraction can be computed with another base material. You can use these attributes to create photorealistic reflections and refractions. By default, the attributes in the Raytrace Options group are available for materials such as Anisotropic, Lambert, Phong, Phone E, and Blinn.

Eccentricity: Controls the appearance of the specular highlight also called hot spots. Eccentricity is related to the width of the highlight. It is a very useful node of the Blinn material. You can choose any value in the range of 0 to 0.9999. Larger values create large highlights, but with smaller values objects appear more finely polished.

Specular Rolloff: Controls the reflection of a surface to the surroundings such as the environment, other reflective objects, or the Reflection Map, when watched from oblique angles. Specular Rolloff value range from 0 to 1 and it does not affect the reflections produced when you render using Ray Tracing.

Cosine Power: Controls the size of the shiny or specular highlights on a surface. The Phong material uses a single input known as Cosine Power. This attribute is only available with the Phong material. The default value for this attribute is set to 20. To get smaller and focused highlights, you must increase the Cosine Power attribute value.

Creating and Applying Materials

By default, Maya applies Lambert material on the object that you create. This material is neutral gray. You can modify the default material by modifying its attributes or applying new materials. There are different methods to apply a material attribute in Maya. The lighting/shading menu allows you to assign new and existing materials as well as modify material attributes; it appears when the menu set is selected as Rendering. You can also use the marking menu that appears when you right-click on a selected object. In addition, you can use the Hypershade window to assign materials. Now you can go ahead and perform the following steps on your computer system to create and apply a material in Maya:

1. **Open** a scene with objects, and **select** an object on which you want to apply material. Then, **select** the Rendering menu set from the menu selected in Status Line which is below File tab at the top left corner of Maya screen.

2. Select **Lighting/Shading> Assign New Material** from the main menu bar. The Assign New Material window appears with the list of materials. Alternatively, the shortcut to open the Assign New Material window is that, you can right-click an object and select the Assign New Material option from the marking menu. The title bar of the window also displays the name of the selected object.

3. **Click** a material from the list. For now, you can click on Blinn. It opens Attribute Editor with new material attributes which allows you to customize the Blinn material as required. Using the Type drop-down list in Attribute Editor, you can select a material type.

4. **Click** the color swatch for the **Color** attribute, and select a color from the compact Color Chooser. For now, you can select the orange color. As you change the attribute value, the selected object updates the default material to the new material in the viewport.

5. **Drag** the slider against the Ambient Color option to set as required. And also, **drag** the slider against the Incandescence option to set as required. Simultaneously, the material on the object is updated with this material.

Similarly, you can modify the default values for other attributes. Attribute Editor displays a thumbnail of the material in the Sample slot. The material applies to all selected objects in a scene. You can also assign a name for the material; the default name is the material name. After creating a material, you can later modify it and assign it to other objects. To apply the material to another object, you can select the object and select Lighting/Shading> Assign Existing Material from the main menu bar, and then, select the name of the material from the list.

Lesson 21
Using the Hypershade Window

The Hypershade window is the central working area of Maya rendering. You can build shading network by creating, editing, and connecting rendering nodes, such as texture, materials, and lights. To open the Hypershade window, you can select Window> Rendering Editors> Hypershade from the main menu bar. The picture 7.1 shows a similar view of Hypershade window. You can also open the Hypershade window in the current viewport by selecting Panels> Panel> Hypershade from the panel menu.

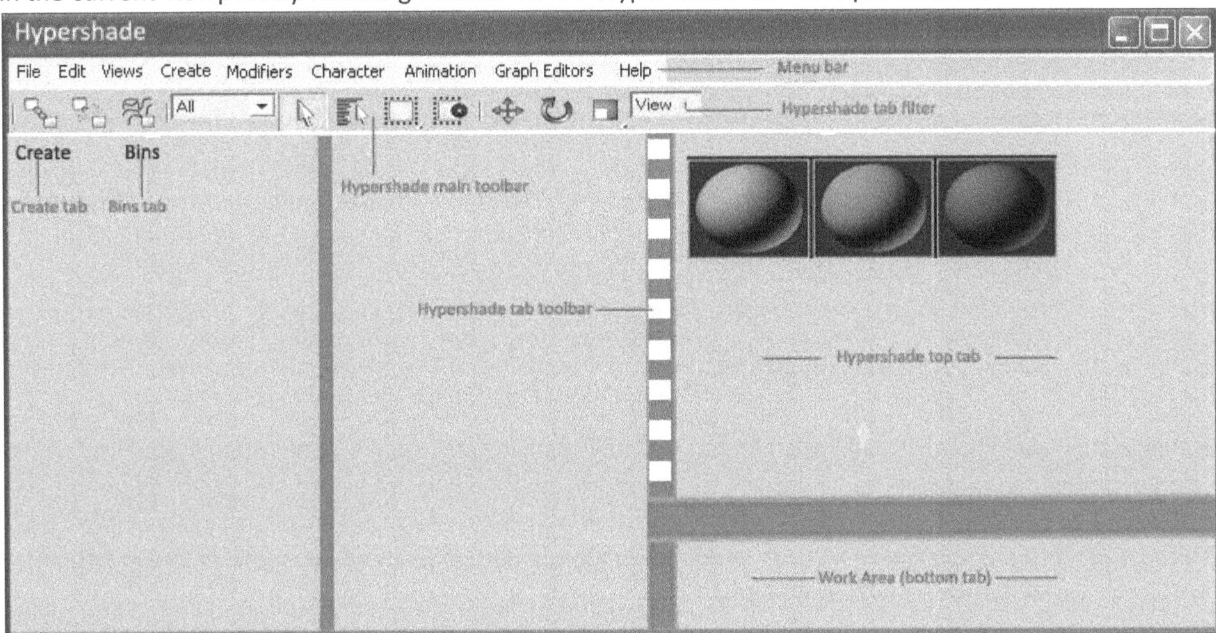

Picture 7.1

Hypershade window contains its own menu, tabs, and tools to perform different actions. Using this window, you can quickly and easily create, edit, and connect rendering nodes. You can also apply textures to the nodes. In the Hypershade window, each node is represented as an icon representing the characteristics of the node. Any changes that occur in the attribute of a node are reflected visually in all the nodes. Now we can discuss about each component of the Hypershade window.

Create Tab

The Create tab is the most important area in the Hypershade window. It appears on the left of the window. Using the bar below of the Create tab, you can generate different types of procedural textures such as fractal noise. There are varieties of icons displayed in the right panel representing different materials, such as Lambert, Blinn, and Anisotropic. In the same (left) panel, there are two categories of nodes: Maya and mental ray. You can click any type of node to create different types of rendering effects. You can also search the render node that you want to create by typing a keyword in the search box. As you type the keyword, the right panel of the Create tab updates in the real-time and displays the render nodes that suit the keyed name.

Bins Tab

The Bins tab is adjacent to the Create tab and displays bins that are containers in Maya. Bins contain shading nodes including materials and textures. Using the icons available at the top of the Bins tab, you can create and organize materials. Placing the cursor over these icons displays a tooltip. The default Master Bin contains all shading information for the current scene.

Tabs

Tabs are the important components of the Hypershade window. There are two types of tabs in the Hypershade window - Hypershade top tabs and Work Area tab (bottom tab). Hypershade top tabs are located at the top right-most panle of the Hypershade window and contain most rendering components that constitute a current scene, such as materials, textures, and lights. Whereas, the Work Area tab contains the shading network (a collection of connected rendering nodes) related to the selected node in the Work Area in the Hypershade window.

Toolbars

There are two types of toolbars in the Hypershade window - Hypershade main toolbar and the Hypershade tab toolbar. The Hypershade main toolbar comprises of different tools to perform various functions. These tools are available in the form of buttons. The various tools available in the main toolbar of the Hypershade window include: Toggle the Create bar On/Off, Show top and bottom tabs, Clear graph, and Input connections. The Hypershade tab toolbar contains different tabs such as View as icons, View as list, and View as small swatch that help in displaying swatches as icons or lists. These tabs also help to sort the swatches by name in alphabetical order, by type (Blinn or Phong), by time (according to the date and time they were created), and in reverse order (reversing the sorting based on name, type, or time when swatch was created).

Hypershade Tab Filter

Using the Hypershade tab filter, you can filter the nodes displayed in different tabs. Each tab contains an implicit filter that is determined by the tab type specified on its creation. The tab only shows the nodes that are passed by this filter. You can filter the nodes in this tab either by name or using the Show button that displays all the available nodes.

Hypershade Menus

The Hypershade menus help to perform various tasks such as creating render nodes, graphing the shading network for a selected node, opening Attribute Editor or Connection Editor, and customizing the display of swatches. You can also create, rename, or remove tabs using the Hypershade menus. Moreover, the Hypershade menus help you to import bitmap images or Maya scenes into the Hypershade window. You can also show or hide the Create tab by selecting Options> Create Bar> Show Create Bar from the Hypershade menu bar.

Now we'll create and apply material using the Hypershade window. The Hypershade window provides another method for creating and assigning materials in Maya. Similar to the Assign New Material window, you must first select the material type, and then modify the default attributes of a selected material. Perform the following steps to apply a material using the Hypershade window:

1. **Open** a scene in Maya which has multiple character models. Then, select **Window> Rendering Editors> Hypershade** from the main menu bar. It opens the Hypershade window.

2. Click **Anisotropic** from the right panel of the Create tab. The Anisotropic material appears in the Work Area.

3. **Double-click** the Anisotropic material in the Work Area. The attributes for the Anisotropic material appear in the Attribute Editor. You can modify the attributes for the material. The changes you make in Attribute Editor are simultaneously reflected in the Hypershade window.

4. **Close** the <u>Hypershade</u> window by clicking the Close icon. Then, **modify** the attributes as required in the <u>Attribute Editor</u>. For now, you can change the color from the Color attribute and increase ambient color value using the Ambient Color slider.

5. After creating a material by changing the attributes, you need to assign the material to the selected objects in a scene. For that, **select** the objects in the perspective viewport, **right-click** on them, and choose **Assign Existing Material> anisotropic 2** from the marking menu. Now you can see on your Maya screen that the selected objects are shaded with the new material in the viewport.

Understanding Textures

In animation technology, a texture is defined as a 2D bitmap image that is uses to create realistic surface material. The process in which you apply a 2D image onto a 3D surface is known as texturing. As Maya is a node-based 3D application, each action performed by creating a node for the action is remembered. Similarly, texture nodes are created while working with textures. Texture node is a type of render node using which you can define the appearances of an object surface when rendered. These nodes are procedural textures generated by Maya, or bitmap images imported into Maya that can be used as texture maps for material attributes and t apply them on the surface of an object. Texture maps on various attributes such as color, bump, and specularity affect the appearance of a material. As you know that a 2D image can be stretched, wrapped, and projected onto a surface in various ways: you can control applying an image to the surface of an object. Now we will discuss about the different types of textures, and then, UV texture coordinates which is used to map a texture onto a surface in Maya.

Exploring Types of Textures

(A) Procedural textures: Represents 2D or 3D plots, which are calculated based on algorithm and mathematical functions without any constraint for resolution (size). Procedural textures also known as procedural maps are CG images used to give a realistic feel to a model. Most 2D and 3D textures of Maya are procedural textures. 2D procedural textures (except images and movies) work by attaching the textures with the UV coordinates of a surface. Whereas, 3D procedural textures do not use UV coordinates of a surface.

(B) File texture: Refers to the saved images that are imported into Maya scene using a File texture node. File textures contain digital pictures and scanned photos. These textures are also generated using 2D imaging program such as Photoshop. All File texture nodes are placed on the surface of objects using a material. Texture mapping is done using the surfaces' UV values. File textures are better than the procedural textures and can give better quality. Unlike, the procedural textures, which tiles (repeats) by default; to tile file textures, you must ensure that edges should match properly to avoid seams on the surface. You can use an imaging program to offset an image, and then, touch up light or dark areas in the offset tile to make sure the edges match exactly. You can apply any bitmap image as a texture map in Maya. Now perform the following steps carefully to apply a texture map onto a surface:

1. **Open** a scene and **select** the surface onto which you want to apply a texture map. Then, you need to **right-click** on the <u>surface</u> and **select** the **Assign New Material** option from the marking menu. The Assign New Material window appears.

2. **Click** a <u>material type</u> button for the surface. For now, you can click the <u>Blinn</u> button. The Assign New Material window closes and Attribute Editor appears with attributes for the selected material.

3. **Click** the checkbox next to Color attributes slider which opens the Create Render Node window. Then, **click** a render node button. For now, you can click the **File** render node in the right panel of Create Render Node window. A File texture render node is added for which you can select a texture map.

4. Click the **Folder** button to select any texture map. The Open dialog box appears; you can browse and select a texture map in the dialog box.

5. **Browse** and **select** a texture map from your hard drive. Then, **click** the Open button at the bottom right side. Right now the texture map does not appear on the selected surface in the viewport. For that, you will have to render the scene.

6. You can display the texture map on the surface in the viewport by selecting the Hardware Texturing option from the Shading menu. For this, select **Shading> Hardware Texturing** from the panel menu. It will display the selected surface with texture map in your viewport.

Mapping UV Textures

UV texture mapping is the process used to create new UV coordinates on a surface. It is necessary to map texture on the surface correctly. Mapping UV texture coordinates indicates to the 3D renderer about placing a 2D map across the geometry, which varies based on the model being created from NURBS or polygons. Parametric mapping is inherent to a surface and is commonly used in NURBS, which are already parametric surfaces. This similarity in surface construction helps the mapping to automatically flow smoothly across the surface. You can move and rotate the positioning of a map on an object to adjust mapping on the surface.

Mapping on polygon surfaces can be done by projecting 2D maps across the 3D surface. This can be done using various projections such as planar, cylindrical, and spherical. Automatic mapping method can also be used for this projection of 2D maps. Planar projections create a smearing effect in the area perpendicular to the direction of the map projection. Cylindrical and spherical projections seem to solve this problem; however, both mapping types have their own drawbacks. For example, you can apply the cylindrical or spherical projection before deformers; later, if you want to change the projection, it is difficult to move the mapping after the deformers. Generally, you must apply the best mapping method for a surface and the visible areas while animating. In complex cases, a combination of automatic mapping, multiple mapping coordinates, and lots of photo editing work can usually fix the problem.

Lesson 22
Exploring Types of Light

Till now, you have learnt modeling, texturing, and animating objects. The next thing you need to learn is adding Maya light in a scene. Basically, lights create mood in a scene and make it more appealing. The overall quality of a final output largely depends on the lights in a scene. Lighting is the process to set-up lights based on time and environment. For example, to show a night scene, light set-up should be dark with minimum lights. The type and number of lights you use in a scene directly affect no just its appearance, but also increase the rendering time. On starting the lighting phase, use lights to illuminate an overall scene, and then, manipulate them to get a realistic output. On most cases, a scene requires highlights (more lights) and shadows (low lights). An excess light in a scene diminishes all other details (materials and shadows); whereas, shortage of light produces a lifeless scene and reduces details. Hence, highlights and shadows must be balanced well to get a realistic output. The traditional approach of lighting starts with the three point lighting technique. Maya uses this technique to differentiate objects from the background. Lights include one fill light (primary light), one key light (secondary light, which is used to create shadows), and one back light (also known as rim light). A key light is the main source of light in a scene and is placed at a location of the main source of light. A fill light is more diffused than the key light and is evenly spread in a scene. Generally, the intensity of fill light is half of the intensity of key light. It fills other objects in a scene with light and works as the source of illumination. And back or rim light is placed behind objects to differentiate it from the background.

In Maya, you find six types of lights – Ambient Light, Directional Light, Point Light, Spot Light, Area Light, and Volume Light. You can create these lights by selecting Create> Lights from the main menu bar, and then, selecting a light type from the submenu. After you create a light, it is placed at the center of the grid. You may need to reposition the light for effective utilization using Move Tool. You can change the default attributes of a light using Attribute Editor after creating it. You can also change light settings by clicking the respective Option box in the submenu. Now you need to perform the following steps carefully to add a light in a scene:

1. **Open** a scene in which you want to add a light. Then, select **Create> Lights> Spot Light> (Rectangle Box**) from the main menu bar. The Create Spot Light Options window appears.

2. **Type** a value in the Intensity text box to set the light intensity. For now, you can type: **4.0000**. Then, **select** a light color from the Color swatch. You can select **red** color for now.

3. **Select** the Cast shadows check box to enable the light to cast shadows. Then, **click** the Create button to create the light. A Spot Light appears at the center of grid, as shown in picture 7.2.

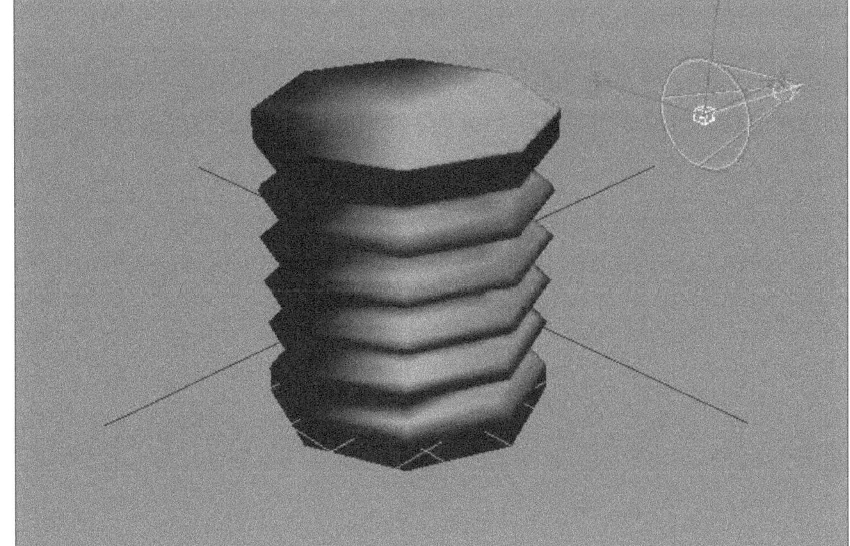

4. **Position** the light object using transform tools as required. When you create a light for a scene in Maya, the scene does not display the light effect, by default; instead, it uses the default lighting. After placing the light in the viewport, you can view the effect by enabling the light for the viewport or by rendering the scene.

Picture 7.2

5. Select **Lighting> Use Selected Lights** from the panel menu. A preview with the effect of Spot Light appears in the viewport.

As you know, to render this scene, you can select Render> Render Current Frame from the main menu bar. In case you want to further modify the light attributes after creating it, you can use Attribute Editor. To open Attribute Editor with the light attributes, right-click the selected light object in the viewport, and select the name of the light at the top of the marking menu. Similarly, you can add other light types in a scene as required.

Exploring Ambient Light

In the discussion of different types of lights and their attributes, we have to start with Ambient Light. It is a combination of both ambient and diffused lights. As it casts an even light across an entire scene, it is typically used to control the overall brightness and color of a scene. When Ambient Light is used in low intensity, it acts as a fill or background light. It illuminates a scene as an Omni-directional light source such as Sun. Therefore, the scene appears flat and wiped out. The Ambient Shade slider in Attribute Editor measures the flatness or unevenness of the lighting effect. Now we can talk about the attributes of Ambient Light as found in Attribute Editor.

Type: Allows you to switch to a different light type from Attribute Editor. You can select the light type from the Type dropdown list. When you change a light type, only those attributes that are common to both types are retained in Attribute Editor. Light-specific values are lost and the attributes specific to the selected light type appear with the default settings. When you change a light type, its position is preserved.

Color: Enables you to select a color of a light in a scene. You can click the color swatch either to change the light color in the Color Chooser window or to map a texture to it. If you map a texture, it is projected by the light based on the light type. The default color selected for the Color attribute is white..

Intensity: Represents the brightness of light. Negative Intensity values remove light from the light influenced area. If the Intensity attribute value is 0, it produces no light; if the value is positive, light is added to a scene. By default, the range of the Intensity slider is from 0 to 10; however, you can specify a larger value in the Intensity text box, for instance, 20. The default value for this attribute is 1.

Illuminates by Default: Illuminates all objects in a scene when selected. If set to off, the light only illuminates objects to which it is linked. The Illuminates by Default checkbox is selected, by default. It works like an on-off switch for lights.

Ambient Shade: Measures the flatness or unevenness of the lighting effect. The slider range from 0 (light comes from all directions) to 1 (light comes only from the position of the light). The default value is 0.45.

Shadow Color: Defines the shadows produced by the light. You can use this attribute to simulate shadows produced by transparent, colored surfaces such as colored glass. The default setting is black. You can also map textures to shadows to create interesting effects.

Exploring Directional Light

A Directional Light casts light in a particular direction evenly across a scene. These lights use parallel rays of light and spread evenly across the entire scene. You can use Directional Lights to simulate sunlight and general indoor lighting. Such simulation is possible only in case of key, fill, and back lights in Maya. Although Directional Lights originate from an infinite large source, they act as a perfect direction sensor. The position of a light is very important similar to the direction of a light. Now we can learn about various attributes for Directional Light in Attribute Editor.

Type: Allows you to switch to a different light type from Attribute Editor, by selecting the type of light from the Type dropdown list.

Color: Enables you to select a color of a light in a scene. The default color selected for the Color attribute is white.

Intensity: Represents the brightness of light. Negative Intensity values remove light from the light influenced area.

Illuminates by Default: Illuminates all objects when selected. If set to off, the light only illuminates objects to which it is linked. The Illuminates by Default checkbox is selected.

Emit Diffuse: Enables diffuse shading results for a light when turned on. By default, this option is selected. You need to render a scene in the Render View to see the effect.

Emit Specular: Enables sepcular shading results for a light when turned on. By default, this option is selected. You need to render a scene in the Render View to see the effect.

Exploring Point Light
A Point Light casts light from a single point in space and spreads evenly from the emission point. You can use the Decay Rate in feature to analyze the decreasing effect of the intensity of a Point Light with an increase in the distance. The effect of a Point Light is similar to a bulb emitting light in the real world. In addition, Point Lights are good for simulating the candle-light effect. You can create a Point Light and modify its attributes by selecting Create> Lights> Point Light> (Rectangle Box) from the main menu bar or in Attribute Editor. Now we can learn about the various attributes for the Point Light in Attribute Editor.

Type: Allows you to switch to a different light type from Attribute Editor, by selecting the type of light from the Type dropdown list.

Color: Determines the color of the light in a scene. You can click the color swatch either to change its color in the Color Chooser window or to map a texture to the light.

Intensity: Represents the brightness of a light. A light with an intensity value of 0 produces no light, while a negative intensity value reduces the light from the area of its influence in a scene. The default range of the Intensity slider is 0 to 10; however, you can type a larger value in the Intensity text box for brighter light (for instance, you can type 20 in the Intensity text box). By default, the intensity attribute value is set to 1.

Decay Rate: Controls the rate at which the intensity of a light decreases with distance. A value less than 1 unit does not affect a scene. No Decay option is selected for the Decay Rate attribute by default.

Illuminates by Default: Illuminates all objects when this checkbox is selected. If the Illuminate by Default checkbox is clear, the light illuminates only those objects to which the light is linked.

Exploring Spot Light
Spot Lights are used to create lighting effects in a scene to real spotlights. In contrast to Directional Light, which emits light from an infinite large source, Spot Light emits in the form of a cone from a specific point and emphasizes more on the direction of the light. You can use Spot Light to create a

beam of light that gradually becomes wider (for instance, a flashlight or car headlight). After creating a light, you can modify attributes in Attribute Editor. You can also modify light attributes before creating it by selecting Create> Lights> Spot Light> (Rectangle Box) from the main menu bar. Now we can learn about a few important attributes for Spot Light in Attribute Editor.

Type: Allows you to switch to a different light type from Attribute Editor by selecting the type of light from the Type dropdown list.

Color: Determines the color of the light in a scene. You can click the color swatch either to change its color in the Color Chooser window or to map a texture to the light.

Intensity: Represents the brightness of a light. A light with an intensity value 0 produces no light, while a negative intensity value reduces the light from the area of its influence in a scene. The default range of the intensity slider is 0 to 10, however, you can type a larger value in the Intensity text box for brighter light (for instance, you can type 20 in the Intensity check box).

Illuminates by Default: Illuminates all objects when this checkbox is selected. If the Illuminate by Default checkbox is clear, the light illuminates only those objects to which the light is linked.

Decay Rate: Defines the gradual fall in the intensity of a light as the distance of an objet from the source of light increases and vice versa. The Decay rate attribute is helpful in setting and maintaining the intensity of light in a scene. The None option is selected as the default Decay Rate.

Cone Angle: Sets the width of a cone, from which light is emitted in case of a Spot Light. A wide cone signifies that the amount of emitted light is intensive.

Penumbra Angle: Specifies the level of intensity of light at specific points on the cone. A negative value signifies that the light is scattered on the cone, and a positive value signifies that the light is emitted far away from the cone.

Exploring Area Light
An Area Light emits light from a rectangular flat shape. In contrast to Point Light which emits light from a single point, Area Light emits light from a specific area. In Area Light, if the light emitted area is large, there is an increase in the brightness of light. You can also control the size of the area being illuminated in Area Light. Such lights are very useful for creating light effects, such as a ray of light falling on an object inside a room from a crack of the door. Area lights help to light specific areas of an object. There are various attributes for Area Light in Attribute Editor.

Type: Allows you to switch to a different light type from Attribute Editor by selecting the type of light from the Type dropdown list.

Color: Determines the color of the light in a scene. You can click the color swatch either to change its color in the Color Chooser window or to map a texture to the light.

Intensity: Represents the brightness of a light. A light with an intensity value 0 produces no light, while a negative intensity value reduces the light from the area of its influence in a scene. The default range of the intensity slider is 0 to 10, however, you can type a larger value in the Intensity text box for brighter light (for instance, you can type 20 in the Intensity check box). The default value for the Intensity attribute is set to 1.

Decay Rate: Controls the rate at which the intensity of a light decreases with distance. The Decay Rate setting as no effect in the scene if the distance is less than 1 unit. No Decay is selected by default for the Decay Rate attribute.

Illuminates by Default: Illuminates all objects in a scene. If set to off, the light only illuminates objects to which it is linked. By default, this option is set to on.

Exploring Volume Light

Volume Light emits light from a 3D volumetric area such as a wall, wood, or stone. It simulates light for a finite distance; for instance, illuminating a candle in a scene. You can control the distance a light reaches by scaling Volume Light in a scene. Proximity (closeness) of Volume Light to an object is important as the scaling of light; hence, considered with using Volume Lights. Now we can discuss about the various attributes of Volume Light in Attribute Editor.

Light Shape: Determines the volumetric shape of a light. You can select the shape of a light from the Light Shape dropdown list, which displays four types of shapes – Box, Sphere, Cylinder, and Cone. The default shape for this attribute is Sphere.

Color Range: Defines the color of a light from the center to the edge of the volume light beam. You can change the color along the defined light direction by changing the values on the ramp (or gradient). By default, the ramp specifies the color from inside to outside. A decay effect is created by interpolating (or blending) the inner color with the outer color. To prevent hard boundary at the edge of Volume Light, you must select black as the outermost color.

Interpolation: Specifies the blending of multiple colors in the ramp. You can choose an option such as None, Linear, Smooth, and Spline for the Interpolation attribute. Linear option is selected by default for the Interpolation attribute.

Volume Light Dir: Indicates the direction of the Volume Light. The options available in the Volume Light Dir dropdown list are Outward, Inward, and Down Axis. The default option selected is Outward.

Using Lighting Effects

Maya has certain attributes of lights that can be manipulated to create special effects. For instance, you can create a beam of light to represent the smoke effect or a glowing effect around an object. All these light effects are visible in the final output while rendering a scene in Maya. Now we can discuss about some lighting effects, such as Fog Effect, Lens Flare Effect, and Glow Effect. These effects can be simulated in Maya.

Creating Fog Effect

You can create the fog effect using the volumetric lighting. The lighting effect in which a flashlight beam shines through a fog is called volumetric lighting. This type f lighting effect is created only when a ray of light shines though a foggy environment. Volumetric light provides light effects based on the interaction of light with the atmosphere (such as for or smoke). The Ambient Light and Directional Light are very weak lights; as both are used for the background and indoor lightings. Therefore, these lights are low intensity lights and they do not work well in foggy environments. Hence, the Volumetric lighting effect is not available in the Ambient Light and Directional Light. Even if the Volumetric lighting effect is used appropriately, it does not render a scene properly due to the foggy environment, as the foggy environment requires proper level of light intensity. However, you can overcome this problem using an artificial source of light, such as beam light from a flashlight. Perform the following steps carefully to add the fog effect:

1. **Open** a scene in Maya and select **Create> Lights> Spot Light** from the main menu bar. This will create a Spot Light first that appears at the center of the gird.

2. **Position** the Spot Light in the scene and transform it as required. To accurately position a light, you can use orthographic viewports. You need to render the scene to see the effect. However, to quickly preview the color without rendering, you can turn on using the Use all lights button in the panel toolbar to see the color of the lighting reflected on the surrounding surfaces.

3. **Open** Attribute Editor which appears with attributes for the selected light. It opens the spotLightShape1 tab selected when you open Attribute Editor, which lets you modify the attributes of the selected light.

4. **Set** the light intensity beside Intensity to **4.000**, Cone Angle (to spread the spot light area) to **55.000**, and Penumbra Angle (to soften the edge of light) to **3.000**.

5. **Expand** the Light Effects group (button) in Attribute Editor by clicking it. Then, **click** the checker button (on right side) beside Light Fog attribute.

6. Now you can **render** the scene to see the effect. For that, select **Render> Render Current Frame** from main menu bar. Keep the scene open for the other steps.

The light fog node is automatically created and connected to the light node and displays its attributes in Attribute Editor. You can see that the Spot Light icon changes in the viewport. This icon represents the position and size of the fog effect. You can change the Color and Density attributes, which are by default set to white and 1.000, respectively. Other attributes present in the Light Effects group are Light Glow, Intensity Curve, Fog Spread, and Fog Intensity. Among these, the Fog Spread and Fog Intensity attributes are used to control the thickness, color, and brightness of the fog.

A Step Ahead for Fog Effect:
When you render the scene, it opens the Render View and you can see that the fog effect ends where the icon ends in the viewport. If you wish, you can continue ahead:

7. **Click** the Minimize icon to minimize Render View, and **select** the Spot Light icon in the viewport. The attributes for the Spot Light shape appears in Attribute Editor.

8. **Scale** the Spot Light icon to pass through the floor object in the scene. You can modify the Spot Light icon to cover the object in the viewport by adjusting its attributes.

9. Set the Cone Angle attribute to 152.000, Fog Spread to 1.500, and Fog Intensity to 1.000. Then, you can render the scene again by selecting **Render> Render Current Frame** from main menu bar.

You can also modify other attributes to fine tune the fog effect. You can also temporarily turn off or permanently remove the illuminated fog from a scene. To temporarily turn off the illuminated fog, you can set the Fog Density attribute to 0 in Attribute Editor.

Creating Lens Flare Effect

In real world, when light shines directly into a camera lens, the light source may appear to glow. In certain cases, the light may reflect off the surfaces of a compound lens of a camera and produce a lens flare. In Maya, the light source does not glow or produce a lens flare, when light shines directly into the camera. However, you can add an optical effect to any light and control the lights that produce a glow or lens flare. The lens flare feature in Maya is disabled, by default. You can perform the following steps carefully to enable the lens flare effects:

1. **Open** a scene and select **Create> Lights> Point Light** from the main menu bar to create a Point Light. Then **position** the light in the scene using Move Tool where you want the lens flare effect to appear.

2. **Select** Point Light and **click** the Show or hide the Attribute Editor button in Status Line to open Attribute Editor for the selected light.

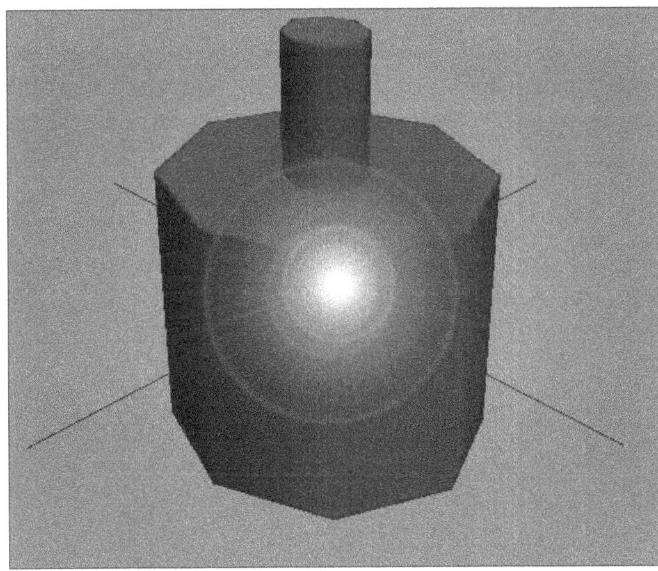

3. **Expand** the Light Effects group in Attribute Editor, and **click** the checker button for the Light Glow attribute to create the light glow node. The light glow node (optical FX node) is created and the attributes of the node appear in the Optical FX Attributes section of Attribute Editor.

4. **Select** the Lens Flare check box and **select** the Exponential option from the Glow Type dropdown list. Then you can render the scene by selecting Render> Render Current Frame from the main menu bar. The lens flare effect appears in the rendered frame. The picture 7.3 shows a similar view of lens flare effect.

Picture 7.3

Maya allows you to add an optical FX node to any type of lights. You can create glow, halo or lens flare effects using this node. Now we can discuss the important attributes from the Optical FX Attributes and Glow Attributes sections of Attribute Editor.

Glow Type: Helps to set the size and shape of a glow from a light. The various options are Linear, Exponential, Ball Lens, Flare, and Rim Halo.

Star Points: Helps to set the number of start points that a glow generates. By default, the optical FX node of Maya creates a four-pointed star with a glow at the center of the light.

<u>Rotation:</u> Helps you to set the rotation of star points.

<u>Radial Frequency:</u> Helps to define the smoothness of a glow. The Radial Frequency attribute is always used in conjunction with the Glow Radial Noise attribute.

<u>Glow Radial Noise:</u> Helps to add noise to a glow, which ultimately creates light and dark patches.

Adding Glow Effect on an Object

You can use glow effect to create glowing effects on objects in a scene. In this case, instead of placing a glow on a light, it is placed on the surface of an object. Whenever a glow effect is set on a light, the light must point towards the camera to visualize the light glow, which consumes more time during the rendering process. Perform these steps to add glow effect on an object:

1. **Select** an object in a scene, **right-click** and **select** the **Material Attributes** option from the marking menu to modify the existing material. The material attributes appear in the Attribute Editor.

2. **Expand** the <u>Special Effects</u> group and type: **0.700** in the <u>Glow Intensity</u> text box to set the glow amount. By the way, the Hide Source check box in the Special Effects group hides the primitive objects and only displays the glow effect. Now you can render the scene by selecting Render> Render Current Frame from the main menu bar. Render view appears with the glow effect.

Understanding Shadows in Maya

Shadows are the integral part of lighting. The lighting does not look realistic and appealing if it is done without shadows. The scene might look flat without shadows. To create shadows, you do not need to model or texture any objet, but you can easily create it with just one click using the attributes for a light in Attribute Editor. There are two types of shadows for light in Maya:

<u>Depth Map:</u> Creates shadows in Maya and is commonly used. When you select the Depth Map shadows in Attribute Editor, shadow maps are created that locate the path of shadows, by following the path of a light backward from the lighted object to the light itself. The Depth Map shadows are easy to render and consumes very less time and lesser CPU power. To add the Depth Map shadow, select the Use Depth Map Shadows check box in the Depth Map Shadow Attributes subgroup of the Shadows group in Attribute Editor.

<u>Raytrace:</u> Calculates the path light travels. It is used to generate shadows using right rays. Raytrace shadows are more accurate, realistic, and take long time to render. It is rendered only in the mental ray renderer. To add the Raytrace shadow, select the Use Ray Trace Shadows check box in the Raytrace Shadow Attribute subgroup of Shadows group in Attribute Editor.

Lesson 23

Understanding Mental Ray for Maya Lighting

Mental ray is originally developed by Mental Images, and was later bought by NVIDIA. It is a photorealistic rendering application for producing production-quality images using ray tracing algorithms. Mental ray lighting and mental ray rendering can be used can be used together to create high quality photorealistic images in Maya. It can be used to create procedural textures, bump and displacement maps, atmosphere and volume effects, environments, camera lenses, and light sources. The following three illumination techniques can be created using mental ray lighting and can be rendered using the mental ray for Maya renderer: (A) Caustic, (B) Global Illumination-GI, (C) Final Gather. These three techniques contribute to the indirect illumination of a scene. Mental ray uses photons to simulate light inter-reflections and caustic effects when using GI or caustic illumination technique. Photons are small packets or energy emitted from a light source into a scene. Mental ray does not use photons; instead, it samples the semi-hemispherical area above every point in a scene to calculate direct and indirect illuminations. As photons are not used in the final gather illumination technique, this technique requires the least rendering time among the three techniques. You can incorporate the three types of light effects (illuminations) in a scene based on the following requirements:

Use GI for numerous bounced or reflected light.
Use caustics for those objects with material that reflect or refract.
Use final gather to include soft lighting to show small details.

Caustic
Caustics are caused by specularly (unlike diffusely) reflected or refracted light. In the real-world, caustics are actually a form of GI; however, they are treated separately by mental ray for Maya, which is easy to control. It is a process in which light is reflected through semi-transparent objects. This type of lighting effect can be commonly observed in liquids, glass objects, and gems. Therefore, caustics should be used for a scene consisting of shiny surfaces that refract and reflect. You can render Caustics only with the mental ray for Maya renderer.

Global Illumination
GI is a natural phenomenon where light bounces off the surfaces in its path. The bounces occur until it is completely absorbed. It is the phenomenon of inter-reflection and multiple bouncing of all lights in a scene, because when they are simulated, one object affects the rendering of another. For instance, if you place a red leather sphere inside a blue box and cast light onto the box, the floor and walls of the box take the color of the sphere. GI effects are subtle, but they add realism to a scene. GI allows you to achieve realistic lighting effects for object and areas of a scene that do not receive direct light. This illumination technique is used to capture indirect illumination inside a scene. You can render GI only with the mental ray for Maya renderer.

Final Gather
Similar to GI, final gather enhances the details in a scene by adding light. However, it has certain limitations as it does not handle multiple bounces of light rays as precisely and efficiently as GI. Final gather consumes less time for rendering amongst the three techniques as it does not use photons. This technique also handles small details better than other illumination techniques. It is used with diffuse materials, such as paper and chalk.

Describing the Mental Ray Attributes
Lights in Maya have several attributes, which are used to define the basic capabilities of the mental ray. These attributes are important for the proper understanding of lighting effects. Note that for the caustics or GI technique to work properly, mental ray light has to emit photons. These photons are emitted from the lights that are enabled to bounce in a scene. This creates indirect lighting such as caustics and GI. Mental ray replicates the phenomenon of light photons bounce off the surface, by tracing photons in your scene. In Maya, mental ray attributes are available only for Point Light, Spot

Light, Directional Light, and Area Light. You can access these attributes for mental ray in the Caustic and Global illumination group of mental ray section. When you open this section on your screen, you will see the different attributes of the Caustic and Global Illumination group, such as Emit Photons, Photon Color, Photon Intensity, Exponent, Caustic Photons, and Global Illum Photons.

Emit Photons

The Emit Photon option when selected emits photon in a scene. These photons bounce off the surfaces of different objects to create indirect illumination in the scene. You can illuminate the whole scene with a single light by enabling lights to emit photons. You need to select the Emit Photons check box in Attribute Editor to enable lights to emit photons. A disabled light cannot emit photons. The quality of the GI effect depends on the number of photons emitted into the scene.

Photon Color

The Photon Color attribute defines the color of photons. When you select a color, it is automatically reflected in the surface of a scene. The color of a photon is white by default, but you can select a different color form the Photon Color swatch to cast a different color effect on the surfaces.

Photon Intensity

Mental ray for Maya uses photons to simulate the caustic effects in a scene. The intensity of each photon affects a scene, if you increase the number of photons, the GI or caustic effect increases. For instance, if the intensity of photons is high in any GI scene, a large amount of bright light is emitted indirectly. The brightness of the GI in a scene is controlled by the Photon Intensity attribute. The light emits the photons into the scene when you render an image. The photons travel throughout the scene, refract through transparent objects, or reflect off reflective surfaces. The renderer stores the illumination that results from this photon emission in a file known as a photon map.

Exponent

The value of Exponent attribute is helpful in adjusting photons intensity. The intensity of photons is based on the relative distance of the source of light from the surface of an object. This is similar to decay, the intensity increases as the value of the attribute decreases. You can decrease the Exponent attribute value to make the indirect lighting reach longer distance. However, noise can occur, if you decrease the Exponent attribute value to less than 1. The Exponent attribute value is 2 by default; this value simulates the natural decay.

Caustic Photons

Caustic photons are employed to generate photons for the caustic effect and stored in the photon map. The greater the number of photons, the accuracy and quality of the render is greater. However, by increasing the number of photons, you can increase the rendering time of a scene considerably. The default value for this attribute is set to 10000, which is suitable for quick and low-quality caustic effect. Generally, when the Caustic Photons attribute is set to 100000, it produces the medium quality of caustic effect; however, when you set the attribute to 1000000, then it produces the high quality caustic effect but takes a huge render time as well.

Global Illum Photons

Global Illum Photons refers to the number of photons that are used to generate the GI effect. Increasing the number of photons automatically leads to greater accuracy and quality in the rendering process. However, more photons mean an increase in the rendering time of a scene.

Lesson 24
Rendering in Maya 2013
Rendering is the final stage in the 3D CG production process. During the rendering process, Maya creates an image or sequence of images by calculating all information in a scene. During the rendering process, the surface properties (materials), lights, shadows, and movement of objects are calculated. In the wider context, the rendering process begins with shading, texturing, and lighting a scene. Rendering is a time-consuming process that uses computer resources, such as memory, processor, and graphics card. The highest quality images typically consume more time to render. To quickly visualize a scene, you can perform test renders with low quality render settings to enable faster rendering. Test renders help to ensure correct image quality that you want for the final output. For rendering, there are various built-in engines called renderers in Maya. Renderers such as Maya Software, Maya Hardware, Maya Hardware 2.0, mental ray, and Maya Vector are available. In Maya 2013, the mental ray renderer has an updated version 3.10. To render a scene, select the renderer and specify settings in the Render Settings window. These settings vary depending upon the renderer selected. You can render a single frame, a region, or an animation. The Batch Render command allows you to render animations. Additionally, you can create and use cameras in a scene that simulate real-world perspectives accurately compared to the default Maya views. Note that these default views are not used while rendering; instead, cameras are created and placed on the creative needs for rendering the final output.

Understanding Rendering Methods

After modeling characters for a scene, applying textures to them, and animating them, you need to render a scene. For this, you must first select a rendering method and then a renderer. Selecting a rendering method depends on the preferred quality of the final output. There are three rendering methods available to render a scene in Maya: (A) Software rendering, (B) Hardware rendering, (C) Vector rendering.

Software Rendering

In Software rendering, all objects and their attributes in a scene for a given frame are gathered. Each object is positioned based on its keyframe translation values at a given frame. However, if the object is a NURBS geometric object, it is first subdivided into polygonal faces. Then, every object is combined with its material to create a shading group node. Later, the shading group node is calculated along with the light to produce shadows, reflections, highlights, and other effects such as fog. The calculations and computations are performed on the central processing unit. As software is not restricted by graphics card, it is more flexible than the other two types. However, it is generally more time consuming, but the images created using this method are good and accurate. There are two software renderers, such as Maya software and mental ray. You will learn more about these renderers in next section.

Hardware Rendering

Hardware rendering uses a graphics (video) card installed in the computer for rendering. If the video card in the system does not support hardware rendering, a warning message is displayed. This type or rendering is used to display geometry, texture, particles, lights, and shadows in the viewport. The quality of the images generated through hardware rendering depends on the graphics card and the drivers of the computer. Mostly, the images are not of good quality compared to those created through software rendering. However, the time taken to render a scene using the hardware rendering method is less compared to the software rendering method. Hardware rendering cannot produce few of the advanced effects including advanced shadows, reflections, and post-process effects. Maya hardware is the only one hardware renderer in Maya.

Vector Rendering

Vector rendering displays objects in scenes as illustrations, cartoons, wireframe, or line art. With vector rendering, you can render scenes to create both bitmap and vector images. In Maya, there is only one vector renderer, namely: Maya vector. It cannot render certain features of Maya, such as bump maps, displacement maps, Maya fluid effects, image planes, lights, materials, particles, fur, or paint effects. Apart from these three (Software, Hardware, and Vector) rendering methods, you can also use third party engines, such as V-ray for Maya, Maxwell, and Pixar's RenderMan for Maya to render a scene.

Understanding Renderers

After selecting a rendering method, you need to select a renderer (or render engine) to render a scene using the Render Settings window or Render View. Maya software renderer is the default renderer. Using this, you can render most of the effects that you create in Maya. However, in Maya, the most commonly used renderer is mental ray, which provides high quality output. There are four types of renderer available in Maya, such as (A) Maya Software, (B) Maya Hardware and Hardware 2.0, (C) Mental ray for Maya, (D) Maya Vector.

Maya Software Renderer

The Maya Software renderer is the default renderer for Maya. It uses the software rendering method to render scenes. It is an all-purpose rendering with extensive features that helps to work with any type of objects and visual effects. It is capable of producing images of premium quality with various optical effects, such as reflections and refractions. It supports true (real-world) raytracing and renders scenes as fast as the Scanline renderer (default renderer in 3ds Max). Maya Software renderer supports Interactive Photorealistic Rendering (IPR), which is a type of the Render View rendering. It allows previewing and modifying lights and materials in the final rendered image. This significantly enhances the productivity of Maya rendering. It stores all information about every pixel of an image and uses the information to update an image quickly, whenever its parameters are adjusted. IPR works with both the Maya Software and mental ray renderers.

Maya Hardware Renderer

The Maya Hardware renderer allows you to render scenes during the hardware rendering method. It uses the graphics card of the computer to convert 3D scenes into 2D images. Compared to the Maya Software renderer, the images produced by the Maya Hardware renderer are of low quality. However, it renders scenes faster than the Maya Hardware renderer. It can render layered textures, polygons and NURBS objects, reflections, shadows, and motion blurs. Maya Hardware renderer uses the existing interface and the workflow for applying materials, textures, particles, and lights on objects in a scene. It does not support subdivision surfaces and point light shadows, and implying shadows are not created for point lights when the Maya Hardware renderer is used for rendering.

Maya Hardware 2.0 Renderer

The Maya Hardware 2.0 renderer was introduced in the previous version of Maya (Maya 2012). Using this, you can perform command line rendering for Viewport 2.0, or to batch render to disc or Render View. You need to select the new Viewport 2.0 before rendering using this type of renderer in Render View. You can select Viewport 2.0 by selecting Renderer> Viewport 2.0 from the panel menu. This renderer supports the File Output settings of the Common tab in the Render Setting window. It also supports rendering from stereo cameras. By the way, it doesn't support render region and IPR in the Render View window, render layers, and depth channels.

Mental Ray Renderer

The mental ray renderer offers certain advanced features including caustic, GI, and High Dynamic Range (HDR) images for rendering. Using these features, you can create images that are more photorealistic and superior compared to those produced by other renderers. To render using the mental ray renderer, you must select mental ray as the renderer in the Render Settings window. To open the Render Settings window, you can select Window> Rendering Editors> Render Settings from the main menu bar. Select the mental ray option from the Render Using dropdown list. Attribute Editor also contains a mental ray section in which you can specify attributes that are used exclusively, while rendering a scene with the mental ray renderer. During the installation process, the mental ray plug-in is loaded by default. However, if you are not able to see the mental ray attributes, you must load it manually. The Plug-in Manager window allows you to enable and disable Maya plug-ins. You can perform the following steps to load the mental ray plug-in:

1. In a new scene of Maya, select **Window> Settings/Preferences> Plug-in Manager** from the main menu bar. The Plug-in Manager window opens with a list of plug-ins.

2. **Scroll down** and **select** the Loaded and Auto Load check boxes for the Mayatomr.mll plug-in. By default, the plug-in is enabled. Then, close the Plug-in Manager window.

Maya Vector Renderer

The Maya Vector renderer allows you to render scenes using complex mathematical calculations; thereby, giving an illustrative appearance to scenes. You can create images in raster such as Tagged Image File Format (TIFF) as well as vector formats, such as Scalable Vector Graphics (SVG) and Adobe Illustrator (AI) using the Maya Vector renderer. These vector images created can be imported directly into vector programs, such as Illustrator and Flash. Moreover, these images are small in size and can be scaled to any size without losing quality. Maya Vector renderer can also produce animated files in the Adobe Flash format such as ShockWave Flash (SWF), which can be directly used in Web pages and animations. However, it is difficult to create a photorealistic image with the Maya Vector renderer. You can use the Maya Vector tab available in the Render Settings window to specify the attribute settings for the Maya Vector renderer. The Maya vector plug-in is loaded by default. But, using the Maya Vector renderer, you cannot render features such as bump maps, displacement maps, Maya Fluid Effects, image planes, lights, Maya Fur, multiple UVs, Maya Paint Effects, particles, materials, and textures.

Lesson 25
Rendering a Scene

You may want to visualize or test render a scene before the final render. You can render a frame, a sequence (number of frames), or entire range of frames. To render a scene, you can use the Render menu or Render View. You can select the type of renderer you want to use from either Render View or the Render menu. After selecting a renderer, you can specify settings such as dimension, output format, and quality or rendering in the Render Settings window. Rendering helps to generate images using predefined and custom settings.

Selecting a Renderer

To render a scene, you first need to select a renderer. When you select a renderer, the user interface is automatically configured to use it. For instance, if you click the Render the current frame button in the Status Line, the selected renderer is used to render the image. Similarly, if you click the Display Render

Setting window button, the Render Settings window appears with specific tabs to the selected renderer. To select a renderer from the Render menu, you can select Render> Render Using from the main menu bar, and then, select the renderer. Alternatively, click the Display Render Settings window button in Status Line, and then, select any renderer from the Render Using dropdown list. Maya 2013 includes five renderers including Maya Software, Maya Hardware, Maya Hardware 2.0, mental ray, and Maya Vector. By default, Maya Software is selected as the renderer. Perform the following steps to select a renderer:

1. **Open** a scene and **select** Rendering menu set from the menu selector in Status Line (at the top left corner, below File tab). The Rendering menu set displays menus specific to rendering, such as Lighting/Shading, Texturing, Render, Toon, Stereo, and Paint Effects.

2. Select **Render> Render Using** and **choose** a renderer from the list of options. Once you select a render, the settings are configured, which are used next time you render a scene.

Using the Render Settings window

With the help of the Render Settings window, you can specify settings for an output image. For instance, you can specify the width, height, and resolution settings for the output image. In the Render Settings window, the settings for the selected renderer appear in tab. If the render is selected as Maya Software, the Render Settings window displays the following two tabs: Common and Maya Software. Using the settings in these tabs, you can render the final output as required. The Common tab is available for all renderers. Using the Render Using dropdown list, you can also select the type of renderer that you want to use in the Render Settings window. In addition, if you have multiple layers in a scene, you can select the layer you want to render from the Render Layer dropdown list. To open the Render Settings window, you can select Window> Rendering Editors> Render Settings from the main menu bar. If you open this window on your screen, you can see the following two tabs:

Common: Allows you to specify settings such as File Output (file name and output image format) and Frame Range (Start frame, End Frame, and By frame). This tab is selected by default. For more settings, scroll down in the Render Settings window.

Maya Software: Allows you to specify settings such as Anti-aliasing Quality, Field Options, Raytracing Quality, Motion Blur, Render Options, Memory and Performance Options, IPR Options, and Paint Effects Rendering Options that are specific to the Maya software renderer.

Using the Common Tab

With the help of the Common tab, you can specify the output settings such as dimension, image format, resolution, renderable camera, and frame range for rendering. The settings in the Common tab remain constant for all the renderers. You can also save a preset of the custom settings that you frequently use to render and use it in future. Perform the following steps carefully to specify the output dimension, quality, and format using the Common tab:

1. **Open** a scene and select **Window> Rendering Editor> Render Settings** from the main menu bar. The Render Settings window appears with the Maya Software renderer and the Common tab selected.

2. **Right-click** in the File name prefix text box to insert keywords in the File Output section, and then, **select** a file name option from the context menu.

3. For now, beside the option <u>File name prefix</u>, you can select the **Insert scene name <Scene>** option, which adds the scene name to the rendered or output image.

4. **Select** an output format from the <u>Image format</u> dropdown list. In this case, you can select **JPEG (ipg)** option. By the way, it allows you to select various formats. If you select the Audio Video Interleave (AVI) for Windows or QuickTime (.mov) for Mac OS X image file format, you can compress the image files by clicking the compression button.

5. **Ensure** the **name.ext (Single Frame)** option is selected for the **Frame/Animation ext** setting to render a static image.

The Frame/Animation ext setting determines whether to render a static image or a sequence. By default, the name.ext (Single Frame is selected. To render a sequence, specify appending of the frame number to the existing file name by selecting a preset. The name refers to the name of the image file and ext refers to the extension of the image file format. If # appears, for instance name.ext.#, it refers to the frame number in a scene. If you have selected a frame number extension option that has #, you can specify the start and end frames for rendering by entering the preferred start and end frame number in the Start frame and End frame text boxes of the Frame Range section, respectively.

6. **Scroll down** to display the <u>Image Size</u> section and **expand** it. Then, **type** in the <u>Width</u> text box: **1280** and press enter. Type in <u>Height</u> text box: **720** and press enter. Type in <u>Resolution</u> text box: **300** and press enter. And then, close the Render Settings window.

In the Renderable Cameras section of the Common tab, you can specify camera settings and use them to render. The default camera used to render scenes is persp (perspective). However, you can select other cameras, such as front, top, or side from the Renderable Cameras dropdown list. You can also render a scene using multiple cameras. For this, make the additional cameras renderable by selecting the Add Renderable Camera option from the Renderable Cameras dropdown list.

Using the Maya Software Tab
As said earlier, the Maya Software renderer is the default renderer of Maya with extensive capabilities. You can create high-quality images with complex shading networks including procedural textures using the Maya Software renderer. This renderer computes materials, lights, or animation applied to an object using the machine processor. You can set attributes specific to Maya Software renderer in the Maya Software tab of the Render Settings window. You can perform the following steps for it:

1. **Click** the <u>Maya Software</u> tab in the <u>Render Settings</u> window to display settings specific to the Maya Software renderer. You may notice that Maya Software tab displayed only when Maya Software is selected as renderer in the Render Using dropdown list of the Render Settings window.

2. **Select** the <u>Production quality</u> option from the <u>Quality</u> dropdown list in the <u>Anti-aliasing Quality</u> section. Then, close the Render Settings window.

You can use default options for the remaining settings and render the scene. There are several other sections in the Maya Software tab that you can use as necessary for the final output that you can access by scrolling down and clicking the section heading to expand the section. Now we can discuss about the sections and the settings they contain.

Exploring Anti-aliasing Quality Settings

The Anti-aliasing Quality section is used to calculate the impact of anti-aliasing on objects in a scene. You can select a preset to set the anti-aliasing settings automatically as required. For instance, the Production quality preset option renders a scene with highest quality settings. This section comprises of the three groups, such as Number of Samples, Multi-pixel Filtering, and Contrast threshold. Anti-aliasing is calculated by selecting an option from the Edge anti-aliasing dropdown list. The Anti-aliasing Quality section contains various settings, which are as follows:

A. Quality: Allows you to specify the quality of anti-aliasing in a scene. The Quality dropdown list contains the following options:

<u>Custom:</u> Allows you to set user-defined values. The Custom option is selected automatically, if any of the anti-aliasing setting does not match any preset setting values.

<u>Preview quality:</u> Sets the values that help to rest render (preview) scenes.

<u>Intermediate quality:</u> Provides better quality rendered images compared to the Preview quality preset.

<u>Production quality:</u> Helps to render a scene without 3D motion blur or low contrasts.

<u>Contrast sensitive production:</u> Helps to test render or final render scenes with high contrast, when you raytrace them.

<u>3D motion blur production:</u> Helps to test or final render scenes with 3D motion blur.

B. Edge anti-aliasing: Contains numerous fields that help in controlling the anti-aliasing of objects. The higher the edge anti-aliasing quality, the smoother the edges of an object appear and vice versa. It contains the following options:

<u>Low quality:</u> Helps in indentifying the visible part of an object by analyzing only 2 points for each rendered pixel, and produces low quality edge anti-aliasing. This setting is the fastest.

<u>Medium quality:</u> Determines the part of an object that is visible by analyzing 8 points for each rendered pixel.

<u>High quality:</u> Analyzes 32 points for each rendered pixel to indentify the visible part of an object. This leads to high quality edge anti-aliasing.

<u>Highest quality:</u> Helps in computing an image in two passes (steps). This option looks for color contrast both within the pixels and outside the pixels. Quality is computed in the first pass; whereas, color contrast is calculated in the second pass.

Exploring Field Options Settings

The Field Options section is used to control rendered images as fields. Maya Software renderer supports only field rendering. Currently, most video systems display individual frames in two stages; by illuminating half of the phosphors on a television screen (every odd row beginning with first row), and then, illuminating the second half of the phosphors (every even row beginning with the second row). These two half-frames are known as fields. The different settings of this section are as follows:

<u>Render:</u> Specifies, whether images are rendered as frames or fields. By default, images are rendered as frames in Maya. When you render an image as field, Maya generates two image files, one for each field. A single frame is rendered at a time x by rendering one field at time x+0.5. The fields that are rendered beginning with the first row are odd fields, and the fields that are rendered beginning with the second row are even fields.

<u>Field Dominance:</u> Specifies, whether odd fields are rendered at time x and even fields at time x+0.5 or vice versa. By default, the odd fields take x time and even fields take x+0.5 time to render. If the Render attribute is set to Frames, the Field dominance options are not available.

<u>Zeroth Scanline:</u> Determines, whether the first line of the first field is located at the top or at the bottom of an image and used in advanced rendering. The At top and At bottom radio buttons help to determine the position of the first line of the first filed. By default, the At top radio button is selected.

<u>Field Extension:</u> Contains various options such as No field extension, Default field extension (o and e), and Custom extension. In this section, the attributes do not take effect if the fields are interlaced automatically.

Exploring Raytracing Quality Settings

Raytracing is an algorithm that generates images by simulating the light rays travelling in a scene, and then, computing their reflection and refraction from the surface and the location of the light source. It generates secondary effects such as reflections, shadows, and GI by adding more rays. However, it consumes much time to render a scene. Using the Raytracing Quality section, you can raytrace during the rendering process. In this section, you can configure raytraced reflections, refractions, or shadows to appear in the final output. By default, these options are disabled. The Raytracing Quality section contains the following options:

<u>Raytracing:</u> produces realistic reflections, refractions, and shadows. Raytracing occurs during the rendering calculations. By default, this option is not selected.

<u>Reflections:</u> Helps in determining the frequency of reflection. Normal range of reflection is from 0 to 10. By default, the Reflections option is set to 1.

<u>Refractions:</u> Help in determining the frequency of refraction. Normal range of refraction is from 0 to 10. By default, the Refraction option is set to 6.

<u>Shadows:</u> Helps in determining the number of times the ray of light is reflected and refracted. An object casts shadow regardless of refraction and reflection. For instance, a Shadows value of 2 implies that the ray of light is reflected and refracted only once.

<u>Bias:</u> Helps to correct 3D motion blurred objects and raytraced shadows during the course of 3D motion, when dark areas or shadows appear on the blurred objects. This can be resolved by setting value of Bias between 0 and 0.05. The valid range for Bias option is from 0.000 to 1.000.

Exploring Motion Blur Settings

Using the Motion Blur section, you can create movement effects by blurring objects. You can turn the motion blur feature on/off from the Render Settings window. The settings or this section are:

<u>Motion blur:</u> Calculates the effect by blurring moving objects. If this option is selected, the 3D Motion blur type is enabled. By default, the Motion Blur option is disabled.

<u>Motion blur type:</u> Represents two types of motion blurs, such as 2D and 3D. By default, motion blur is of 3D type. The 2D Motion blur is a post-process phenomenon, as the blurring effect occurs after the rendering process is completed. The 3D Motion blur takes more time to render compared to the 2D Motion blur.

<u>Blur by frame:</u> Helps in calculating the intensity of blurring of moving objects.

<u>Blur length:</u> Helps in scaling the intensity of blurring of moving objects. Optimal range of Blur length is from 0 to infinity. By default, the Blur length option is set to 1.

<u>Smooth and Smooth value:</u> Helps in blurring the edges of static objects.

<u>Keep motion vectors:</u> Helps in blurring rendered images using vector data in addition to 2D Motion blur.

<u>Use 2D blur memory limit:</u> Helps in calculating the maximum amount of memory required for the entire process of rendering. By default, the memory value is 200 MB. You can increase the memory limit using the fields provided in the Render Settings window.

Exploring Render Options Settings

The Render Options section includes four groups, such as Post Processing, Camera, Lights and Shadows, and Color/Compositing. You can use these groups to perform several functions; for instance, simulating the effect of particles dispersed in the air. When a ray of light is passed through these particles, the light is diffused, resulting in an increased depth of a scene. The settings under different groups of the Render Options section are described as follow:

Environment Fog: Creates an environment fog node, which is used to simulate various effects in the air such as fog, smoke, or dust.

Apply Fog in Post: Renders the fog as a post-process. This option is disabled by default.

Ignore Film Gate: Renders the area of a scene that is visible in Resolution Gate. It represents the area of a scene that the camera actually renders. This option is selected by default.

Shadow Linking: Reduces the rendering time required for a scene. It links lights with surfaces, which includes specified surfaces in the calculation of shadows (shadow linking) or illumination (light linking), by a given light during the rendering process.

Gamma Correction: Corrects the color of rendered images. The default value of this option is 1 (no color correction). This behavior of the Gamma correction option for the Maya Software renderer is the reverse of the mental ray renderer. A higher gamma value lightens the mid-tones of an image in Maya Software renderer.

Clip Final Shaded Color: Helps in determining the color value in the range of 0 to 1.

Jitter Final Color: Helps in reducing the bending effect in those areas with smooth gradation.

Premultiply Threshold: Controls the amount of edge anti-aliasing, if the Premultiply check box is selected.

Exploring Memory and Performance Option Settings

Using the Memory and Performance Option section, you can control rendering of a scene. The settings available in this section help you to optimize the rendering process and render scenes much faster. This section has three groups, such as Tessellation, Ray Tracing, and Multi Processing. The different groups available in the Memory and Performance Option section are described as follows:

Tessellation: Specifies, handling of tessellation information for surfaces. You can use various settings such as Use file cache, Optimize instances, Reuse tessellations, and Use displacement bounding box to specify subdividing objects while rendering.

Ray Tracing: Helps in controlling the global setting of raytraced objects in a scene. It contains three settings – Recursion depth, Leaf primitives, and Subdivision power.

Multi Processing: Helps to use all available CUPs for rendering. You can also set a value for the number of CPUs using the slider. This is done only in case of multiprocessor machines.

Exploring IPR Options Settings

Using the IPR Options section, you can render materials, lighting effects, shadow maps, or even 2D motion blur for the IPR Render. You can also increase the performance of rendering, by disabling unnecessary settings in this section.

Exploring Paint Effects Rendering Options Settings

Using the Paint Effects Rendering Options section, you can render stroke, oversample, or oversample post filter for Maya Paint Effects. The Paint Effect strokes cannot be rendered, if the Enable stroke rendering check box is not selected. Using the Read this depth file setting, you can calculate the Z depth information while compositing images. You can also turn the Oversample setting on/off in the Paint Effects Rendering Options section. The Oversample setting helps to increase the quality of paint effects strokes while rendering. The Oversample and Oversample post filter settings are used for rendering Paint Effects, fur, or hair in Maya.

Lesson 26
Rendering a Frame
In the previous lesson, we have discussed about specifying various settings for the final output. Now you are going to learn about either rendering a single frame or a sequence of frames. By default, the current frame is rendered. To render the current frame, you can also click the Render the current fame (current renderer) button in Status Line or select Render> Render Current Frame from the main menu bar. Both methods open Render View and render the entire frame. The rendering image is automatically saved to the image directory of the current project. Render View is ideal for rendering a single frame or a single frame of an animation. Perform the following steps to render a frame:

1. **Open** a scene and **specify** the settings in the Render Settings window. Then, **select** the Rendering menu set in the menu selector (at the top left, below File tab).

2. Select **Render> Render Current Frame** from the main menu bar. The current frame is rendered in Render View.

Rendering a Region using Render View
If you render a whole frame, it consumes a lot of time for a production quality output. To save time, you can render a small region to analyze to analyze the quality of the output. Smaller region renders much faster than the whole frame. You can also use region rendering feature to render a specific region to test the resulting output of an effect, such as caustic or glow. In Render View, you can define an area that you want to render by dragging a marquee. The defined area is indicated by a red outline. After defining the region, click the Render region button in the Render View toolbar. Perform the following steps carefully to render a specific region using Render View:

1. **Open** a scene and **click** the Open Render View button in Status Line. Render View appears with the previously rendered frame. Render View has a menu bar as well as a toolbar. The Maya Software renderer is selected by default in the toolbar.

2. **Define** the area by dragging a marquee selection around the area that you want to render. Then, **release** the mouse button, which turns the marquee selection to a red outline.

3. **Click** the Render region button in the Render View toolbar. The rendering is completed in a few seconds.

Render View also displays the attributes of a rendered image that you had set at the bottom of the window. You can also perform advanced rendering using the IPR feature available in Render View. This feature is used to work with textures, lighting, glows, optical effects, depth-map shadows, motion blurs, and depth of field. Sometimes, scenes and image files with large sizes may run out of memory while rendering. In this case, you can use batch rendering to reduce memory usage.

Working with Render Layers

Using Render layers, you can render objects separately. It allows you to place objects in separate layers and render each layer separately. Each layer can have different types of shading and rendering attributes. Using layered objects, you can organize rendered images properly for the output. Render layers also help in further processing of rendered images. If you modify multiple scenes, you need to make changes only in those layers that constitute these scenes, which is an easy and convenient approach. A master layer of a scene always appears in Render Layer Editor. This master layer contains all objects and materials of a scene. It is only visible in Render Layer Editor, if there is more than one layer (in which case it is non-renderable by default). Now we can discuss about creating a render layer from selected objects.

Creating Render Layers

Using render layers, you can create multiple images for each frame. You can include objects into a single layer, multiple layers, or all layers while creating it. Later, you can assign selected objects to a new layer. To create a render layer, use Render Layer editor. You can display Render Layer editor by clicking the Render tab in Layer Editor. You can also change the characteristics of each layer or object on a layer by overriding its materials. However, you cannot override the characteristics of the master layer. Perform the following steps to create render layers with objects:

1. **Open** a scene with multiple objects and select those objects that you want to place in a separate layer. Then, **click** the Render tab in Layer Editor to show Render Layer Editor. Alternatively, you can select Window> Rendering Editors> Render Layer Editor from the main menu bar to display Render Layer Editor.

2. **Click** the Create new layer and assign selected objects button in Render Layer Editor. A new layer named layer1 (Normal) is created in Render Layer Editor and appears above the master layer. By the way, the word 'Normal' within brackets represents the blend mode for the layer, which is the default mode. To change the blend mode, click the down arrow and select a blend mode from Render Layer Editor.

3. **Double-click** the newly created layer layer1 (Normal) to rename it. Then, **type** a name for the layer and press enter.

You may notice that other objects in the scene are hidden when layer1 (Normal) is selected. It happens because the hidden objects are not associated with this layer. This kind of segmenting objects helps to keep track of objects in Maya. You can also add objects to an empty layer after creating it by selecting Layers> Create Layer from the Selected from the Render Layer Editor menu bar. To exclude a layer while rendering, click the icon that appears before the name of the layer. Similarly, you can add other objects of the scene to layers as required.

Rendering Specific Layers

To render a specific layer, first what you need to do is that you have to select the layer in the Render Settings window. From the Render Layer dropdown list, you can select the layer that you want to render. By default, the masterLayer option is selected in the Render Layer dropdown list. If a scene has multiple render layers, they are listed in the Render Layer dropdown list. After selecting the render layer from the dropdown list, you can render the scene. Perform the following steps carefully to render a specific layer:

1. **Open** a scene with multiple render layers and select **Window> Rendering Editors> Render Settings** from the main menu bar to display the Render Settings window. The Render Settings window appears with the masterLayer option selected for the Render Layer dropdown list.

2. **Select** the layer that you created in the previous section of the lesson from the Render Layer dropdown list, and then, close the Render Settings window.

3. Select **Render> Render Current Frame** from the main menu bar. The Rendered output will appear in the Render View.

Using the Mental Ray Renderer

Mental ray is a very important application of Maya. It is basically merged with the Maya interface to provide photorealistic rendering, and it allows you to batch mental ray rendering from the Maya UI. Menu items specific to the mental ray renderer are listed in the Render menu. There are several settings specific to the mental ray renderer that you can modify in Attribute Editor or the Render Settings window. To render using the mental ray renderer, you must change the default renderer (Maya Software) to mental ray. For this, select Render> Render Using> mental ray from the main menu bar. You can also select it from the Render Settings window. Perform the following steps carefully to render a scene using the mental ray renderer:

1. **Open** a scene and select **Window> Rendering Editors> Render Settings** from the main menu bar to display the Render Settings window. The Render Settings window appears.

2. **Select** the mental ray option from the Render Using dropdown. The settings specific to mental ray appear in various tabs.

These tabs are: Common, Passes, Features, Quality, Indirect Lighting, and Options. In the Common tab, you can specify the size, name, or quality of the output image. If retains the settings values specified when the Maya Software renderer is selected. Using the Features tab, you can enable lights to cast shadows in the scene. By default, Shadows and the Raytracing settings are enabled in the Features tab. You need to have at least one light source in a scene that emits photons for mental ray to compute GI. To enable emission of photon, select a light and open Attribute Editor, and then, select the Emit Photons checkbox available under the Caustic and Global Illumination section. Similarly, in the Indirect Lighting tab, you can add a sun effect to create a day scene, which can make the output video realistic and beautiful.

3. **Click** the Features tab in the Render Settings window and **select** the Global Illumination checkbox for the Secondary Effects setting in the Rendering Features section.

4. **Select** the Final Gathering checkbox for the Secondary Effects and select **Render> Render Current Frame** from the main menu bar to render the current frame.

There are various factors that determine the effect of GI and final gathering such as position of light objects, the type of lights, or intensity of lights. The Global Illumination and Final Gathering settings bounce the light reflections and refractions multiple times. Now we can discuss about these two attributes:

Global Illumination: Produces realistic output due to the natural phenomenon, where light bounces off any surfaces in its path until completely absorbed.

Final Gathering: Produces scenes, where the indirect illumination changes slowly.

Selecting the Global Illumination and Final Gathering checkboxes uses the default values for rendering, which you can later modify in the Indirect Lighting tab. While rendering an exterior scene, you need to add an Image Based Lighting (IBL) or a Physical Sun and Sky, also referred to as environments. You can click the Create button next to the Image Based Lighting option to create a new IBL environment node. Now as we have learnt new things in this section, we can proceed to render the above scene with an environment effect by adding a sky and sun to it:

5. **Click** the Indirect Lighting tab in the Render Settings window and **click** the Create button for the Physical Sun and Sky setting in the Environment section. The settings for the Physical Sun and Sky setting appear in Attribute Editor, which you can modify, if required.

6. **Close** the Render Settings window and select **Render> Render Current Frame** from the main menu bar to render the scene with the default values.

Exploring Render Nodes

In Maya, render nodes are building blocks that are used to create a render (final image). For instance, you start with an image node (in which you select the stating image), and then, add effects and modify nodes. Render nodes could be image processing effects including blur, sharpen, distort, or displacement (in 3D programs). These render nodes are individual components that are interconnected and used for creating any kind of rendering effect. In Maya, there are various types of nodes such as transform nodes, shape nodes, and rendering nodes. You can also animate on the render nodes. The following are the types of render nodes available in Maya: Texture nodes, Placement nodes, and Material nodes.

All the three render nodes along with their basic input and output connections help in defining attributes of the last rendered image. Special effects can be created by connecting various nodes in different ways. Nodes can be shared by objects in a scene to have efficient rendering. For instance, if the appearance to tow objects is similar, you can share a single texture node, so that both objects appear the same. Sharing nodes help to use less memory and renders faster. You can work with rendering nodes in the Hypershade window. Now we can discuss the different types of render nodes:

Texture Nodes

Texture node can help to create textures, such as 2D Textures, 3D Textures, Env Textures (Environment texture). You can also create textures such as Layered Texture. They appear in the Create tab of the Hypershade window. 3D textures allow objects to appear as carved out materials, such as marble, rock, wood. 3D textures are displaced when the 3D Textures node is selected in the Create tab. To create a 2D texture node, you can click a 2D texture in the right panel. The selected texture node appears in the Work Area.

Placement Nodes

Placement nodes are available under the 2D and 3D textures shown in the Create Maya Nodes group in the Hypershade window. These nodes help to determine the position of 2D and 3D textures. Actually, they specify the location for these textures to be placed in the Work Area, as textures can be relocated as well mapped with each other as projections. You can also place 2D textures in a scene using the surface UV (where U represents the horizontal axis and V represents the vertical axis) space (local); whereas, 3D textures can be placed using the world space. Placement nodes play a key role while texturing multiple surfaces. You can also use the Position manipulators for repositioning textures or labels interactively. You can scale (repeat), move (position), or rotate a texture node to specify the appearance of the texture on the surface. A 3D placement node defines a 3D texture or environment (Env) texture positioning and orientation in the world space. 3D placement nodes help to texture multiple surfaces. You can reposition 3D textures with numerical precision in the place3dTexture node Attribute Editor, or you can use manipulators to reposition textures or labels interactively.

Material Nodes

Material nodes help to define the appearance of objects surfaces while rendering. In Maya, the main function of material nodes is defining the reaction of surfaces to light. Different types of material nodes are Surface, Displacement, and Volumetric. You can set the material node attribute such as color, specularity, and transparency to create a variety of images of wider perspective. All material nodes can be created in the Hypershade window. Different types of material nodes are described as follows:

Surface Material: Represents the types of surfaces onto which you can map textures. Surface attributes such as shininess, matte, reflectivity, and glossiness depend on the types of materials. For instance, if the texture requires a shiny surface such as chrome, use a Phong material rather than a Lambert.

Displacement Material: Helps to use images for specifying the surface relief on objects. Surface relief is the number of depressions and elevations on the surface of an object.

Volumetric Material: Describes the physical environment where scenes are created. Volumetric materials describe the physical appearance of phenomena, which occupy a volume of space (for instance, fog, smoke, dust, or other fine particles). You can produce various effects such as displaying light fog through mirror reflections by raytracing volumetric materials.

Lesson 27
Working with Cameras

The Maya cameras, in some cases, may be more creative than real-world cameras. For instance, Maya cameras are not restricted by size or weight, so you can move cameras to any position in a scene, even inside the smallest objects. In Maya, there is a default perspective camera for viewing scenes. However, you can also view scenes using the three orthographic cameras: front, top, and side. These four cameras (one perspective and three orthographic) are primarily used to view scenes while modeling, animating, shading, texturing, or lighting objects. However, these default cameras are not used while rendering; instead additional cameras are created and placed based on the creative needs for rendering the final output. Maya cameras simulate real world views more accurately than the default Maya views (cameras). Maya provides the three types of cameras:

Camera (one-node camera): Allows you to render static scenes and simple animation such as panning out of a scene.

Camera and Aim camera: Allows you to render slightly more complex animation. For instance, an animation in which the animated object moving along a wavy path.

Camera, Aim, and Up camera (three-node camera): Helps you to render an animated scene by specifying the end of the camera to face upward. It is useful to render complex animations. The Camera, Aim and Up camera is similar to a basic camera, but contains the aim-vector control and up-vector control for rotating the camera.

You can use the Options window for a camera to set various attributes before creating the camera. You can set attributes such as Center of interest, Focal length for Lens Properties, and Shutter angle for Motion Blur. The focal length of a camera is measured in millimeters. If a camera has a high focal length, the objects appear bigger; whereas, if the camera has a low focal length, the objects appear smaller. Maya also allows you make changes in the camera attributes using Attribute Editor after creating a camera.

Creating a Camera

Camera plays an important role in rendering and allows viewing a scene in interesting perspectives. You can create several cameras for viewing and rendering a scene from various angles. After creating a camera, you can transform it by moving, rotating, and scaling to view and eventually render a scene. To create a basic camera in a scene, you can select Create> Cameras> Camera from the main menu bar. You can perform the following steps to create a basic camera in a scene: 1. **Open** a scene and select **Create> Cameras> Camera** from the main menu bar. The new camera always appears at the center of the grid, which can be viewed by zooming in. 2. **Transform** the camera using <u>Move Tool</u> and <u>Rotate Tool</u>, and position it in any location.

Viewing a Scene through a Camera

A scene is always viewed through the perspective camera, which is the default camera view in Maya. Additionally, you can add cameras and view objects in a scene using these cameras. You can view a scene only through a single camera at any point of time. As the camera is created at the center of the grid, you must reposition it appropriately to view a scene. Let's perform these steps to view a scene through a camera:

1. **Open** a scene and select **Create> Cameras> Camera, Aim and Up** from the main menu bar to create a three-node camera. The new camera appears selected at the center of the grid.

You can see on your computer screen that the camera has small knob-like controls attached to it. These aiming controls are used to aim the camera at a particular object in a scene. You can adjust the aiming control of the camera using Move Tool. When the aiming control moves, the camera moves accordingly. Note that you cannot move a camera using Move Tool through which you are currently viewing the scene.

2. **Select** <u>Move Tool</u> from Tool Box and **move** both the camera and its <u>Look At Point</u> to position the camera as required.

3. **Select** the camera and go to **Panels> Look Through Selected** from the panel menu. The current view changes to project the scene through the selected camera.

4. **Click** the <u>Smooth shade all</u> button on the panel toolbar to view the scene in shaded view. The current view is shaded in the viewport.

The name of the camera (camera 1) appears at the bottom of the camera view. You can navigate in a camera view similar to navigating in the perspective viewport using the combination of mouse button and keys. If you want to revert to viewing the scene through the perspective or any of the orthographic cameras, select a camera by selecting Panels> Perspective> persp or Panels> Orthographic from the panel menu.

Making a Camera Renderable

As stated earlier, you can render a scene using any of the default camera views (perspective or orthographic). However, these default camera views do not give an aesthetic feel to the final render. You can create a new camera and use it to render scenes for more creative angles. To use a newly created camera to render scenes, you first need to make it renderable. Let's perform these steps to make a camera renderable:

1. **Select** a camera through which you want to render a scene. For now, you can select camera1. Then, select **Window> Rendering Editors> Render Settings** from the main menu bar to open the Render settings window.

2. **Scroll down** and **click** the Renderable Cameras section in the Common tab to expand it. Then, **select** the name of the camera from the Renderable Camera dropdown list. For now, you can select camera1.

3. **Close** the Render Settings window and select **Render> Render Current Frame** from the main menu bar to render the scene.

The selected camera view renders using the active rendered and shows in Render View. You can create multiple cameras and make one renderable, by selecting it in the Renderable Camera dropdown list.

Adding Depth of Field

Depth of field is an artificial environment in which objects included in the range of a camera are in focal view, while objects that fall outside the range of a camera appear blurred. You can add depth of field to a selected camera and render a scene using this camera. The Maya Software and mental ray renderers are mainly used for setting depth of a field for rendering. Perform the following steps to add depth of field to a camera:

1. **Open** a scene with cameras to add depth of field. Then, **select** the camera, and for now, select **Panels> Look Through Selected** from the panel menu to view a scene through the camera.

This way, we want to show those objects away from the camera appear blurred. That can be achieved by adding depth of field to the selected camera.

2. **Click** the Show or hide the Attribute Editor button to open Attribute Editor. Then, **scroll down** and **click** the Depth of Field section to expand it.

3. **Select** the Depth Of Field check box to enable depth of field. Then, **type: 40** in the Focus Distance text box and press enter. Now you can render the scene by selecting Render> Render Current Frame from the main menu bar.

You can see on your computer screen that the objects that are closer to the camera appear clear and those farther from the camera appear blurred, which implies that the camera only focuses within a specific range. This range is controlled by the Focus Distance attribute.

Adding Motion Blur

Motion blur allows you to create the effect of movement in a scene by blurring objects. It represents an optical illusion when an object moves fast before a camera. This phenomenon happens because the iris of the camera is not able to capture the image of an object during its course of motion. The motion blur feature helps to add a non-stop motion effect in a scene; thereby, allowing the camera to capture a clear image of the object. As the effect is caused by the relative motion between camera, objects and a scene, motion blur may be avoided by panning the camera to track those moving objects. There are two types of motion blur in Maya, which are supported only by the Maya Software renderer.

2D motion blur: Calculates the blurring effect after the frame is rendered. It is a post process that looks more uniform; hence, not quite as realistic as 3D motion blur. 2D motion blur is ideal for surfaces far away from a camera, where level of detail is not much important.

3D motion blur: Calculates blurring effect based on a camera shutter angle and the motion blur frame step, while a frame or a sequence is rendered. 3D motion blur is ideal for surface, when it is moving and revealing another surface behind it. It is slower as compared to 2D motion blur, but fetches a better quality effect than 2D motion blur.

When rendering a scene with several objects, select those objects to be blurred. If you apply motion blur on all objects in a scene, the rendering time will increase. Now you can perform the following steps to render a scene with motion blur:

1. **Open** a scene with an animation and select **Window> Rendering Editors> Render Settings** from the main menu bar to open the Render Settings window. The Render Settings window appears.

2. **Select** the Maya Software renderer from the Render Using dropdown list. Then, **click** the Maya Software tab and **scroll down** and **click** the Motion Blur section to expand it.

3. **Select** the Motion blur check box to enable it. **Type: 10** in the Blur by frame text box and press enter.

The Blur by frame setting controls the amount of blurriness rendered for 2D and 3D motion blur. The higher the number, the greater is the blur effect. The Shutter Open and Shutter Close settings are active only if the Use Shutter Open/Close check box is enabled. To increase the motion blur effect, increase the difference between the Shutter Open and the Shutter Close values.

4. **Select** the Use Shutter Open/Close check box and **type: -1** in the Shutter Open text box and press enter. Then, **type: 1** in the Shutter Close text box and press enter. Now we will render the animated scene as a video file. To render an animation you need to select a video format such as avi from the Image format dropdown list.

5. **Click** the **Common** tab and **select** the AVI (avi) option in the Image format dropdown list. Then, **expand** the Frame Range section.

6. **Type: 32** for the end frame of the animation in the End frame text box, and press enter and close the Render Settings window.

7. Select **Render> Batch Render** from the main menu bar to render the animation. The animation is rendered with the Maya Software renders and based on the number of frames and the quality of the output, a completion message appears in Command Line. The video file is saved in the movies folder of the current project that you can access and play to see the motion blur effect.

Using Stereoscopic Camera

Stereoscopic cameras are used to create 3D renders with the illusion of a 3D depth of field. You can use them while rendering a movie to be seen using special 3D glasses. These cameras have two or more lenses. Multiple lenses help them to capture 3D images. The stereoscopic cameras also help you to create the depth of field in collaboration with the 3D interface. You can also create a multi-camera rig of two or more stereo cameras using Multi-Camera Rig Tool. You can use the camera rig to interactively change the focus distance of a camera. Rigging is the process of creating an organized system of deformers, expressions, and controls applied to an object to easily and efficiently animate it. Camera rigs can also be customized using Maya Embedded Language (MEL), Python scripting, or Custom Stereo Rig Editor. Perform the following steps to use a stereoscopic camera:

1. **Open** a scene and select **Create**> **Cameras**> **Stereo Camera** from the main menu bar. The stereoscopic camera appears at the center of the grid. An icon containing three cameras appears, and by default the center camera is used to view a scene.

2. **Move** and **rotate** the stereoscopic camera to position anywhere, and then, select **Panels**> **Stereo**> **stereoCamera** from the panel menu to switch to the stereo mode.

You can switch between different viewing modes such as Horizontal Interlace or Anaglyph by selecting Stereo> <viewing mode> from the panel menu. When you render a scene with a stereoscopic camera, the individual left and right camera images are also rendered. The images have to be composited to apply any stereo effect.

3. Select **Render**> **Render Current Frame** from the main menu bar. The rendered frame appears in Render View.

Note that all 3D simulations of stereoscopic camera work only if the high end graphics card is used. In Render View, you can change the render output to other stereo mode by selecting Display> Stereo Display> <type of render output> from the Render View menu bar.

Niranjan Jha Showman
Trainer, Author, Physician, Entrepreneur, Filmmaker, Activist
Cromosys Corporation
Education and Technology Research Center
www.facebook.com/cromosys
+91-9561450045
Nallasopara (W), Mumbai, India

NIRANJAN JHA SHOWMAN

Founder - Niranjan Jha Showman

Education and Technology Research Center

Patankar Park, Nallasopara (W), Mumbai. +91-9561450045

Education, Technology, Publication, Healthcare, Newsmedia, Realtor, Filmmaking

www.facebook.com/cromosys

Cromosys Publication
Teach
Yourself
German
NIRANJAN JHA SHOWMAN

Cromosys Publication
Teach Yourself French
NIRANJAN JHA SHOWMAN

Cromosys Publication
Teach
Yourself
Spanish
NIRANJAN JHA SHOWMAN

Cromosys Publication

English
Voice
Accent and
Pronunciation

NIRANJAN JHA SHOWMAN

Teach
Yourself
Autodesk
MAYA

Cromosys Publication

NIRANJAN JHA SHOWMAN

Cromosys Publication
Teach
Yourself
Autodesk
3ds Max
NIRANJAN JHA SHOWMAN

Cromosys Publication
CRIMINAL FACTORY
NIRANJAN JHA SHOWMAN

Cromosys Publication
FOCAL DISASTER
NIRANJAN JHA SHOWMAN

Cromosys Publication
Your talents will not help you succeed without your skill of using them.
NIRANJAN JHA SHOWMAN
BE
MILLIONAIRE
LIKE
ME

Copyright Office
Government of India

सत्यमेव जयते

Extracts from the Register of Copyrights

Dated : 22/07/2022

1.	Registration Number	: **T-86782-2022**
2.	Name, address and nationality of the applicant	: NIRANJAN JHA SHOWMAN, CROMOSYS PUBLICATION, 001, JAYSATYAM, PATANKAR ROAD, NALLASOPARA (W), MUMBAI, MAHARASHTRA - 401203. INDIAN
3.	Nature of the applicant's interest in the copyright of the work	: AUTHOR
4.	Class and description of the work	: LITERARY / BOOK
5.	Title of the work	: **Teach Yourself Autodesk Maya**
6.	Language of the work	: ENGLISH
7.	Name, address and nationality of the author and if the author is deceased, date of his decease	: NIRANJAN JHA SHOWMAN, CROMOSYS PUBLICATION, 001, JAYSATYAM, PATANKAR ROAD, NALLASOPARA (W), MUMBAI, MAHARASHTRA - 401203. INDIAN
8.	Whether the work is published or unpublished	: UNPUBLISHED
9.	Year and country of first publication and name, address and nationality of the publisher	: N.A.
10.	Years and countries of subsequent publications, if any, and names, addresses and nationalities of the publishers	: N.A. SAME AS ABOVE
11.	Names, addresses and nationalities of the owners of various rights comprising the copyright in the work and the extent of rights held by each, together with particulars of assignments and licences, if any	:
12.	Names, addresses and nationalities of other persons, if any, authorised to assign or licence of rights comprising the copyright	: N.A.
13.	If the work is an 'Artistic work', the location of the original work, including name, address and nationality of the person in possession of the work. (In the case of an architectural work, the year of completion of the work should also be shown).	: N.A.
14.	If the work is an 'Artistic work', whether it is registered under the Designs Act 2000 if yes give details.	: N.A.
15.	If the work is an 'Artistic work', capable of being registered as a design under the Designs Act 2000.whether it has been applied to an article though an industrial process and ,if yes ,the number of times it is reproduced.	: N.A.
16.	Remarks, if any	:

Diary Number :   7396/2020-CO/T
Date of Application :   05/05/2020
Date of Receipt :   05/05/2020

DEPUTY REGISTRAR OF COPYRIGHTS